Voices from the Asylum

Four French Women Writers, 1850–1920

SUSANNAH WILSON

OXFORD
UNIVERSITY PRESS

OXFORD

UNIVERSITY PRESS

Great Clarendon Street, Oxford ox2 6dp

Oxford University Press is a department of the University of Oxford.
It furthers the University's objective of excellence in research, scholarship,
and education by publishing worldwide in

Oxford New York

Auckland Cape Town Dar es Salaam Hong Kong Karachi
Kuala Lumpur Madrid Melbourne Mexico City Nairobi
New Delhi Shanghai Taipei Toronto

With offices in

Argentina Austria Brazil Chile Czech Republic France Greece
Guatemala Hungary Italy Japan Poland Portugal Singapore
South Korea Switzerland Thailand Turkey Ukraine Vietnam

Oxford is a registered trade mark of Oxford University Press
in the UK and in certain other countries

Published in the United States
by Oxford University Press Inc., New York

British Library Cataloguing in Publication Data

Data available

Library of Congress Cataloging in Publication Data

Data available

Typeset by SPI Publisher Services, Pondicherry, India
Printed in Great Britain
on acid-free paper by
MPG Books Group

ISBN 978–0–19–957935–8

1 3 5 7 9 10 8 6 4 2

Acknowledgements

This book is based on a doctoral thesis submitted in 2005 that was made possible by an award for postgraduate study from the Arts and Humanities Research Board. The project was also assisted financially by the Faculty of Medieval and Modern Languages at the University of Oxford, and Jesus College, Oxford.

My first debt of thanks is owed to my doctoral supervisor, the late Professor Malcolm Bowie, whose kind support and vigorous intellectual engagement with my work guided the project to completion. Professor Michael Sheringham took over the supervisory role in the final stages, and his input was generous and invaluable. Alison Finch, Toby Garfitt, Miranda Gill, Ruth Harris, David Haycock, Anthony Pilkington, Gabrielle Townsend, and Caroline Warman, as well as my anonymous readers, have read parts of the book and provided very useful comments. The staff at Jesus College, Oxford; the librarians at the Taylor Institution, Bodleian, and Radcliffe Science Libraries in Oxford; the Bibliothèque nationale de France; and the Parisian archives have provided friendly and professional assistance with this research. I am also very grateful to the editors at Oxford University Press for their efficient and responsive handling of this project.

I thank those friends and family members who have provided moral support and informal intellectual discussion throughout my studies, as well as generous hospitality during periods of research in Paris. I am grateful to my parents, Mavis and Mark Wilson, whose support from the beginnings of my interest in French Studies to the completion of this book has been beyond measure. Finally, special thanks to David Haycock for his constant loving support, and to Nathaniel, our little boy, who is a source of continual joy and has focused and distracted my mind in equal measure.

Contents

List of Abbreviations

BNF	*Bibliothèque nationale de France*
DBF	*Dictionnaire de biographie française*
EU	*Encyclopædia universalis*
GD	*Grand dictionnaire universel du XIXe siècle*
GL	*Grand Larousse encyclopédique*
SB	*La Sainte Bible*

Note on Presentation

Page references to the four primary texts are given in parentheses after quotations in the main text and footnotes. When several quotations from the same page appear in succession within the same paragraph, the page reference is given after the final citation. Ellipses in square brackets, i.e. [...], and emphases in quotations in bold type are my own, in order to avoid confusion with the multiple ellipses and the use of italics and underlining for emphasis in the original texts.

In presenting this research, a significant amount of space has needed to be dedicated to prefatory material. Chapters 2–5 each include an introductory section covering the following ground: a biographical sketch of the author; information on publication and the textual corpus used; a review of secondary literature; and case-historical and diagnostic material. The remainder of each chapter is devoted to an extended close exploration of the text in question. Some excerpts of text are quoted at length in the main discussion, and Esquiron's *Mémoire* is reproduced in its entirety in an appendix to the chapter. These inclusions are justified in order to give the reader access to rare texts that, with the exception of the correspondence of Camille Claudel, have never been reprinted or translated.

Introduction

*Si les malades ont parfois parlé, on n'a pas assez fait compte de ce
qu'ils ont dit.*

J.-J. Moreau de Tours, 1845

Among the thousands of women committed to French psychiatric
hospitals between 1854 and 1943, only a tiny number left written
accounts documenting their experiences prior to and during incarceration. The identities and stories of most survive only as names in
admissions registers, or as initials in the case studies of their observers.
Four women in particular, however, left vivid personal records that have
survived: the Parisian musician Hersilie Rouy; the feminist activist
Marie Esquiron; the self-proclaimed mystic and 'stigmatisée' Pauline
Lair Lamotte; and the well-known sculptor, and lover of Auguste
Rodin, Camille Claudel. All four were subjected to psychiatric treatment, though with only limited success.

Mémoires d'une aliénée (1883) is Hersilie Rouy's account of her
experience of treatment in a range of French psychiatric hospitals
between 1854 and 1868. The title of Marie Esquiron's memoir sums
up her complaint: *Mémoire adressé à Monsieur le Ministre de la Justice
par Madame Esquiron, née de Gasté, Séquestrée dans la Maison de santé de
M. le docteur Goujon, 90, rue de Picpus, à Paris, Où elle réfute elle-même
l'imputation d'aliénation mentale et le rapport de MM. Les aliénistes
Mottet, Magnan et Voisin* (1893). Pauline Lair Lamotte was a patient
of the renowned French psychiatrist Pierre Janet; her untitled writings,
composed between 1896 and 1904, were published in the first volume
of his treatise *De l'angoisse à l'extase: études sur les croyances et les sentiments* (1926). Finally, Camille Claudel corresponded regularly with a
number of friends and family members throughout her long incarceration, and described the artistic stasis of her mental illness and the restrictions of the asylum regime. Her collected letters were not published

until 2003.[1] As I will show in this book, these women all resisted the
reductive process of contemporary psychiatric diagnosis, and their
memoirs are unique documents, offering an alternative view of the
treatment of mental illness during the heyday of alienist medicine.

In 1838 a law was passed in France that integrated into French law a
post-Revolutionary solution to the problem of insanity, in recognition of
the emergence of psychiatry as a medical discipline at the beginning of the
nineteenth century. The 'loi des aliénés' offered a medico-legal conception of madness as both a pathological state requiring treatment by
medical professionals and a danger to society necessitating the incarceration of those afflicted.[2] It is perhaps ironic, from the point of view of 'les
malades', that Moreau de Tours should have recommended listening
more to what they had to say: between 1838 and 1870 the number of
French women incarcerated in psychiatric institutions doubled, and
during the 1860s and 1870s writing by patients protesting against their
incarceration increased markedly.[3] The voice of the patient has arguably
been neglected by historians and literary critics, and these accounts will
here be read as representing the unacknowledged counterpoint to theoretical and clinical writings by medical professionals. It will be argued
here that psychiatry was a socially coercive form of treatment that
functioned—intentionally or unintentionally—as a medico-legal arm of
a misogynistic society. Patients' writings are by contrast rare and compelling surviving voices of resistance against this process. Close textual
analysis of utterances deemed psychopathological by medical experts
will reveal that a case can be made for reading the construction of a

---

[1] Rouy (1883); Esquiron (1893); Janet (1926); Rivière (2003).
[2] Ripa (1986a: 75) writes: 'Cette loi met un terme au vide législatif que la
Révolution, bannissant les lettres de cachet et chaînes, avait instauré face à la folie.
Elle établit les rapports entre la société et son fou, rebaptisé aliéné, terme plus médical
et moins péjoratif.'
[3] Ripa (1986b: 9) found that in France as a whole, from 1845 to 1849, 9,930 women
were incarcerated in psychiatric asylums. By 1871 this had risen to 19,692. The
Salpêtrière, the women's public asylum in Paris, housed 800 women in 1838, rising to
1,400 in 1860. The distinguished alienist J.-J. Moreau de Tours was most famous for his
treatise on cannabis, *Du hachisch et de l'aliénation mentale* (1845: epigraph citation taken
from p. 133). Rigoli (2001: 413) charts the rise of writing by patients. Many outside the
asylum also raised grave concerns about the power of the alienist doctor enshrined in the
law of 1838. A glance through the *Annales d'hygiène publique et de médecine légale* from
the 1860s and 1870s reveals a range of articles discussing such protest documents
(patients' accusations of 'false commitment'), the criticism of the press, and the defence
of the psychiatric profession. Casimir Pinel's comments (1864) are evidence of a
profession closing ranks in response to this criticism.

delusional narrative as a legitimate strategy for coping with and mitigating an unbearable real-life situation, and as a means of preserving a sense of self. In this sense, 'insane' writings that evince historically false claims, such as specific accusations of persecution or grandiose delusions, can be read as metaphorical representations of real suffering, and compensatory devices created to ensure the survival of the self. Writing that resists the process of oppressive pathologization represents an important emancipatory attempt that announces later feminist revisionist histories of the asylum, and indeed the anti-psychiatric movements of the twentieth century. These were typified by critics of the normalizing function of medical treatment for mental illness, such as the Surrealists and radical psychiatry.[4]

The first chapter of this book will discuss in detail how these texts relate to the historiography of psychiatry, the specific ways in which they have been used before, and how they can be placed within a broader literary context. This study also takes its place in the context of a significant body of critical work on the theme of madness and women's writing. Many women writers have in recent decades been discovered or rediscovered thanks to the efforts of feminist literary criticism and 'gynocriticism', the specific study of women authors.[5] The work of Elaine Showalter and others to revive interest in nineteenth-century English-language women writers has been reflected in French cultural studies by scholars such as Béatrice Slama, Diana Holmes, Alison Finch, and Rosemary Lloyd.[6] Finch has provided the most comprehensive critical survey to date of women's writing during this period, and has demonstrated that women writers were active and appreciated in nineteenth-century France, but their work was quickly forgotten after their deaths. Lloyd, as co-editor of the volume *Women Seeking Expression*, demonstrates that in post-Revolutionary France 'women struggled against the multiple restrictions and limitations imposed on them by convention, society and the law, and found means of expression that were to shape much future thinking about literature, music, art, science, education and self-definition.'[7]

---

[4] Breton (1924: 312) criticizes the French law in his *Manifeste du Surréalisme*: 'Chacun sait, en effet, que les fous ne doivent leur internement qu'à un petit nombre d'actes légalement répréhensibles, et que, faute de ces actes, leur liberté [...] ne saurait être en jeu.'

[5] Showalter (1978, 1979).

[6] Slama (1980); Holmes (1996); Finch (2000); Lloyd (2000); Lloyd and Nelson (2000).

[7] Lloyd and Nelson (2000: 5).

A logical extension of this increased focus on women writers has been renewed critical interest in forms of self-writing traditionally—although not exclusively—associated with women and the private sphere of the home and intimate relationships, increasingly treated seriously as literary genres: autobiography, correspondence, diaries, memoirs, and devotional writings. The work of Philippe Lejeune, Michael Sheringham, and Kathleen Hart has contributed much to the discussion of women's autobiography, by highlighting the way in which nineteenth- and twentieth-century women engaged with the world in which they lived, through relating personal experience to the public and political realms.[8] Hart shows that women writers such as Flora Tristan, George Sand, and Louise Michel tended to link personal narratives to the process of socio-historical change, and thus to make the personal political. Sheringham observes the female autobiographer's tendency to define herself in relation to significant others, and the pattern of 'the achievement of freedom through writing itself'.[9] The four texts to be examined here demand a contrasting approach, however; although they do comment indirectly on the political status of women in French society, they are to a great extent introspective and characterized by a turning away from the world in on the self. Nevertheless, we shall see that, in common with other women writers of their time, these authors did offer a form of commentary on the dynamic era in which they lived.

The research presented here adds to this body of knowledge by bringing to light a fascinating but still largely unacknowledged tradition in the history of women's writing: the 'psychiatric memoir'. The generic status of each of these writings is far from fixed, however, and each incorporates a number of the above-mentioned forms. But the reasons for reassessing these texts are dissimilar to those commonly given for the re-evaluation of published women writers: like literary works they offer, as Finch argues, an 'alternative perspective on familiar themes of the time'; in contrast to literature, however, they are not noticeably accomplished,

---

[8] Lejeune (1975, 1993); Sheringham (1993); Hart (2004). Although Lejeune does not specifically discuss women's autobiography as a distinct category, his definition of autobiography in terms of a 'pact' with the reader is useful when considering how women writers approach their addressee. Lejeune (1998: 125) writes: 'J'appellerai ici "autobiographie" tout texte régi par un pacte autobiographique: l'auteur s'engage à tenir sur lui-même un discours véridique. Un autobiographe, ce n'est pas quelqu'un qui dit la vérité sur lui-même, mais quelqu'un qui dit qu'il la dit.'

[9] Hart (2004: 11); Sheringham (2000: 188–9).

and are not always easy or pleasurable to read.[10] The form of writing studied here is, in contrast, rather constrained and repetitive, and its strength rhetorical rather than aesthetic. As we shall see in Chapter 1, these writings have been acknowledged and validated by feminist historians of the asylum, who have touched upon the issue of the voice of the patient. Regrettably, however, they have been exposed to little or no textual analysis, having been treated primarily as documentary sources or clinical case material.

Critics such as Showalter, Gordon Claridge, and Lisa Appignanesi have carried out important research on the subject of the patient's self-expression in the English-language field. This has gone some way towards redressing the current imbalance in favour of the clinician.[11] Susan Hubert's *Questions of Power: The Politics of Women's Madness Narratives* examines a range of autobiographical writings penned by incarcerated women in the nineteenth and twentieth centuries in the United States. She argues that nineteenth-century women used writing as a form of rebellion against incarceration, but draws on Gail Pheterson's theory of 'internalized oppression' in order to suggest that twentieth-century women were more likely to adopt a submissive stance in acceptance of their diagnoses.[12] These conclusions take account of the differences in medical treatment that came about in the later period, as well as the increased respect commanded by the psychiatric profession. However, in my opinion the approach taken by Hubert does not go far enough. In this project, therefore, I have sought to engage with the text of the patient as a meaningful utterance, whether delusional and outspoken or characterized by quiet resignation. At present in French Studies no such study has been carried out, and this research contributes importantly to knowledge in the context of the experiences of French women.

The well-known work of Showalter on women and madness, as well as that of Sandra Gilbert and Susan Gubar, has led to the almost universally accepted feminist critical position that female madness is a subversive strategy of resistance against patriarchy.[13] Other theorists in the French-language feminist tradition, such as Hélène Cixous and Julia Kristeva, have also in varying ways sought to validate the language of unreason and that which is pre-linguistic. Their ideas have been widely

---

[10] Finch (2000: 4).
[11] Showalter (1987); Claridge (1990); Appignanesi (2008).
[12] Hubert (2002: 26); Pheterson (1986).
[13] Gilbert (1979); Showalter (1987).

used in the interpretation of the madwoman's incomprehensible bab-
bling, and indeed her silences, as subversive of oppressive patriarchal
closures.[14] However, critics of the view that the madwoman's position is
subversive argue that since she is silenced, imprisoned, and unseen she
cannot exercise any effective form of resistance. Marta Caminero-Santangelo casts doubt on the idea that there is any value in reading
madness as a metaphor for resistance, because insanity is 'characterized
by the (dis)ability to produce meaning—that is, to produce representations recognizable as meaningful within society.'[15] There is much
validity in this interrogation of the ethically questionable championing
of the speech of the madwoman, since meaning is not easily discerned
from her utterances. But whilst it is true that there is an important
distinction to be made between speaking out and being heard, it is also
arguably the case that an act of resistance is not defined by its perceived
success or failure. Rather, we shall see that the madwoman did speak,
and that what she said was meaningful when read as a metaphorical
commentary on her life experiences.

In addition to the work of historians, a vast body of work exists on the
subject of 'la folie' in French literature, whether in relation to the use of
the term and the depiction of characters in fictional texts or to the
writings of mentally disturbed authors, such as Gérard de Nerval and
Antonin Artaud.[16] Critics such as Shoshana Felman have sought a
means of 'giving voice' to the literary representation of madness that
traditionally has been viewed as defined by its silence and very lack of
discursive position.[17] Alistair Swiffen has written on the theme of
treating psychosis in the writings of Nerval, Desnos, and Lacan. He
views these writers as forming a broadly anti-psychiatric literary tradition that is 'radical in its call for greater sensitivity on the part of the sane
to the experience of the mad'.[18] The authors presented here can also be

---

[14] Cixous's notion of 'écriture féminine' celebrates that which is non-rational in
language as representative of a peculiarly feminine form of empowerment, and Kristeva's
concept of the prelinguistic 'semiotic' can be used to illustrate the hope that women's
silence and non-linguistic expressions can be read as subversive of rational, patriarchal
discourse. See Cixous (1975) and Kristeva (1977).

[15] Caminero-Santangelo (1998: 9).

[16] André Breton celebrated the madness of Nerval and Artaud as representing a form
of metaphorical release. Other critics such as Prendergast (1986: 168) reproach this view
as foolish and irresponsible.

[17] Felman (1978).

[18] Swiffen (2002: iii).

read as taking a place within this tradition, although their experiences are here read in the context of the general status of women.

Since the 1960s, discussion of the idea of madness and society's treatment of the insane has been dominated by the figure of Michel Foucault. His most important work on the subject, *Folie et déraison: histoire de la folie à l'âge classique*, argues that the Age of Reason brought with it an intolerance of the insane, and a concomitant grand-scale incarceration of the afflicted.[19] Foucault constructs what he terms an 'archaeology of silence', arguing that the insane were silenced, incarcerated, and physically restrained, and in the nineteenth century their suffering medicalized through psychiatric observation. However, since my research is concerned with the idea that the incarcerated were sometimes vociferous and active, Foucault's assertion in his later work on the nineteenth century, *Histoire de la sexualité*, that sources of power are complex and multifarious, and that power will always engender resistance, is more pertinent to the present analysis.[20]

The widespread introduction of anti-psychotic drugs and surgical interventions in the twentieth century meant that patients could be pacified and truly silenced.[21] Prior to these developments in the field of psychiatric medicine, the period during which these women were writing was arguably a unique time that allowed voices of resistance to rise up. Although in the second half of the twentieth century so-called anti-psychiatric thinkers strongly criticized the ideology of the treatment of mental illness, this almost always occurred in the context of clinicians raising concerns on behalf of patients: in practice, this usually meant that men spoke on behalf of women.[22]

The period when the women considered here were active as writers was, by contrast, a precarious time during which the psychiatric profession was attempting to establish itself. The extreme tension this provoked

---

[19] Foucault (1961).

[20] Foucault (1976: 125).

[21] The use of psychosurgery (frontal leucotomy) to modify the symptoms of psychiatric illness was pioneered in 1936 by Moniz. This was widely practiced until concerns were raised about the adverse side effects of the procedure and advances in pharmacology made it possible to treat disorders using drugs (Gelder 2001: 716; Baruk 1951). The use of psychosurgery followed the same pattern in France (Bertrand 2002). Anti-psychotic drugs were introduced in 1954 (Lieberman 1995).

[22] Although writers such as Laing have analysed madness as a female strategy within the family, Showalter argues that it remains the case that 'women are spoken for but do not speak for themselves' (1987: 250). On madness as a 'strategy' within the family, invented by a person in order to live in an unliveable situation, see Laing (1967).

over the issue of medical authority is palpable in these texts. The latent threat perceived consciously or unconsciously by clinicians meant that contemporary medical discourse came to be inflected with anxiety, and the clinician's position defended, in part, by denying the insane the possibility of subjectivity. The relative insecurity of the profession reflects the political upheavals of the era: the four texts discussed deal with the period from the crumbling of the Second Republic and the emergence of the Second Empire, through the turmoil of the Franco-Prussian war, the 1871 Paris Commune, the Belle Époque, the First World War, and the establishment of the Third Republic. These episodes, important as they are, arguably had less influence on the narratives produced by these authors than the enduring effect of the 1838 'loi des aliénés' and the Napoleonic Civil Code, and the collusion of the medical profession with a misogynistic legal system that kept women in a subordinate position throughout the nineteenth and early twentieth centuries.

The later nineteenth and early twentieth centuries were a brief moment in history when some patients spoke out for themselves. While Freud and Breuer treated hysterics and began the crucially important process of giving voice to the patient, in other places women were expressing themselves whether or not this was endorsed by clinicians. Freud's patient 'Anna O.' can be credited with the invention of the 'talking cure', and his major discovery was that 'a symptom's apparent meaninglessness could be illuminated by placing it in a very specific, "traumatic" past context, when it did have meaning'.[23] In a similar way, the authors examined here found a means, through writing, of mitigating their absolute disempowerment and of reclaiming a sense of individuality and autonomy apart from their mental illness. Though they enjoyed varying degrees of success, their ostensibly meaningless or deranged utterances can be placed in a context that gives them meaning.

The research presented here therefore finds its place at the crossroads of several heterogeneous bodies of knowledge, both within and beyond the field of French Studies: feminist literary criticism; gynocriticism; the feminist critique of patriarchal society; the historiography of women's experience of the asylum; clinical writings by psychiatrists and psycho-analysts; and literary analysis of the theme of madness and of writing by 'insane' authors. Each chapter begins with an introductory section

---

[23] Forrester (1980: 20). Freud (1893–5: 30) says: 'She aptly described this procedure, speaking seriously, as a "talking cure", while she referred to it jokingly as "chimney-sweeping".'

outlining the state of historical and literary scholarship in relation to each individual discussed. These texts are approached from a closely textual point of view, in order to draw general conclusions about a specific historical occurrence, and these disparate individuals are viewed as part of a writing tradition inspired by a common source experience.

A project of an interdisciplinary nature has necessary limitations within each of the areas of knowledge to which it contributes. The focus will be on the writings of women, because it can be argued that the way in which male and female patients were treated and pathologized was gender-specific. It therefore says little about the experiences of men under asylum conditions.[24] I do not suggest that men suffered less as a result of acute mental illness and psychiatric treatment, but merely that their words and actions were less likely to be viewed as pathological because they deviated from traditional sex-role stereotypes: these were deeply ingrained in French society through the establishment between 1800 and 1804 of the Napoleonic Civil Code. This gave women the same legal status as minors and the insane, and enshrined in law their subordinate status. Women owed their husbands obedience in exchange for protection, while divorce remained illegal between 1816 and 1884. For unmarried women, birth control was unreliable, abortion risky and illegal, and until 1912 it was impossible to pursue legally the father of a child; women also only gained the right to vote in 1944. Education for women was substandard, and a regular system of secondary education for girls set up as late as 1880.[25] For the latter reason, among others, the textual corpus used here is relatively small: these women were inevitably all bourgeois, educated individuals, despite the fact that illiterate working women made up the majority of the female asylum population.

The rarity of these accounts can be compared to the unusual documents studied by the medieval historian Emmanuel Leroy Ladurie. These were written records of confessions extracted by force from ordinary peasants in the village of Montaillou in the fourteenth century. Such historical sources as these are precious, for rarely do we have access to authentic records presenting the human voice in document: the voice

---

[24] According to Prestwich (1993: 116) many more men than women were admitted to Parisian asylums from 1860 onwards. Roubinovitch (1897: 262) makes the unsubstantiated claim that despite the fact that more men are placed in asylums, there are more madwomen in society.

[25] On the position of women in France during this period, see Zeldin (1973: 343–62); Parry (2002: 106–10); Slama (1980: 219).

of unremarkable, ordinary people that survive only as a result of fortuitous circumstances:

Ce qui manque parfois, c'est le regard direct: le témoignage, sans intermédiaire, que porte le paysan sur lui-même. [. . .] Par chance pour nous, par malchance pour eux, un homme, au XIVe siècle du plein démographique, a donné la parole aux villageois, et même à tout un village en tant que tel.[26]

Although the authors studied here can hardly be said to be unremarkable, these documents are similarly valuable because the vast, silent majority of women who passed through the asylum were never given a voice. The narrative of those incarcerated is rare and precious because, as Chambers identifies, 'sauf quelques rares exceptions [. . .] la parole du fou interné ne parvient pas à l'extérieur'.[27]

   This study also departs significantly from analyses of famous cases of female hysterics, such as the extensive discussion surrounding the case of Freud's 'Dora'.[28] This is because the women studied here exhibited symptoms that place their mental disorders primarily in the realm of what today is termed psychosis and personality disorder, rather than hysteria. The term 'psychosis' describes in clinical language, both psychiatric and psychoanalytical, what is broadly meant by 'madness' and 'insanity' in lay terms. In psychiatric practice it has proven to be an unsatisfactory term, broadly denoting the most severe mental disorders in contrast to the neuroses, which group together 'less serious' mood and emotional disorders. One straightforward criterion of psychosis is the patient's perceived inability to distinguish between subjective experience and reality.[29] This rupture with reality manifests itself in delusional beliefs and ideas that are confused with the shared truths of the sane: notions not recognized as being 'true' by 'normal' people.[30] Psychoanalysis consistently describes psychosis in terms of a major confusion between the 'external world', the shared reality of others, and the 'internal world' of unconsciously held beliefs. Whereas a healthy individual is able to mediate between the internal world and objective

---

[26] Leroy Ladurie (1975: 9).
[27] Chambers (1983: 76).
[28] For a more detailed discussion of this case, see Chapter 3.
[29] Gelder (2001: 90–1).
[30] See also Jeanneret (1980: 61): 'La folie marque dans l'être une rupture radicale; elle correspond à une modification profonde des mécanismes psychiques et entraîne un bouleversement fondamental de la personne, que le psychiatre doit essayer de saisir dans son irréductible différence.'

reality, in the psychotic mind unconsciously held beliefs come to predominate. This results in an absolute turning in on the self and separation from the external world of time, space, reality, and relationships.

A major problem occurs when an appreciation of ideas as 'normal' or 'delusional' is skewed by sexist attitudes, where the truth of an individual's situation is overridden by prejudicial assumptions regarding how she ought to behave, and what she ought reasonably to expect. This study reveals that when, in the cases of female patients, delusional beliefs coexist with a sense of ambition, artistic or personal aspirations could easily be incorporated into a diagnosis of mental illness. Patriarchal society was essentially pathogenic: psychiatric practice was an integral part of that oppressive society, and it disempowered creative and independent-minded women in a comparable way. If the experience of oppression was a contributing factor in psychotic breakdown, and women might literally have sought 'asylum' or refuge in delusional stories about themselves, then treatment in asylums frequently, if paradoxically, exacerbated their problems. The clinical psychologist Dorothy Rowe explains how the process of disbelieving patients can be so damaging:

People who believe that they know what is best for other people are denying other people's truths. Whenever our own truth is denied, ignored or invalidated we experience the greatest fear we can ever know: the threat of the annihilation of our self. Terrible though death is, we can come to terms with the thought of our death when we feel that our lives have significance and that some important part of ourselves—our soul, or our children, or our work—will continue after we are dead. But if our self is annihilated, our life has no significance, for we have never existed, and there is nothing left for us to carry on. Facing this threat, we have to protect ourselves.[31]

It is my contention that a process of self-protection takes place textually in the writings of these four women, in which delusional or disturbed ideas are promoted in order to preserve the self from extinction. The fact that they survive means that, despite their personal tragedies, they found a measure of success.

The psychoanalytical tradition offers useful precedents for any analysis of the writings of psychotic patients. Clinicians have engaged theoretically with the text of the patient: Freud wrote a compelling analysis of the memoir of Judge Schreber; Lacan's doctoral thesis on paranoid

---

[31] Dorothy Rowe, in foreword to Masson (1997: 17).

psychosis bases its assertions on the examination of the case of the patient 'Aimée'; Jung discusses the word associations of his schizophrenic patient Babette Staub, and argues that delusions function as a compensatory defence that makes sense when viewed in the context of the patient's history.[32] Although these analyses are in various ways problematic they can be favourably contrasted to the psychiatric analysis of patients' writings, which does little more than to describe, classify, and prescribe means to pacify. Psychoanalysis, on the other hand, attempts to make sense of the internal world of the writing subject. Indeed, the application of the psychoanalytical model of the mind as a tool of textual analysis will reveal that these texts may be read as 'appropriate' responses to unbearable life situations: if delusions represent a reliable means of preserving the self, and actual reality offers little worth holding on to, it is in the interest of survival that some humans retreat into the internal psychic world.

One explanation offered by the psychoanalytical tradition is indeed that psychosis is a mental process of attempted reparation. As Laplanche has written: 'Psychoanalysis sees the common denominator of the psychoses as lying in a primary disturbance of the libidinal relation to reality; the majority of manifest symptoms, and particularly delusional construction, are accordingly treated as secondary attempts to restore the link with objects.'[33] Psychoanalysis holds that in a 'healthy' mind the ego mediates between the id and reality, but that in psychosis the ego comes under the sway of the id. The weakened ego, having lost contact with the external world, constructs a delusional, 'new' reality in line with the desires of the id. Psychoanalysis therefore offers not only a theoretical model that describes becoming a 'normal' human subject as a process of loss and separation, but also an explanation for the disintegration of the subject that occurs in psychosis; it also gives us a version of subjectivity that ascribes meaning to unconscious thoughts.

A characteristic of the texts presented here is extreme introspection, a turning away from the world and obsessive concentration on the subject's own feelings and beliefs. This peculiar feature sets the texts apart from others in the autobiographical tradition, which as we have seen engage with the world at large and the realms of politics and the family.

---

[32] Freud (1911); Jung (1907); Lacan (1975a).

[33] Laplanche (1988: 370). Laplanche and Pontalis are quoted in English to maintain clarity and consistency of terminology (other psychoanalytical theoretical texts are all cited in English translation).

These authors, too, define themselves in terms of significant others, but these others frequently appear in imaginary form, perhaps as persecutors or long-lost parents in 'family romance' scenarios, with the effect of driving the writing subject further towards the annihilation that she unconsciously dreads. These heterodox voices may therefore appear to exist in isolation: there is no hint of awareness that others might have shared the same experiences. Nevertheless, we shall read these texts as a clear writing tradition that expresses the nature of a common trauma.

Despite their writings technically belonging to different genres, and the authors having different apparent objectives and potential readers, we can read their texts as having a certain communality of purpose in the extent to which they, like other women writers, reflect and offer an indirect commentary on the times in which they lived: a contradictory era of great political upheaval and yet of stasis. Despite the revolutionary nature of nineteenth-century France and the multiple changes of regime, and although some progress was made in the areas of education and divorce legislation, it has been shown that hope for major change in the status of women was repeatedly frustrated.[34] The women studied here experienced severe mental distress as a reaction to the limitations of an unequal society. Their texts offer us a window onto the paradoxically changing and yet enduring dynamic of the times.

These texts can be contextualized within the mainstream literary tradition of the nineteenth-century *roman personnel*, or autobiographical novel. Authors such as Chateaubriand, Constant, and Stendhal presented alienated heroes that embodied the social and political malaise, or *mal du siècle*, experienced by different social groups as a result of the 1789 Revolution, Empire, and the Restoration in 1815. Margaret Waller has convincingly shown that women writers such as George Sand, Germaine de Staël, and Claire de Duras subverted this genre through the creation of heroines whose own *mal du siècle* was feminist in nature, and who can therefore be construed as proto-feminist figures. She argues that Sand's *Lélia* is a work in which 'the exceptional being who embodies the modern malaise is a woman not a man, and her mal du siècle, far from a crisis in male identity, is largely a symptom of her explicitly feminist discontent.'[35] The writings introduced and examined

---

[34] See the two chapters on women's writing in this era by Rosemary Lloyd, 'The Nineteenth Century: Shaping Women' (120–46) and Alex Hughes, '1900–1969: Writing the Void' (147–67) in Stephens (2000).
[35] Waller (1993: 137).

here may be read as following in this tradition of the literary represen-
tation of a specifically feminist malaise. Waller further argues that the 'male malady' of the masculine *mal du siècle* is actually a fiction of impotence that uses 'disabled subjectivity [as] an integral part of an empowering (authorial) male identity'. She contrasts this with the iconoclastic agendas of the female-authored novels: 'The feminocentric novels [...] use the loss of absolutes to criticise the gender and power arrangements of the old and new orders.'[36] In the chapters that follow, we shall examine the way in which the four texts to be analysed follow this radical critical tradition through the commentary they offer on the position of women through the period 1850–1920. As these feminocentric novels are iconoclastic and critical of the limitations society imposed upon women, so the texts composed by female psychiatric patients, which are to some extent delusional, may be read as fictions of empowerment created in response to those same constraints.

Rouy's *Mémoires* is a Second Empire text, composed in the wake of the final dissolution of the French monarchy and the failed Revolution of 1848. In the context of the politically repressive and conservative reign of Napoleon III, dominated by the anti-feminist ideas of thinkers such as Proudhon on the left, and Michelet on the right, Rouy's fragile textual self reflects the frail sense of identity of those abandoned by such a regime, such as women and the remnants of the aristocracy. Esquiron's text is set firmly in the context of the established Third Republic and the Belle Époque. Her determined struggle to be released reflects the femi-nist hopes of the era, and there is some evidence she took an active role in the women's movement.[37] By the time of her writing some progress had been made in the legalization of divorce, enabling Esquiron to at least attempt to free herself from the constraints of a loveless marriage. The writings of Lair Lamotte, although also technically a text of the same relatively stable political period, are different in tone. They are inflected with the despairing memory of the upheavals of the 1870s: the Paris Commune; the humiliation of the Franco-Prussian war and the fall of the Second Empire; the establishment of the Third Republic and its renewed

---

[36] Waller 183; 176.

[37] Marie Esquiron is recorded as having given a speech entitled 'Sur la violation de la loi au détriment des femmes' at the *Congrès français et international du droit des femmes* (Paris: E. Dentu, 1889: 247–8) two years prior to her incarceration. She is named as 'Mme Esquiron (née de Gasté)', confirming it as the same author.

rejection of Catholicism. Claudel's writing was produced in the same context of the relative optimism of the post-1870 era, and her letters also touch upon the later upheaval of the First World War. We shall see that Claudel's attitude reflects the disappointment of cautious, turn-of-the-century French feminism. As Claudel hopes for emancipation, feminists hoped for change and, despite some minor improvements, further reforms were frustrated and, unlike in Great Britain, women failed to gain the vote at the end of the First World War.[38]

In the discussion that follows, we shall see in further detail how each of these writers embodied the frustrations of her era and how she reflected the dynamic of her time through parallels with literary movements and women's writing. As we have seen, Rouy's text can be read as a direct contemporary of Sand and mid-century literary Realism, following closely in the tradition of the feminist *mal du siècle* novel. The later writers, in their concern with late nineteenth-century ideas such as moral degeneration, embody aspects of *fin de siècle* literary traditions such as Decadence and Symbolism.

This volume amalgamates three important strands of research: the writing of women back into literary and social history by bringing to light an important but largely unrecognized writing tradition; aspects of an institutional and disciplinary history of psychiatry and psychoanalysis; and the theoretical perspectives of contemporary and current psychoanalytical theory and radical psychiatry. Close textual analysis is used to examine texts not conventionally viewed as 'literary' in order to suggest that medical history needs to be rewritten from a local point of view, giving the voice of the patient prominence where previously it has been sidelined. Engagement with the patient's account on a textual level reveals the voice of the patient to be a complex linguistic construction that exposes important truths about painful human experiences. As we shall see, many of those who have written sympathetic appraisals of these cases have emphasized those parts of their stories that sound sane. It is my view, however, that the most profound and useful conclusions are reached when the reader appreciates the complexity of a text not easily resolved in the sane mind.

The texts are dealt with in chronological order, according to when they were composed, rather than when they were published. Chapter 1 is a contextualizing and historicizing introduction. It situates the texts in

---

[38] See note 34.

terms of recent historical scholarship on women, madness, and the asylum in France; contemporary psychiatric thinking on 'les écrits des aliéné(e)s'; and the literary context of the 'fou littéraire'. Chapter 2 examines the question of how Hersilie Rouy's *Mémoires* offers simultaneously the inadequate and constrained perspective of a voice in isolation, and that of a dynamic, compelling voice in dialogue. It argues that Rouy succeeds in constructing a vivid description of the exasperating experience of being disbelieved, and produces a document that stands as a convincing indictment of the orthodox means of managing mental illness. Chapter 3 analyses the *Mémoire* of Marie Esquiron, and considers the extent to which the author's claim to insight into her own case is as valid as that of her doctors. It argues that the reasoning process of her incarcerators is fraught with irrational agendas. Chapter 4 focuses on the writings of Pauline Lair Lamotte, a patient of Pierre Janet at the Salpêtrière who went by the name of 'Madeleine Lebouc': it considers how this woman's quasi-mystical writings can be read simultaneously as pathologically introspective, and as a dynamic voice engaged in animated debate with the clinician. Chapter 5 examines the case of the sculptor Camille Claudel, and the fine line she trod between brilliant creativity and devastating mental illness. This chapter considers the paradoxical nature of her text, which presents delusional, paranoid ideas that will be read as metaphorical representations of real experience.

These five chapters consider in detail the way in which these individuals were pathologized, and in some cases how their struggles were exacerbated by the treatment they received. The asylum is overtly or inadvertently presented in these texts as an integral part of a society that oppressed women and made them less than second-class citizens. There is much historical evidence that these institutions were intended to be therapeutic in nature: these memoirs offer verification of the counter-argument that in practice this was far from being the case. In this context, delusional narratives will be read as meaningful utterances, and texts produced by mentally disturbed women can be held to be uniquely insightful despite their manifold internal inconsistencies, paradoxes, and tensions. Complex levels of reality exist in texts too frequently dismissed as purely delusional by medical experts, and these truths can only be appreciated when the hegemony of consciousness and reason is challenged.

1

Women's Writing and Women's Incarceration

Historical and Theoretical Approaches

The law of 1838, the contemporary practice of psychiatry, and the subordinate status of women in wider society all contributed to the creation of social conditions that motivated writing by psychiatric patients. These voices took a heterodox position in relation to the authority of the medical profession, pre-empting later feminist revisionist histories of psychiatry that present nineteenth-century French society as a precipitating environment for the mental suffering of its female citizens. In this preliminary analysis, the texts to be examined in subsequent chapters will be set in their historical context and shown to form a tradition in the history of women's writing in France. A first section, entitled 'Psychiatric medicine and the incarceration of women', will examine the implications for women of the 1838 'loi des aliénés' and some of the specific ways in which nineteenth-century psychiatry was complicit in the oppression of women in French society. The second section will consider the phenomenon of 'les écrits des aliéné(e)s', and will compare and contrast writings produced by men and women under asylum conditions. The third section will consider the precedents set by literary study, which has given a voice to the insane by bringing obscure authors to light. The latter will be examined with particular reference to the theme of writing the experience of madness and the literary tradition of the nineteenth-century 'fou littéraire', as researched by the twentieth-century Surrealist novelist and poet Raymond Queneau.

PSYCHIATRIC MEDICINE AND THE INCARCERATION OF WOMEN

The 1838 *loi des aliénés* stated that each *département* was required to have a public asylum. French alienist medicine had been based in Paris since its inception, and therefore established centres of treatment (or containment) such as Bicêtre, for men, and the Salpêtrière, for women, already existed in the capital city. The aim of the law was to centralize and standardize psychiatric medical practice and for all regions to offer the same possibility of treatment for those afflicted by madness.[1] The new law created two forms of admission: the perhaps misleadingly titled 'placement volontaire', and the 'placement d'office'. In the first case, admission of a person to an asylum was at the request of a relative with the agreement of two doctors: one to certify illness, and one from the medical establishment confirming the diagnosis a fortnight after admission ('certificat de quinzaine'). The second type of admission was effected by police authorities in the case of 'toute personne, interdite ou non interdite, dont l'état d'aliénation compromettrait l'ordre public ou la sûreté des personnes'.[2] In the case of the 'placement volontaire' the patient was not free to leave without the agreement of her family, and in that of the 'placement d'office' without a doctor's assessment that she was 'cured'. The difference between the two forms of admission was in the person of the complainant, and the effect for the patient, if judged insane, was the same.

Coincident with the official creation of the asylum came the blossoming of psychiatry as a new branch of medicine. Although the term 'psychiatrie' only came into use in 1842, its roots lay in the inception of 'alienist' medicine at the end of the eighteenth century, with Philippe

---

[1] Goldstein (1987: 297–9). This commitment to a national network of asylums was theoretical rather than a reality: although the provision of asylums was prescribed, Calemard de Lafayette, a physician and deputy from the Auvergne region, argued while the law was being debated in 1837 that 48 out of the 86 *départements* lacked the resources to provide them. There are still some French *départements* where the obligations of the law were never fulfilled.

[2] A transcription of the 'loi du 30 juin 1838 sur les aliénés' is given in Castel (1976: 316–24) (citation from 319). Ripa (1986b: 18) found that the 'placement d'office' had become the norm by 1853 (80% of all commitments in this year), indicating that most admissions were police decisions, and the majority of asylum residents women who were likely to have contact with the law: prostitutes, the poor, the destitute insane, the disabled, etc.

Pinel's mythical gesture of liberating the mad from their chains, immortalized in the 1849 painting by Charles Muller, displayed in the Académie nationale de médecine in Paris, 'Pinel fait enlever les fers aux aliénés de Bicêtre'.[3] The law of 1838, redefined the 'fou' or 'folle' as 'aliéné(e)', a sick person in need of medical intervention. During the first half of the nineteenth century, much hope was placed in the potential of the 'moral treatment' to cure mental illness. However, with the rise of Bénédict-Augustin Morel's degeneration theory during the more pessimistic post-1848 era, by the later half of the century, when these texts were composed, asylums were moving farther away from the therapeutic ideal of curability and contained an increasingly chronic population.[4]

Traditional 'Whig' histories of psychiatry, which are generally held to have dominated intellectual discussion before the 1950s, view the nineteenth century as a period when psychiatric treatment became more enlightened. Roy Porter and Mark Micale assert: 'Whig narratives were presentist, progressivist, and tenaciously internalist. They typically presented a dual historical movement, from cruelty and barbarism to organized, institutional humanitarianism, and from ignorance, religion, and superstition to modern medical science.'[5] These narratives emphasize the emancipatory role of alienist pioneers such as Pinel and his successor Esquirol in France, and William Tuke in England, who famously introduced the so-called 'moral treatment', which embraced the hope of curability and was supposed to replicate family care, in place of inhumane physical constraints.[6]

However, these views came to be fiercely contested from the 1960s onwards, with voices such as Michel Foucault in France, Thomas Szasz in the United States, and R. D. Laing in the United Kingdom

---

[3] The dictionary *Le Petit Robert* suggests that the term 'psychiatre' dates from 1802, and 'psychiatrie' from 1842. Goldstein (1987: 6–7) points out that the 1802 listing of the term was limited to scholarly discourse, and she found no evidence of the use of the term 'psychiatre' before 1900, and the earliest use of 'psychiatrie' in 1847. Scipion Pinel (1836), son of Philippe Pinel, claims the famous scene of Pinel liberating the mad from their chains occurred in 1792. For a critical analysis of the founding myth of Pinel see Swain (1997: 151–93) and Weiner (1994).

[4] See Morel (1857).

[5] Porter (1994: 6). Such suggestively titled texts as Selling, *Men Against Madness* (1940) and Semelaigne, *Les Pionniers de la psychiatrie française avant et après Pinel* (1930–2) are examples of Whig histories.

[6] See Fournet (1854); Esquirol's discovery was held to be that 'la folie est souvent une maladie purement morale' (Leuret 1841: 3).

presenting revisionist assessments that challenged this vision of the progressive and benign nature of psychiatry. Foucault's central argument is that in the 'Age of Reason', the 'Classical Age' of the seventeenth and eighteenth centuries, the treatment of the mad came to be characterized by exclusion and confinement, and that subsequent nineteenth-century reformers such as Pinel introduced a radically new idea when they equated madness with illness.[7] Foucault further argues that alienist medicine, heavily rooted in the philosophy of the Enlightenment, denied the insane the possibility of true subjectivity. This is because madness entails a rupture with rational thinking, and therefore with true meaning. This view was later challenged by the insights of psychoanalysis, to be discussed later, which validated the non-rational realm of the unconscious.

The trajectory of the asylum began in the seventeenth century with the creation by Louis XIV of the 'hôpital-général' in each city of the realm, and the subsequent great confinement of lunatics, the poor, and vagrants. These establishments had no medical remit, but rather functioned as instruments of social control, alongside the workhouse that was set up in 1764. By the late eighteenth century, the Enlightenment idea of the curability of mental illness became a real possibility.[8] The new asylums of the nineteenth century were intended to be healing spaces, but in reality the legacy of the past proved difficult to shift. The role of the asylum remained ill-defined, and the nature of the 'placement d'office' as a police decision meant that these institutions continued, to some extent, to function as a repository for those rejected by society.[9]

Thomas Szasz and R. D. Laing, in their works of radical psychiatry, *The Myth of Mental Illness* and *The Politics of Experience*, mirrored Foucault's suggestion that the nineteenth century saw the replacement of physical constraints with the sinister, moral control of the asylum that continued into the twentieth century.[10] Szasz argues that mental illness does not exist at all, but is instead a construct designed to control society's unwanted; Laing describes schizophrenia as an appropriate response to living in an insane world. In terms of the nineteenth

---

[7] Foucault (1961).

[8] Goldstein (1987: 41–2).

[9] Ripa (1986b: 17–18) argues that the asylum replaced the 'hôpital–général' and that although its official remit was the treatment of mental illness, it also functioned as a poor house and a hospice for the chronically ill, the disabled, and geriatrics.

[10] Szasz (1961); Laing (1967).

century, Robert Castel brought these radical ideas to the history of French psychiatry in 1976, in his book *L'Ordre psychiatrique*.[11] Castel argues that the insane, as an important locus of post-Revolutionary social disorder, needed to be neutralized by the law and contained within the new social structure of the asylum that conferred upon the mad person the status of a minor. These later revisionist approaches, write Porter and Micale, 'fatally challenged what they perceived as the shallow and idealizing historiography of previous generations and unveiled Whig medical history as the ideology of medical progress that it was'.[12]

In their emphasis on the morally normalizing function of psychiatry, these revisionist accounts have great implications for the assessment of the position of female psychiatric patients in nineteenth-century France. Indeed, feminist writers of history in the 1970s and 1980s were important contributors to this intellectual revision by extending the remit of the approach to examine the specificity of women's experiences at the hands of the psychiatric profession. This approach is exemplified by authors such as historian Yannick Ripa in France, and psychologist Phyllis Chesler in the United States.[13] Chesler's thesis, regarding the nineteenth and twentieth centuries, is that women have been systematically disempowered by psychiatric treatment. She argues that this has been inherently sexist in its refusal to take seriously what women say, and that women are pathologized and punished for deviating from traditional sex-role stereotypes.[14] Similarly, Yannick Ripa's groundbreaking empirical research into women and madness in nineteenth-century France has produced the single most important work of social history, treating the issue of female incarceration in this cultural context. Ripa's conclusion is that psychiatry was a form of medical treatment that was inevitably complicit in the oppression of women in a society that relegated its female citizens to the status of minors.[15]

Ripa's in-depth examination of archive material concerning the incarceration of both sexes between 1838 and 1860 revealed that although women were less likely than men to be placed in asylums, the alienist project allowed women in general to be more easily labelled 'mad'. She argues that this is because the boundaries between normality

---

[11] Castel (1976).
[12] Porter (1994: 8).
[13] Chesler (1974).
[14] Felman (1975: 4) argues that the rhetorical power of Chesler's book comes from the fact that she 'gives voice to the woman'.
[15] Ripa (1983).

and madness were more blurred in the case of women, and the pathological considered closer to the essence of femininity.[16] She notes that,
since men were more immediately essential to the economic functioning
of society, although they were quick to be admitted under the 'placement
d'office' they were also much more likely to be released at the request of
their families. Ripa found that women were easy to replace (through
remarriage, or older female children), and the widowed or single woman's
absence from society did not leave empty any economic function, which
meant they were much less likely to ever leave the asylum.[17]

Crucial to Ripa's findings is the assertion that female madness in
nineteenth-century France was a cultural phenomenon, not a natural
one. This is supported by the discovery that the madness of working
women differed considerably from that of the bourgeois woman. The
medical profession constructed female madness as a logical consequence
of what Ripa terms 'la nature féminine indomptable'. Therefore, 'sou-
mission et passivité sont pour eux synonymes de guérison'.[18]

Female madness was necessarily distinct from its male equivalent, because
as cultural models of normality were based on dissimilar criteria, so the
appreciation of what was deemed pathological or dangerous was different:

la femme normale est une bonne ménagère, attentive à offrir à son époux une
maison accueillante, elle est vouée à rester au foyer pour y élever les enfants dans
les règles et dans la morale définies par la bourgeoisie. Elle ne peut et ne doit être
intéressée ni par la culture, ni par la politique; une instruction minimale lui est
nécessaire pour ne pas être le jeu des préjugés populaires teintés d'une religion
désuète et donner à sa progéniture à travers laquelle elle existe, les bases morales
indispensables.[19]

---

[16] An appreciation of what was considered 'normal' is crucial to understanding
cultural constructs of sickness. Foucault (1963: 36) writes of the nineteenth century:
'Lorsqu'on parlera de la vie de la race, ou même de la "vie psychologique", on ne pensera
pas seulement à la structure interne de *l'être organisé*, mais à *la bipolarité médicale du
normal et du pathologique*.' On the notion of femininity as 'normal pathology' see
Bardwick (1971).
[17] These results are summarized in the conclusion to the thesis (Ripa 1983: 515–18).
Ripa charts the increase in the asylum population after 1838, and the relative numbers of
men to women (p. 8); she shows that every year from 1842 to 1860 a higher proportional
number of men were released than women (on average 13.8 women and 16.83 men for
every 100 patients of each sex) and that from 1854 to 1860 more men than women were
released deemed cured. Men were also marginally more likely to be released even if not
cured (Ripa 1983: 485–7).
[18] Ripa (1983: 517).
[19] Ibid. 518.

Ripa demonstrates that the principle criterion of normality for men was the ability to work: 'En tant que soutien de famille, il est plus vite réclamé par les siens. [...] Être capable de travailler est le critère déterminant pour la sortie d'un aliéné. La femme ne bénéficie pas de cet avantage inattendu!'[20] A man's ability to work was frequently enough to secure his release, whereas a number of other criteria enter the picture for women: 'Chez les femmes, la docilité, l'application au travail, la propreté et les marques d'affection pour leur entourage sont les preuves de la guérison.'[21]

Given these differences in the assessment and treatment of male and female madness, the case histories of our authors are what we might expect them to be. All transgressed the gender stereotypes laid down by patriarchal society in several important ways. All failed in their functions as 'normal' bourgeois women. They were all childless, and we know that Rouy and Claudel engaged in sexual activity outside of marriage, and probably lost infants or had abortions or miscarriages.[22] Rouy, Claudel, and Lamotte were never married, and Esquiron rebelled against the husband she despised and sought to divorce. They were interested in art, culture, and learning and in branching out of the roles carved out for them by society and into the public sphere. Rouy was a talented musician, who studied at the Conservatoire; Claudel was a sculptor of genius; Lamotte was, despite a limited education, a reasonably accomplished writer with an enthusiastic interest in spiritual and theological matters; Esquiron was also a very competent writer and a feminist activist, who sought the freedom to manage her property and investments. It cannot be denied that these were exceptional women. The individual case histories at the beginning of each chapter will show that each of these authors was alienated within society, having failed to meet the requirements of culturally constructed feminine normality, before being alienated from herself through serious mental illness.

---

[20] Ibid. 490.

[21] Ibid. 493. It should also be noted, however, that the relapse rate for men was also slightly higher (48% of women compared to 50% of men in 1853). Ripa (1983: 497) suggests that many men may, therefore, have been released whilst still too vulnerable to manage a successful reintegration into society. Incurability was a deciding factor in the recommendation to continue Rouy's incarceration (Rouy 1883: 443). However, two examples of male authors who were, by contrast, released deemed 'incurable', in the mid-nineteenth century, are Auguste Comte in 1838 (Pickering 1993: 391) and Gérard de Nerval in 1841 (Murat 2001: 70–5).

[22] See the case histories given in Chapter 2 and Chapter 5 for the details of these events.

It would seem that Chesler and Ripa have reached similar conclusions in their studies of the psychiatric treatment of women. The argument that the pathologization of women followed the same pattern as the oppression of women in society at large suggests that there was a special link between the cultural construct that we call 'femininity' and female madness. There is much validity in both these arguments, but as subsequent new historians of the asylum have argued that the picture painted by Chesler is too simplistic a vision of the experience of female psychiatric patients, so Ripa can be shown to present only a part of the story. Discussing the case of the United States, these new historians acknowledge the use of nineteenth-century mental hospitals as a means of social control, and confirm the strongly patriarchal, socially conservative nature of its therapeutic rationale, but reject the suggestion that all clinicians and superintendents were misogynistic or cruel.[23] Indeed, historian Aude Fauvel paints a picture of an institution—the network of asylums in France—buckling under the pressure of increased admissions over the course of the nineteenth century.[24] Although there appears to be some inherent sexism in the way in which women were diagnosed and treated, we should also be wary of suggesting that clinicians were motivated to commit and detain women out of pure misogyny. The aim of the asylum was to cure people, and the fact of overcrowding meant that there was a real possibility of release if deemed healthy. The problem, it seems, is that the idealistic alienist movement of the early part of the century underestimated how difficult it could be to truly cure patients afflicted with mental illness.

The writings examined in this volume are simultaneously exceptional and exemplary, because they confirm the truth of the account given by historians such as Ripa, but they add to it significantly by being evidence of the existence of a strong emancipatory programme. The image depicted by Ripa is a tragic one, and one true for the vast, silent majority of female asylum residents in the period studied. However, there is a more

---

[23] Here I am paraphrasing Nancy Tomes (1994) on the ambiguous account given in the new social histories of the asylum, which did not concentrate solely on the issue of gender. See Dwyer (1988) and McGovern (1986).

[24] Fauvel (2002) brings to light the fascinating case of 'Le crime de Clermont': in 1880, a resident of the asylum at Clermont was murdered by the 'gardien–chef' of the institution. An enquiry was held, and asylum residents were interviewed in exceptional circumstances. Their voices were heard in the absence of their usual intermediary—the psychiatrist. The resulting document provides a unique window onto the experience of incarceration for the patient, and the investigation brought about a wide public debate in the press and among politicians on the reform of the law of 1838.

complex story to be told, and there is arguably more to the truth than oppression and silence. Voices of resistance did manage to make themselves heard, and these acted as crucial precursors to the revisionist account of the social history of the asylum by identifying the same reasons why the trajectory followed by psychiatric medicine in the nineteenth and early twentieth centuries was not entirely enlightened or humanitarian.

'LES ÉCRITS DES ALIÉNÉ(E)S'

It is my contention that the texts uncovered by this research are exceptional, and that it is likely that they are among the only surviving texts of this kind in the French language.[25] Ripa has carried out the principal in-depth, empirical research on this subject and has found that such documents are extremely rare: she mentions the case of Hersilie Rouy, but does not comment at all on the other three authors. In her bibliography she cites just four examples of writing by female psychiatric patients: only two of these are French, and one of them falls outside the time frame of her thesis. In addition, only one example of a letter of complaint penned by a woman, such as that written by Marie Esquiron, is given in her analysis of 'Réactions à l'internement'.[26]

Ripa's analysis of the frequency of writing by psychiatric patients has shown that many more men than women wrote while incarcerated.[27] Because of the destruction in the 1960s of much precious archive material we cannot know exact numbers, but the remaining proportions might be an indicator of how likely it was for female patients to produce protest writing.[28] Ripa proposes three explanations for this: first, higher illiteracy and ignorance of the right to appeal among women; second, the lax application of the law by asylum authorities (although this does

---

[25] Some contemporary examples of 'madness narratives' from the United States are Metcalf (1876); Smith (1879); Packard (1866); and Lathrop (1890) (discussed in Hubert 2002).

[26] Ripa (1983: cxxxvii) cites in her bibliography only the cases of the Americans Elizabeth Packard (1866) and Zelda Fitzgerald, Hersilie Rouy's *Mémoires*, and the letters of Camille Claudel as examples of writing by patients.

[27] This is confirmed in Séglas (1892: 204): 'D'une façon générale on peut dire que les fous écrivent beaucoup [. . .] Les femmes écrivent beaucoup moins que les hommes et leurs écrits revêtent le plus généralement la forme de lettres, qui est, d'ailleurs, plus en rapport avec leur caractère, leur éducation antérieure.' He terms such patients 'graphomanes'.

[28] The Archives de la Préfecture de police destroyed a large number of records relating to asylums in 1961. This is confirmed in Ripa (1983: cxiii).

not explain why the same would not be true of male patients); third, the suggestion that women, already used to their subordinate position in society, accepted more readily their diagnoses and chose more covert means of revolt if they did protest. It was also found to be the case that men were generally more likely to exhibit insubordinate behaviour; for example, men's attempts to escape from Bicêtre were more common than similar behaviour from their female counterparts at the Salpêtrière.[29]

This confirms the initial proposition that these texts are exceptional rather than representative of the self-expression allowed most women under these conditions. They also survive as the result of fortuitous circumstances: Hersilie Rouy found a protector who published her memoirs; Marie Esquiron had sufficient personal wealth to publish her story; Pauline Lair Lamotte was the subject of the intense fascination of a famous clinician, who subsequently published some of her writing; Camille Claudel's fame, and indeed that of her brother and her lover, ensured that care has been taken over the years to conserve and publish her correspondence where others' has fallen into obscurity.

Such writings also provide case-historical material for psychiatric treatises, and while historians highlight the need for historiography to take account of the point of view of the patient, few serious studies of this kind have been attempted, and in psychiatric writing the patient's utterances are rarely acknowledged as indicative of any level of reality. Theodore Zeldin acknowledges that 'medical history is inevitably written largely from the point of view of the progress of knowledge; it tells more about the doctor than the patient, and it is more concerned with general demographic results than with the details of how individuals bore their sufferings'.[30] We shall see an example of this in Chapter 2, where I discuss how Rouy's memoirs were used widely as evidence in emergent discussions of what came to be called paranoia, the 'délire

---

[29] Ripa 1983: 457–8.

[30] Several historians have highlighted this lacuna in writing the history of the mad. See Zeldin (1977: 823) and Goldstein (1987: xii): 'They [the patients] deserve a book of their own, but in this book they appear only as the objects from which a science of psychiatry was drawn.' Porter (2002: 161) also urges historians to listen to the voice of the patient: 'In his *The Interior of Bethlehem Hospital* (1818), Urbane Metcalf, a former inmate who claimed he was heir to the Danish throne, painted Bethlehem as corrupt and brutalizing. For their part, the Hospital's records identify him as a troublemaker. In such cases, historians must read between the lines and judge for themselves: contested readings of reality afford windows on to inter-subjectivities that never were univocal.'

d'interprétation'.[31] Women's writing was, in addition, unlikely to be viewed as accomplished. Using the example of the Swedish author August Strindberg, writer of an autobiographical memoir entitled *Plaidoyer d'un fou*, Sérieux and Capgras argue: 'l'éclosion d'un délire d'interprétation, même très actif, n'est nullement incompatible avec l'existence des plus brillantes qualités intellectuelles. Raison et délire marchent ici de pair, génie et folie peuvent même s'associer'.[32] There do not appear to be any examples of such parallels being made in the case of women's writing, and Sérieux and Capgras's analysis of Rouy's *Mémoires*, as we shall see in Chapter 2, is not so flattering.

The writings of Lamotte are one of the central sources of information for the formulation of Pierre Janet's ideas on belief and feelings, and in particular his theory of 'délire psychasthénique'. Claudel's writing has been the subject of retrospective diagnosis by present-day psychiatrists, and Esquiron's memoir could conceivably receive the same treatment, but has been little studied. Patients' spoken and written utterances were an important indicator of the manifestation of mental disturbance. As such they were frequently used in the formulation of ideas about mental pathology, but not in the appreciation of the human experiences that lay behind them.

The vast majority of writing by male patients did not enjoy comparisons with uniquely insightful states of mind such as genius, however, and psychiatry would have us believe that the delusions at the centre of such texts are symptomatic of illness, and not indicative of reality. Authors of medical treatises tell us that paranoid patients, 'persécutés', are often plausible and apparently sane to the untrained observer. Since it is the doctors themselves who are frequently held to be part of the conspiratorial system, it seems to have been in their interest to play down complaints by patients if they were to protect their profession from accusations of misconduct.[33] Writing by females, however,

---

[31] Sérieux and Capgras (1909: 351–66) refer extensively to patients' written productions in their explanation of the theory of 'la folie raisonnante'. Particular examples are given in an appendix entitled 'Le délire d'interprétation dans quelques œuvres littéraires', which cites Strindberg's *Plaidoyer d'un fou* (1895) and *Inferno* (1898), which is 'écrit sous forme de mémoires' (355).

[32] Ibid. 366.

[33] A text by a male 'persécuté' frequently cited is an 1821 text by Berbiguier de Terre-Neuve du Thym (1990), *Les Farfadets, ou Tous les démons ne sont pas de l'autre monde*, in which a patient of Pinel narrates in intricate detail his perceived life-long persecution by superior figures—kings, princes, and emperors—called 'farfadets' and described as agents of Satan. His doctor, unable to cure him, is placed at the head of this persecutory

appears as doubly pathological, because the process of writing and creating was for them considered an unnatural activity, being tradition-ally viewed as the unique preserve of men. Some interesting case studies appear in a treatise by Morel in 1860, in which he outlines the specific dangers of intellectual hyperactivity in women, which, as we shall see in Chapter 3, is also a concern of the doctors who treated Esquiron. In a discussion of his '*Observation de tendances maladives d'excentricités, de délires dans les actes, développées chez les femmes sous l'influence de l'élément héréditaire*', Morel lists three case studies of women who used their writing skills in ways deemed inappropriate. 'Madame Charlotte P . . .' is a young woman who developed 'masculine' tastes early, such as drinking and hunting with her father, and who is guilty of leaving her husband without valid reason. She subsequently 'fabriquait elle-même des lettres renfermant des déclarations d'un amour excentrique, désordonné, et qu'elle supposait lui avoir été écrites par des personnages distingués'.[34] 'Madame P . . .' is further chastised for her literary ambitions:

Elle se fit auteur elle-même, et publia des romans dont le style, les idées et les sentiments reflétaient les dispositions maladives de son esprit, et qui, il faut le dire à la honte d'une époque avide de productions de ce genre, trouvèrent des lecteurs et même des admirateurs. M. P . . . eut beaucoup de peine à faire renfermer sa femme, dont les réponses *lucides et raisonnables* ne semblaient pouvoir donner prise à un diagnostic de folie.[35]

This patient proved recalcitrant when forced to undergo treatment, and set to work creating 'projets chimériques, récriminations de toutes sortes contre son mari et sa famille, rédaction de lettres, de mémoires pour prouver qu'elle n'était pas aliénée'.[36]

---

hierarchy. His case is discussed in Legrand du Saulle (1871: 365–7) and Lévy-Valensi (1911). Another case is Léon Sandon, *Plaidoyer de Me Léon Sandon, avocat, ancien avocat général, contre les médecins Tardieu, Blanche, Parchappe, Foville, Baillarger & Mitivié, prononcé à Paris, devant la Première Chambre, le 9 mai 1865*). Sandon (1865: 3–4) writes: 'Je plaide donc contre les médecins qui m'ont fait mettre à Charenton, Je soutiens que leur certificat qui me déclarait atteint de délire ambitieux, de tics nerveux, de paralysie, de perte de sens commun était le produit d'une erreur grave, le produit de leur servilité, de leur complaisance coupable envers un ministre tout–puissant.' See also Foucault (1973) and Maître (1994) for discussions of mental disturbance and its autobiographical expression.

[34] Morel (1860): 555–6. This assessment resonates with the suspicion with which doctors treat Rouy's claims of associations with distinguished persons, as we shall see in Chapter 2.

[35] Ibid. 556.

[36] Ibid.

Another patient, 'Madame C...', compromised the comfortable position of her husband with her verbal creations: 'Madame C...alla jusqu'à écrire au procureur impérial que son mari se rendait coupable de malversations.' She was confined to the asylum because, in line with Ripa's assessment of women's societal function, of the 'impossibilité de se conduire sensément au dehors et d'élever ses enfants, en raison [...] d'un véritable trouble des sentiments qui ne peut qu'exercer une action funeste sur la santé des enfants'.[37] Other women patients are also presented as inexhaustible in the erroneous deployment of their intellectual faculties, such as 'Madame X...', who acts as advocate in the fight against asylum authorities on behalf of weaker, illiterate patients:

Elle recevait leurs plaintes, leurs réclamations, rédigeait pour ses compagnes d'infortune des lettres, des mémoires, comme aurait pu faire le meilleur avocat; elle analysait, commentait les motifs qui les faisaient agir, rectifiait parfois leurs erreurs de perception avec une lucidité et un bon sens qui nous étonnaient; [...] elle était, en un mot, dévorée d'une activité fébrile qui surexcitait ses facultés intellectuelles.[38]

All of these women were daughters of mad mothers, so Morel's conclusion is predictable: 'La transmission héréditaire des tendances maladives délirantes similaires m'a paru plus complète chez les femmes que chez les hommes.'[39] In blaming hereditary degeneracy, no mention is made of the possibility that the repetition of the oppressive social conditions of mothers in the next generation could result in the same mental health problems being exacerbated by the intolerance of women's intellectual activity. Morel, like so many of his contemporaries and successors, did not understand the fundamental frustrations of women's existence: 'Quelques-unes, sans commettre aucun de ces actes répréhensibles, étaient incitées, *poussées*, comme elles disent, à quitter leurs maris, leurs enfants, leur famille, et à changer de milieu sans but préconçu.'[40] It was beyond the bounds of possibility that women might be less than satisfied with the narrow role dictated by society: as Germaine Greer would assert a century later, 'The housewives' life is not real. [...] The refusal to accept this as a rewarding life is not a refusal to accept reality.'[41] These examples are the postulations of just one psychiatric thinker, but they are representative to

---

[37] Ibid. 557–8.
[38] Ibid. 559.
[39] Ibid.
[40] Ibid. 560.
[41] Greer (1999: 312).

a great extent of the profession as a whole. We shall see this attitude reflected in comments made by numerous doctors about the individual cases presented here. This might corroborate Ripa's suggestion that the boundaries between what was considered normal and pathological were more fluid and ambiguous in the cases of women. One clear example of this is the abundance of female case studies—which far outnumber those of men—in analyses of hybrid and borderline forms of madness, such as Ulysse Trélat's *La Folie lucide*.[42]

In alienist discourse we find a paradoxical attitude towards the writing of patients: on the one hand, as in the case of Rouy, writing is prohibited completely; on the other, writing by patients is seen as a useful diagnostic tool. Since patients are often held to 'dissimulate' when speaking to doctors, for fear that they will not be believed, it is commonly noted that the patient's writing is sometimes the place where delusions show up most clearly. Pinel first noted this tendency in 1800, observing that 'la crainte de se trahir leur inspire une sorte de réserve', and the theme of dissimulation in the verbal communications of 'les aliénés' became commonplace in psychiatric literature in the nineteenth century.[43] Marcé notes that the patient is frequently pulled in two directions: either wanting to express herself to the world at large, or seeking to conceal as much as possible her verbal output:

[Ils] rédigent ces lettres, ces pétitions, ces mémoires volumineux, dans lesquels ils exposent leurs réclamations, leurs griefs, leurs souffrances et la longue série de persécutions dont ils sont l'objet. [. . .] Tantôt les malades les adressent aux autorités, aux personnages en vue, aux hommes d'affaires, à tous ce qu'ils rencontrent; tantôt, au contraire, ils les cachent au fond de leurs poches, dans la doublure de leurs vêtements, dans la profondeur de leurs armoires, attachant une importance mystérieuse aux faits qu'ils ont révélés et qu'ils veulent cacher à tous les regards.[44]

And Legrand du Saulle describes how he encouraged patients to write in order to assess their states of mind:

Lorsque je me trouve en présence d'un malade qui s'observe, se contient et se défie, je temporise, je fais laisser à sa disposition du papier, des plumes et de

---

[42] Trélat (1861).

[43] Pinel (1800: III).

[44] Marcé (1864: 87). On the question of delusional complaints and the widespread accusation of 'séquestration arbitraire' see also Legrand du Saulle (1871: 362–4); Séglas (1892: 217); and Simon (1888: 322), who notes 'Les persécutés sont les plus prodigieux consommateurs de lettres, cahiers, carnets que contiennent les asiles'.

l'encre, et j'attends. Au bout d'une heure ou au bout de huit jours, quelques phénomènes d'excitation intellectuelle apparaissent, et un irrésistible besoin d'expansion remplace la fausse attitude théâtrale.[45]

Standard practice seems to have been that once such evidence was produced, writing by patients was actively discouraged and even prohibited: written expression was used as a diagnostic and not a therapeutic tool. Rouy's account of her treatment in the asylum corroborates this, and indicates why patients may have sought to hide their writings, among their only possessions in a depersonalizing space:

Ne pouvant comprendre par quel moyen j'avais écrit [...], on poussait les fouilles jusqu'à emporter mes jupons, à peigner mes cheveux bouclés, à écarter les bouffettes de mes pantoufles, afin de s'assurer qu'un bec de plume ou un crayon n'y était pas caché. Les malades [...] me donnaient des chiffons de papier, en les attachant à un fil que je faisais descendre par ma fenêtre; d'autres m'en glissaient sous la porte en passant dans le corridor. Je collais ces morceaux ensemble; à défaut d'encre, j'avais mon sang.[46]

Given the sheer level of adversity involved in trying to write under such conditions, it seems an astonishing feat that Rouy ever managed to publish her memoirs. This final act of emancipation came, ironically, after her death and was effected by a male protector.[47]

The picture created by clinicians about the verbal productions of patients is that, despite its strictures, protest writing was rather common. Indeed, it is unsurprising that some of those who engaged in this activity took their protest to the level of publishing their stories: 'Il est beaucoup d'adhérés qui ne se contentent pas d'écrire, mais qui font imprimer leurs productions.'[48] We shall see in the next section of this chapter that the publishing of these stories aligns our authors with writers outside the confines of the asylum, and blurs the distinction between authors considered insane and those judged merely eccentric or bizarre, all subsumed in the category of the 'fou littéraire'.

What this brief excursus on the subject of writing by psychiatric patients allows us to provisionally assert is that the texts studied here are both typical and original. They tell a story of the injustices and

---

[45] Legrand du Saulle (1871: 334–5).

[46] Rouy (1883: 137–8).

[47] See the introduction to Chapter 2 for more information regarding the publication of Rouy's memoirs.

[48] Séglas (1892: 224).

miseries of the asylum that has been told repeatedly by both men and women through the whole history of the institution. However, they are also unique voices, simply due to the fact that they survive, having resisted attempts to silence them. They are typical because it has been observed that such patients wrote a huge amount, and because it was not uncommon for them to seek to publish their accounts; they are original because women allegedly wrote far less than men, and were less likely to write memoirs. In the cases of those texts that did come to the attention of clinicians and theoreticians, the process of writing was never validated as a therapeutic or emancipatory process: it was only judged as evidence of symptoms then placed within classificatory frameworks of mental pathology. In the course of this research no examples were found in psychiatric discourse, prior to the twentieth century, of clinicians attempting to make sense of delusions as meaningful human utterances. Although such theorists thought it necessary, when faced with a delusional individual, to 'entrer dans son délire', this was viewed as a means to a diagnostic end, and most diagnoses predicted the onset of dementia.[49]

LITERARY PRECEDENTS: VALIDATING THE 'INSANE'

Jules Séglas notes that the publishing of writing by those patients who would later be called 'revendicateurs' by Sérieux and Capgras was common:

Les malades qui portent [. . .] leurs œuvres à la connaissance du public, y sont généralement poussés par deux ordres d'idées, des idées de persécution ou des idées de grandeur. Leur but est d'exposer, par exemple, des découvertes de tout genre: inventions, théories politiques, religieuses, scientifiques, etc. . . . ou d'attirer l'attention générale sur les souffrances qu'ils endurent, sur les manœuvres de leurs ennemis. Ces imprimés revêtent toutes les formes possibles: affiches, articles de journaux, recueils de poésies, de chansons, brochures, romans, autobiographies en un ou plusieurs volumes. On y retrouve la plupart des particularités que nous venons d'exposer.[50]

Into this category fall the writings of Rouy and Esquiron, who went to considerable lengths to make sure that their texts were published in

---

[49] Lachaux (1893: 77).
[50] Séglas (1892: 224).

some form. This fact places our texts on a continuum of literary production, which ranges from the certified, incarcerated insane to those in the outside world considered mad: the 'borderline' mad and eccentrics who evaded the asylum. These texts embody proto-feminist, anti-psychiatric voices, and prefigure later literary figures and movements critical of psychiatry, such as André Breton and the Surrealists.[51] As iconoclastic voices they can also be aligned with women writers who spoke out against the patriarchal establishment, and who encountered the hostility of its members.[52]

An article that appeared in the revue *La Révolution surréaliste* in 1925, entitled 'Lettre aux Médecins-Chefs des Asiles de Fous', argues against the arbitrary powers of psychiatric medicine and in favour of the view that madness is a legitimate human experience that ought to be validated, not punished:

On sait,—on ne sait pas assez—que les asiles loin d'être des *asiles*, sont d'effroyables geôles, ou les détenus fournissent une main-d'œuvre gratuite et commode, ou les sévices sont la règle, et cela est toléré par vous. [. . .]

Nous affirmons qu'un grand nombre de vos pensionnaires, parfaitement fous suivant la définition officielle, sont, eux aussi, arbitrairement internés. Nous n'admettons pas qu'on entrave le libre développement d'un délire, aussi légitime, aussi logique que tout autre succession d'idées ou d'actes humains.[53]

This category of writers has been transformed into a nineteenth-century literary tradition by Raymond Queneau, in his analysis of what he terms 'fous littéraires' in *Les Enfants du limon*.[54] His research into the writings of unconventional and 'mad' authors searches out the likelihood of inspired genius in such works, but ultimately abandons this possibility, concluding that they are, for the most part, misguided eccentrics. In this conclusion, Queneau departs from the assertions of the Surrealists who inspired him by actually reinforcing the view of the medical profession: that there is no value in listening to these voices. Following this attempt, André Blavier created a form of encyclopaedia of 'fous littéraires',

---

[51] As well as the letter cited below, the *Second manifeste du Surréalisme* (Breton 1930: 850–63) is followed by an important critique of psychiatry through André Breton and Paul Éluard's 'Essai[s] de simulation' of various forms of mental illness.

[52] Specific parallels with other literary women writers will be drawn in subsequent chapters.

[53] Breton (1925).

[54] Queneau (1938). Similar cataloguing of eccentrics was carried out by Champfleury (1852). See also Gill (2009) for a discussion of the cultural phenomenon of eccentricity in France.

dividing the authors studied into categories such as: 'Cosmogones, philosophes de la "nature"'; 'Prophètes, visionnaires et messies'; 'Persécutés, persécuteurs et faiseurs d'histoires'; 'Les savants'; 'Médecins et hygiénistes'; 'Inventeurs et bricoleurs'; 'Romanciers et poètes'; and writers who comment on 'La condition asilaire'.[55]

Hersilie Rouy is mentioned in the last category, and our three remaining authors are not mentioned at all. This is possibly because only Rouy and Esquiron were published, and because the latter's memoir was not rediscovered until 2001. Some other women authors from this period mentioned in *Les Fous littéraires*, who were considered cranks by many but never certified insane, and who wrote and published their own work, are science writers Céline Renooz and Clémence Royer.[56] These two authors are mentioned in the section dedicated to 'Cosmogones, philosophes de la "nature"', and were active between the late 1880s and the early 1900s. Royer was, according to Blavier, a 'femme d'un rare génie pour certains, hétéroclite pour d'autres' whose writings 'réfute[nt] la théorie de l'attraction universelle, au bénéfice de la répulsion mutuelle des éléments cosmiques'.[57] Renooz also published an article in the journal *La Religion laïque* in 1888, in which she describes a quasi-mystical—though not specifically 'religious'—experience of 'révélation', where she receives inspirational ideas about certain aspects of evolutionary theory without the aid of scientific experimentation and observation.[58] The common ground between these perhaps spurious scientific writings and the writing produced by psychiatric patients is the feeling of isolation they evoke, and the sense of frustration experienced by women whose ideas, deemed eccentric or categorically deluded, were dismissed by the male establishment. Royer is quoted as complaining of the lack of interest in new ideas

---

[55] Blavier (1982: 7).

[56] Works by these authors quoted in Blavier are Clémence Royer, *La Constitution du monde. Dynamique des atomes. Nouveaux principes de philosophie naturelle* (1900) and Céline Renooz, *La Force* (1895), which among other points argues that electricity is composed of oxygen and that carbon is not an element but a form of nitrogen.

[57] Blavier (1982: 280–1).

[58] Renooz (1888: 267). Some of Renooz's arguments are that science should become more 'feminine', in other words less empirical, and that Darwin's theory of the origin of species is fundamentally flawed. James Smith Allen (1999: 282) argues that she echoes other critiques of positivism: '[H]er version of evolution was symbiotic and functional rather than competitive and conflictual. Nature for her was not animals fighting for survival but plants cooperating in harmony. [. . .] Renooz's early anti–Darwinism was at the heart of a new scientific epistemology, one of many similar critiques of nineteenth-century positivism.'

by other scientists: 'Je me heurte partout à l'indifférence ou au mauvais vouloir de nos savants officiels, qui ne semblent pas vouloir admettre que je puisse avoir quelque chose à leur apprendre et que j'aie trouvé une vérité qu'ils ignorent.'[59] Similarly, Renooz's article, inflected with a latent inflation of the importance of her ideas, demonstrates an awareness that her ideas will not be universally accepted or understood:

Bientôt, le besoin de communiquer à d'autres la grande nouvelle, commença à me tourmenter. [...] Mais personne autour de moi, ne pouvait comprendre l'état de mon esprit. Ceux qui m'entouraient, des gens du monde ou des bourgeois, peu instruits—des femmes surtout—tous, étrangers aux études que j'avais entreprises, m'auraient certainement accusée de folie, si j'en avais parlé. Je savais qu'à une époque de scepticisme comme la nôtre, le récit que je fais ici, serait d'abord accueilli par l'incrédulité, la raillerie, je savais que je ne pourrais être comprise que par les personnes—peu nombreuses—d'une intelligence très élevée.[60]

It remains the predictable fact, however, that there were many more 'misguided' scientific opinions proposed by male thinkers. This is evidenced in the fact that the overwhelming majority of the authors catalogued by Blavier are 'fous littéraires' rather than 'folles littéraires'.[61] Few of the women writers cited in this volume were ever incarcerated, and the close parallels between eccentric texts and those produced by asylum patients, such as Hersilie Rouy, suggest that it was possible for mentally disturbed women to function reasonably successfully in the outside world. Their desire to be released ought therefore to have been recognized, even if not all their beliefs could be said to be true. One of the recurring themes in my discussion will be that, to an important extent, these women knew themselves and their own needs better than their 'carers'.

Indeed, what might be termed writing the experience of madness was, it would seem, a far more problematic enterprise for women. The female insane could not afford to have insight into their own madness

---

[59] Blavier (1982: 280).

[60] Renooz (1888: 267).

[61] In a nine-hundred-page catalogue of examples of 'fous littéraires', only thirty examples of women's writing are given. These include the authors already mentioned. Some other examples of 'folles littéraires' in the period here studied are Fontaine (1852); Fusnot (1854); Hanin (1934); Jomiaux (1895); Jousselin (1895); Saint-Rémy (veuve Teissier) (1899). Two other cases, Sophie Adélaïde and Maria Stella Chiappini, whose writings are examples of 'délire de revendication de filiation' are discussed in Chapter 2 in relation to Hersilie Rouy.

because the implications of this realization were more far-reaching than for men. The fact that we do not read these authors now is not because their voices did not formulate convincing discourses of resistance. Rather, it is because they were suppressed during their time and they are suppressed now. James Smith Allen, commenting on Céline Renooz's autobiographical writings, argues that madness or eccentricity is no reason not to listen to these voices:

Ultimately [...] posterity's judgment of Renooz and her ideas does not matter. Marginal, eccentric, paranoid—whatever the adjective—Renooz was no more so than many of her better-known contemporaries. Just a generation earlier these same terms apply to Auguste Comte, for example, whose colleagues at the École polytechnique disdained him, whose spiritualist visions he systematized, and whose erratic behaviour required institutional treatment.[62]

Just as Comte could be much derided and yet is now still widely read, while authors such as Renooz never emerged out of their obscurity, literary writers such as Gérard de Nerval are judged to have produced highly significant works despite, and partly because of, mental disturbance. Nerval's *Aurélia* is the archetypal 'journal de folie', in which is traced one individual's descent into the recesses of an acutely disturbed mind is traced. Dr Blanche is said to have commented that through this narrative, Nerval 'voyait sa folie face à face', and as a man who was able more easily to embrace the possibility of the 'cure', Nerval is allowed the possibility of looking back on the experience with insight, and of seeing the true nature of his waking dream.[63] By contrast, female authors such as those studied here seem less likely to have this healing insight, for to own one's madness had different consequences for single, isolated women without the support of a family network and no economic or public artistic function in the world.

The findings of this opening analysis suggest that these texts function as the vehicles of exceptional voices for a constellation of reasons. First, it seems that women suffering from borderline forms of madness were more likely than men to find themselves committed to the asylum. This, as we shall see in subsequent chapters, is due in part to the role of the

---

[62] Smith Allen (1999: 295–6).

[63] Gérard de Nerval, 'Aurélia' (1966: lxiii). The editor notes: 'S'il est vrai que la destinée et par conséquent l'œuvre de Gérard sont essentiellement marquées d'une dualité cyclique, le parcours dont *Aurélia* retrace le mouvement rassemblé est bien ce cycle achevé du rêve et de la vie, de la démence et de la conscience, du désespoir et de la foi, du mystère et de la lucidité.' (751).

patriarchal family in decision making regarding its female members. Second, women who were incarcerated were less likely to write, more likely to be prohibited from writing if they did, and stood less chance of being released and therefore of being able to tell their stories. We can assert at this stage that male and female discourses of the asylum— emanating from patients and clinicians—differ in their extremity: women's narratives are clustered around the borderline, and men's are placed at the extremes of delusion (patients) and reason (doctors). Women like Rouy and Esquiron, in this respect, followed stereotypically male patterns of authorship, while ones such as Claudel and Lamotte created textual productions more in line with the stereotype of women's personal writing, such as letters and diaries. Because of the likelihood of female-authored texts to be more 'borderline' in nature, in other words less transparently delusional but also less sane sounding than the writings of their incarcerators, they stand as subtle, bewildering utterances in which the distinction between reality and madness cannot easily be drawn. In psychoanalytical terms, the confusion between the external and internal worlds of the subject that psychosis entails is less complete, in these cases at least, and the retrospective insights afforded by recovery are less accessible because the distance between sickness and the cultural construct of feminine normality is not so great.

2

Mémoires d'une aliénée by Hersilie Rouy

'Où est la folie là-dedans?'

Mémoires d'une aliénée by Hersilie Rouy, published posthumously in 1883, is a first-hand account of the experience of treatment in French psychiatric hospitals between 1854 and 1868. It tells the story of a Parisian musician who for fourteen years was detained against her will, at the request of her family, in six different asylums in Paris and the surrounding provinces. All the time vociferously denying she was insane, from the moment she was incarcerated until the day she died she fought for her sanity to be recognized and to pursue legally those responsible for her committal. Having been declared illegitimate by her family, in the asylum this woman was robbed of the surname she had always held, and the vestiges of a fragile sense of identity were systematically obliterated by the pathologizing methods of alienist medicine. Doctors despaired of her rebellious behaviour, and were wearied by her intransigence in protest against the authority of the medical profession.[1] After her release, Rouy dedicated the remainder of her life to writing up her memoirs for publication and fighting for

---

[1]   In the part of this chapter that deals with a close analysis of the text, I refer to the author and first-person narrator as 'Hersilie' because among the names she is given (or gives herself) this one is the most stable indicator of her identity. The current discussion of this case owes much to the previous work of Matlock (1991); Ripa (1983, 1986a, b); Roche (1998); Soulayrol (1988); and Cura (1993).

Édouard Le Normant des Varannes, 'receveur des hospices' at Orléans asylum, would become Hersilie's protector and most crucial ally (273, 362). He published Hersilie's text as *Mémoires d'une feuille de papier écrits par elle-même* a year previously in 1882 under the pseudonym Édouard Burton. The title given refers to the little scraps of paper used by Hersilie to write whilst incarcerated, and is mentioned in the preface to *Mémoires d'une aliénée* as her chosen title (iii). Its young heroine, a musician called Eucharis Champigny, is locked away in an asylum and passed off as dead by her family. This considerably stranger, fictionalized version of Hersilie's memoirs develops at length the 'family romance' scenario presented in a toned-down version in the later text.

compensation, which eventually she won. She died on 27 September 1881, and was buried with the name she fought to retain and the recognition that she was her father's legitimate daughter.[2] The allegation of false commitment made in *Mémoires d'une aliénée* caused quite a stir at the time in both the press and the psychiatric establishment. Unlike most of her female contemporaries in the asylum, Rouy was vindicated: declared 'cured' (despite also having been judged incurable), released, and compensated for her troubles.[3]

The most informative primary material regarding this case can be drawn from two distinctly different sources: Hersilie's own *Mémoires*, and an article published in 1910 by psychiatrists Sérieux and Capgras, entitled 'Roman et vie d'une fausse princesse'.[4] These present radically different accounts of the same story, from two perilously problematic points of view: one written from memory by a person deemed insane, the other from medical case notes by doctors concerned with sustaining the credibility of the psychiatric profession in the face of widespread public criticism of the handling of the case. Taking these heterogeneous documents together we can attempt to establish something resembling a reliable biographical picture concerning the case of Hersilie Rouy.

Hersilie's story, which is in a state of flux throughout the text, is initially that she was born in Milan in 1814 to French parents. Her father, Charles Rouy, was an astronomer who had worked all over Europe, eventually settling in Paris in 1823. He had an older son from a previous marriage, Claude-Daniel, and Hersilie was the eldest of five subsequent children. Their mother died in 1830, and in 1845 Hersilie's sister Dorothée married Jean Rouy, son of Claude-Daniel and her own half-nephew, having apparently been given a 'reconnaissance d'enfant naturel', thereby suggesting some irregularity concerning the parents' relationship (1–11). Hersilie does not explain further, and

---

[2] The editor of Hersilie's *Mémoires* writes: 'Elle fut déclarée fille légitime dans son acte de décès, à la mairie comme à l'église' (491).

[3] A significant public debate ensued surrounding this case. *France Médicale* published a piece defending the health professionals concerned on 12 August 1871, and a response from Hersilie Rouy was also printed (369–73). Francis Magnard wrote in the *Figaro*, 28 July 1871: 'Une demoiselle Hersilie Rouy, pianiste de talent, qui, en 1854, fut enfermée à Charenton, *sous le nom de Joséphine Chevalier*. Quatorze ans se passèrent sans que la malheureuse, colportée d'asile en asile, pût faire entendre ses réclamations' (363–73). The favourable reaction of the press is also noted elsewhere: 'Les journaux de la région narrent les odieuses persécutions subies par cette victime d'une déplorable erreur, d'un crime inouï. Elle devient l'héroïne du jour' (Sérieux 1910: 221).

[4] Sérieux (1910).

indeed her version of events does leave a number of gaps. By the time Charles Rouy died in 1848, Hersilie had fallen out with her siblings over her right to inherit, and eventually severed ties with her family (24–30).[5]

Hersilie was a talented pianist, and had studied at the Conservatoire from the age of ten. At the time of her incarceration she was working as a musician, teaching and giving private concerts. However, feeling let down by her family she grew increasingly fearful of the outside world. A series of strange events led Hersilie to believe that someone wanted rid of her, to put her in an asylum and pass her off as dead. As if in fulfilment of her own prophecy, an unknown man took her from her home on 8 September 1854, and admitted her as a 'placement volontaire' to the private asylum at Charenton (50, 80). On 30 November of the same year she was transferred to the Salpêtrière and admitted as a 'placement d'office' under the name 'Chevalier-Rouy', a name that she had never had and which she refused to acknowledge, protesting that she had been admitted under a false name (87, 96–8). According to the 'pièces justificatives' reproduced at the end of the *Mémoires*, which record her mother's maiden name as 'Chevalier', the conferral of this name is not as arbitrary as is suggested. Hersilie's complaint of 'séquestration arbitraire' was, however, at this point entirely justified: it would later transpire that her admission to Charenton was technically illegal according to the law of 1838. There were two administrative irregularities in this case: first, the 'certificat d'internement' was signed by the same doctor who admitted Rouy, when the law required that one doctor certify illness, and a different person request admission; second, this Doctor Pelletan was unknown to Hersilie, and not a friend as the admission records note.[6] This error would enable Hersilie to mobilize a campaign that resulted in her definitive release fourteen years later.[7]

---

[5] Of the six children mentioned, only three survived (2). The two remaining siblings are Claude-Daniel, a legitimate son and Hersilie's half-brother, and Dorothée, who managed to secure herself the name of Rouy by marrying a relation.

[6] Ripa (1986a: 76).

[7] Sérieux (1909: 386). An extended footnote here gives a resumé of Hersilie's case, ranged in Sérieux and Capgras's thesis among the case studies of 'fous raisonnants' who dupe the non-specialist:

On voit dans ce livre à quel point des administrateurs et des magistrats peuvent se laisser impressionner par la vivacité intellectuelle de ces 'fous raisonnants', par la correction de leurs écrits et l'habileté de leurs réticences; ils arrivent même à justifier un délire ambitieux étrange, mais établi exclusivement sur des interprétations. [...] Après un séjour de quatorze ans [...] elle fut mise en liberté grâce à l'intervention du receveur et des membres de la Commission des hospices d'Orléans où se trouvait la malade. Elle

Sérieux and Capgras's account differs little in the initial details, and they agree that an administrative mistake was made at the time of Hersilie's first committal. They also agree that Hersilie was 'très intelligente et douée d'aptitudes musicales'. There is no doubt in their mind that Hersilie was seriously mentally afflicted, though, and they add that Hersilie's father was mad also, a 'persécuté' who died demented, as was one of her brothers: 'L'un de ceux-ci semble avoir également été un dégénéré.' Charles Rouy had married his second wife, 'une demoiselle Chevalier', without divorcing the first, meaning that all the children after Claude-Daniel were illegitimate. This was the cause of the family rift, which would prove a crucial turning point for Hersilie, who, 'livrée à elle-même, vit en artiste, tantôt dans la gêne, tantôt dans le luxe'. According to her brother, 'elle contracta alors des relations avec une personne très haut placée dont elle se considérait comme la fiancée'. Sérieux and Capgras report that she gave birth to a baby girl in 1848, and lost the child soon afterwards.[8]

A series of traumatic experiences appears to have led to the first signs of serious mental illness: the loss of her mother at a formative age; the death of her beloved father; the shame of being declared illegitimate; the loss of her inheritance; the precariousness of the artist's life; being left pregnant by a rogue lover; and the loss of her only child. At the age of thirty-four, according to Sérieux and Capgras, having lost everything that meant anything real to her, Hersilie isolated herself in her home, and began to construct a whole new story for herself. This would be based on the delusional interpretation of her certificates of birth and baptism, through which she developed ideas of persecution and delusions of grandeur about what her 'true' origins might have been. Sérieux and Capgras conclude:

Le commissaire, averti par les concierges, vient frapper à sa porte et, comme elle ne répond pas, fait ouvrir de force par un serrurier [. . .] Des amis préviennent

---

parvint à obtenir de l'État une indemnité de 12000 francs et une allocation annuelle de 3600 francs pour séquestration illégale (des prescriptions de la loi de 1838 avaient été effectivement négligés lors de son premier internement).

[8] Sérieux (1910: 195–6). Although Hersilie's *Mémoires d'une aliénée* do not mention the loss of a child, the event is alluded to in *Mémoires d'une feuille de papier* (Burton 1882: 351). In a letter attributed to the fictional character who appears to represent Claude-Daniel Rouy, the following statement is made: 'On venait de tous côtés me dire qu'Eucharis [Hersilie] était folle à lier; elle avait dressé dans sa chambre, au milieu de tentures noires, un autel surmonté d'une boîte à violon qu'elle prenait pour un cercueil d'enfant, et sur lequel elle versait d'abondantes larmes.'

son frère, un médecin vient l'examiner et la trouve agenouillée devant des boîtes recouvertes de draperies noires et entourées de cierges allumés. Elle est conduite à Charenton.[9]

Once committed, Hersilie adopted as her own the popular legend that the duchesse de Berry, mother of the Bourbon heir, gave birth to a girl who was taken away and replaced by a boy child in order to ensure the succession of a male heir. Hersilie signs letters 'Sœur du roi Henri V', and says that 'sa ressemblance frappante avec la duchesse de Berry étonnait tout le monde' (169). This story, that Hersilie claims not to believe but never quite disavows, is evidence of the double bind in which she and her fellow writers found themselves: ultimate proof of her madness for her doctors, but a means of drawing attention to her case for the powerless patient: '[Ils] en ont fait leur grand cheval de bataille, parce qu'*elle fait effet*; comme moi, de mon côté, je me suis servie de cette légende invraisemblable dans le même but' (112).[10] In this battle, though, it is Hersilie who won through in the end.

Hersilie spent much of her time writing while incarcerated. Despite being discouraged by doctors and having writing materials confiscated, she wrote using whatever was available, even her own blood (224). These pieces of writing, recorded on whatever scraps of paper she could find, would eventually form the text of *Mémoires d'une aliénée*, published by Ollendorff in Paris in 1883.[11] The text runs to over five

---

[9] Sérieux (1910: 196, 204). This description also reiterates the above-mentioned allusion to Hersilie grieving for a lost infant.

[10] Hersilie's own variation on this story is that the duchesse de Berry gave birth to twins, a boy and a girl, and that the girl was taken away and adopted by Charles Rouy. This enables her to claim to be the real sister of the Bourbon heir, Henri V, without challenging his legitimacy, and the legitimate daughter of the man she knew as her father. The rumour of a child substitution had come into existence because the duc de Berry had fathered only daughters before his assassination, but his wife was pregnant when he died. The eagerly anticipated 'miracle baby' produced was a boy, crucially for the continuation of the Bourbon line (Merriman 1985: 53–7).

[11] Ollendorff produced a wide range of books from the late 1870s to the 1920s, from literature, drama, and literary criticism to special-interest history and leisure. It includes a number of women writers among its clients, Hersilie's *Mémoires* being one of its earliest publications. Ollendorff also published a text by a woman claiming to have been substituted for Queen Victoria: Sophie Adélaïde, *Histoire contemporaine* (1887). Another case of 'délire de revendication de filiation', published earlier in the century, which bears a curious and ironic resemblance to the story of Hersilie Rouy through the name 'Stella' and the Italian connection, is that of Maria Stella Chiappini. She wrote *Maria-Stella ou Échange criminel d'une demoiselle du plus haut rang contre un garçon de la condition la plus vile* (1830), in which she claimed to be the true daughter of Philippe-Égalité, pretender to the throne of Louis-Philippe (Blavier 1982: 884).

hundred pages, with approximately the first half dealing with Hersilie's incarceration. This part of the book gives detailed descriptions of life as an asylum resident, and reproduces a vast amount of interesting primary material: diagnostic statements by doctors; letters to friends, strangers, and the authorities; and reported dialogue. The second part of the book recounts the legal process following her release, culminating in the almost unparalleled achievement of the female patient's word finally being given precedence over that of the medical experts.[12]

Secondary commentary on the case of Hersilie Rouy falls somewhat predictably into two camps: first, that of psychiatrists who used her memoirs as case-historical material in treatises on afflictions that would now be discussed under the broad headings of paranoia and personality disorder; second, that of critics and re-evaluators of nineteenth-century French psychiatry, as well as feminist revisionist historians, who have reconsidered her case in recent years as a case in point of the suffering many women endured at the hands of alienist medicine.

The first category is represented by theorists such as Sérieux and Capgras, who celebrate Hersilie's *Mémoires* as taking a place among the 'classiques dans la littérature psychiatrique'.[13] As well as the mention—or dismissal—Hersilie's case receives from these doctors she appears as a case study in Ulysse Trélat's treatise *La Folie lucide*, which describes a range of (largely female) cases of 'folie lucide': patients who might appear sane to the layperson, but whose madness is revealed in their behaviour.[14] Hersilie also appears as a 'fou littéraire' in Raymond Queneau's *Les Enfants du limon*, an account based on Sérieux and Capgras's observations, and through the reference in Queneau she gains a mention in André Blavier, *Les Fous littéraires*. Queneau does

---

[12] Aboville, Loiret deputy and investigator of the case, concludes:

Sans avoir commis aucun acte de folie constaté, sur les simples récits de son portier, Mlle Rouy, dans la maturité de l'âge et en pleine expansion de son talent de pianiste, a été enlevée de son domicile par le docteur Pelletan, à la prière de son frère de père, M. Claude-Daniel Rouy. Elle a été reçue à Charenton en violation formelle de la loi, sans aucune demande signée et sur le certificat médical de l'homme même qui l'amenait; inscrite sous un nom qu'elle n'avait jamais porté; dépouillée à Charenton et privée pendant huit ans des papiers établissant son état civil; [. . .] Sans doute il est impossible de lui rendre ces vingt années, brisées d'abord par des tortures morales et physiques, puis par les anxiétés de la misère; mais on doit du moins, par une pension régulière, assurer le pain de ses vieux jours contre les vicissitudes de la politique (412–13).

[13] Sérieux (1910: 193).

[14] Trélat (1861: 183–6) (case number 50). Hersilie Rouy also features in Broc (1863) (observation X).

little more than reiterate Sérieux and Capgras's assessment and in no way bears out the specificity of Hersilie's experiences, other than pinpointing how her story is delusional.[15]

The unwarranted success of Jeffrey Masson's polemic *Against Therapy*, despite its manifold historical inaccuracies and distortions, brought Hersilie's *Mémoires* to the attention of the English-speaking world, as a case of 'false commitment' in a review of the prehistory of psychotherapy.[16] In France, Yannick Ripa, Anne Roche, and Laurent Soulayrol have all contributed useful studies that take seriously Hersilie's description of her experiences in the wider context of the social history of women's incarceration in the nineteenth century.[17] These commentators have validated Hersilie's text as a primary historical source in the writing of a psychiatric history of women, in contradistinction to the psychiatric account that uses the account in theoretical works without reflecting on the experience from the point of view of the patient. They have provided pertinent analyses that take up the issue of the pathologization of women's behaviour, but with the exception of Masson all concede that we cannot take at face value Hersilie's claim to be sane. All these analyses have taken Hersilie's side by emphasizing those aspects of her writing that have the ring of sanity, and authenticate this feature of her written production, but pay less attention to the arguably more problematic 'delusional' aspect of her text.

---

[15] Queneau (1938: 254–9); Blavier (1982: 882–3).

[16] Masson (1997: 52–64). Masson claims that Hersilie was admitted under the name (Chevalier) of one of the doctors who admitted her, ignoring the more plausible explanation that this was her mother's maiden name.

[17] See n. 1 for bibliographical references to these works. Rouy's case is now well documented, and researchers may find a large number of brief references to her story in a range of historical and literary texts. In the main, these tend to be brief secondary references to the primary investigations (by Ripa, Soulayrol, Roche, Matlock, Sérieux and Capgras) cited here, for example Preez (2004), or popularizing summaries of her case based on a factual and straightforward reading of the beginning of her memoirs, for example Fontaine (2005: 161–4). It is a sign of the singularity of her case that Rouy is from time to time resurrected and cited as a useful case study in popular works such as Appignanesi (2008) and in the French press. See, for example, Richard de Vendeuil's article 'Les grandes affaires d'Orléans: Hersilie R., internée et militante', in *L'Express*, 21 June 2007. The general pattern in these works is to document her case as a historical source that informs us with an account from the point of view of the patient. With the exception of Matlock, there has been little close and rigorous engagement with the text of Rouy's memoirs. Too frequently critics such as Appignanesi use secondary references to Rouy through questionable sources such as Masson's *Against Therapy* (1997), therefore simplistically presenting his arguably dubious interpretation without returning to the original text.

One exception to this is a thoughtful analysis of Rouy's memoirs by Bernard Cura, a modern French psychiatrist.[18] Cura convincingly corrects the bias of his nineteenth-century predecessors by using the insights of psychoanalysis, particularly Freud's ideas on narcissism, in an attempt to explain the meaning and function of Rouy's delusional ideas in the context of her family history. He notes and validates the long sections of text where Rouy appears to maintain complete lucidity, and contrasts these with the delusional elements of her story. Cura bases his analysis on Foucault's argument that nineteenth-century psychiatry was dominated by Cartesian philosophy, which denied the possibility of subjectivity to the insane, because of the breakdown of their reasoning faculties. Since psychoanalysis challenges this model of the mind by hypothesizing the existence of the unconscious, the possibility of interpreting the utterances of the insane becomes real. Cura's analysis misses some of the background provided by Sérieux and Capgras, however, and bases his interpretation solely on Rouy's text. Neither does he consider the wider context of the position of women in French society at this time. His approach complements the reading of Rouy's memoirs offered here, although the biographical picture he creates is perhaps less complete. Cura understands Rouy's delusions as being based in an overinvestment of affect in the relationship with her father, and reads this intense attachment—and indeed its rupture with his death—as the principal pathogenic agent in the story.[19] While Cura's reading of the narcissistic nature of Rouy's delusions mirrors my own, I interpret her ideas with reference to a broader range of precipitating factors, including the unequal power relationship between the male and female characters in her story.

In addition to these assessments of Hersilie Rouy's written word, Jann Matlock has carried out literary analytical work on these memoirs, which recognizes Hersilie's strength in the face of adversity as coming from her use of writing as a means of outmanoeuvring her incarcerators. She considers the problems of attempting to inscribe one's sanity from within a system that defines the subject as mad; how writing of this kind destabilizes interpretive strategies and theories of writing of the self; and the way in which Hersilie's own self-analysis leaves us unable to know

---

[18] Cura (1993).
[19] Cura (1993) writes: 'Il semble bien que la libido libérée par l'objet d'amour, que représentait le père, n'ait pas eu à être consommée dans un deuil. Elle fut directement réinvestie dans un système délirant.'

whether she was sane or insane. Matlock convincingly demonstrates that Hersilie's incarceration can be read as 'an extension of the limited status of women in her society', which is an argument taken up in this chapter, but chooses to leave the question of sanity undecidable.[20]

The present analysis builds on and departs from these previous studies, by developing the argument that social alienation is in this case an antecedent cause of mental alienation. It is possible to take Hersilie's side by engaging textually with the insanity of her writing as well as with its sanity, in order to trace the patterns of alienation that occurred in her life. None of the previous analyses have made use of Sérieux and Capgras's detailed write-up of the case, and those which make passing reference to the prior text, *Mémoires d'une feuille de papier*, fail to problematize this version of the story as a text. One clear limitation of former discussions of this case is that the only commentators to have actually read and analysed *Mémoires d'une feuille de papier* alongside *Mémoires d'une aliénée* are Sérieux and Capgras, whose conclusions are in radical need of reconsideration. As Matlock views Hersilie's textual 'doubling' as a strategy to evade the asylum, I read this phenomenon with a psychoanalytical slant as a technique of preservation against the extinction of the self.[21] This analysis re-evaluates the case of Hersilie Rouy: it deals closely with a text that exhibits much evidence of severe mental distress in order to postulate that this case, without being an example of a sane person being called insane, represents an instance of the widespread real persecution of women that occurred in nineteenth-century France, and which precipitated mental alienation.

Rouy's writing was produced in the context of the post-Romantic era in France, where literary Realism had triumphed. As Flaubert, in *Madame Bovary* (1856), represented in his anti-heroes an alternative to the gentlemanly lovers of women's popular fiction, so women writers, including Rouy, expressed dissatisfaction with a woman's lot in a man's world.[22] In the earlier feminist *mal du siècle* novels, the heroines of Sand's novels *Indiana* and *Lélia*, as well as Duras's *Ourika* and Staël's *Corinne*, expressed the dissatisfaction of unhappily married women and

---

[20] Matlock (1991: 187).
[21] Freud (1919: 234–5) cites an idea first posited by Otto Rank, that 'the "double" was originally an insurance against the destruction of the ego'.
[22] See Alison Finch's discussion of Realism in Unwin (1997: 81).

the waste of female potential in society.[23] As the story of Hersilie Rouy reflects, these narratives deconstruct the myth of romantic love and the promise of protection by men offered to women in the terms of the Napoleonic Code. Contemporaries such as Marie d'Agoult, writing under the nom de plume Daniel Stern, in the confessional novel *Nélida* (1846) present protagonists who discover their freedom after doing away with a male lover; d'Agoult was also highly crtical of the conservative regime of Napoleon III that displaced the optimism of the aborted 1848 Revolution. Rouy's iconoclastic agenda reflects that of her feminist foremothers, who used the trope of melancholia in order to illustrate the limitations of women's position in society. This is particularly relevant in an era dominated by Morel's theory of degeneration, which resulted in the mentally ill being increasingly viewed as incurable.

Other near contemporaries of Rouy in the tradition of women's autobiography include Flora Tristan, *Pérégrinations d'une paria* (1838), and George Sand, *Histoire de ma vie* (1854). Tristan recounts the story of her escape from a forced marriage and subsequent wandering lifestyle, and, influenced by the socialist movements of Saint-Simon and Fourier, aims to lead women into a new era of social justice. Sand, argues Hart, is an example of a 'culturally transgressive and politically subversive woman' who also eschewed the constraints of marriage and created for herself the existence of an honorary male through the adoption of a masculine pseudonym and the lifestyle of an independent writer. Hart also argues that there is a public–private conflict in Sand's autobiographical writing, which acts as 'the scene of Sand's struggle to reaffirm her participation in the historical process, while also demonstrating her conformity to certain cultural standards of womanhood'.[24] Sand took an active role in the 1848 Revolution, and both she and Tristan link their personal narratives to the political events of their times. We shall see, by contrast, that Rouy's text is extremely introspective in its concern with the author's own life and predicament. However, it will also become clear that she does exhibit aspects of this autobiographical tradition by linking her own story to that of the Bourbons, and indeed by appealing to the Empress Eugénie in her correspondence. Whilst Rouy does not seem to adopt an explicitly socialist agenda, and indeed she does not overtly concern herself with the position of women in general, her memoirs do express concern about

---

[23] Waller (1993: 137) argues that these novels express a specifically feminist *mal du siècle* that is 'a symptom of [their] explicitly feminist discontent'.

[24] Hart (2004: 93; 98).

her treatment as a woman by men (psychiatrists) and in this sense they reflect the concerns of other women writers of her era. It could also be argued that her pathological attachment to such obsolete hierarchical figures reflects the upheavals of an era rooting for an enduring sense of identity and political stability that would only finally be delivered with the emergence of the Third Republic in the 1870s.

Upon first contact with doctors Hersilie tells us: 'Monsieur le docteur me déclara "que j'avais l'imagination vive, des idées de persécution"' (58); Pelletan's diagnosis is 'monomanie aiguë avec hallucinations' (80); Doctors Calmeil and Lasègue record a verdict of 'délire partiel' (92); Trélat's initial diagnosis is 'délire multiforme en voie de démence', and he adds, 'en cet état, [elle] est dangereuse pour elle-même et pour les autres' (99). These assessments appear to be based upon identifying delusions of persecution, largely because of Hersilie's vociferous objection to her committal. However, this point of view soon shifted to emphasize the presence of delusions of grandeur, termed 'monomanie ambiteuse' (122), because of Hersilie's supposed inflated sense of self-importance and attachment to the story of the Duchesse de Berry.[25]

For Sérieux and Capgras, Hersilie is the perfect specimen with which to demonstrate their 'folie raisonnante' thesis. According to their account her writing evinces evidence of both a 'délire de revendication' and a 'délire d'interprétation': she is a paranoid, pathological complainer. In current psychiatric thinking the former is expressed in theories of personality disorder: patients who appear plausible, articulate, and perceptive, but who exhibit maladaptive and inflexible character traits, making them unable to function 'normally' in society.[26] Personality-disordered patients are widely considered to be incurable, like Hersilie Rouy. Payen describes his patient as:

Une [. . .] intraitable pensionnaire, et de la pire espèce, par le trouble qu'elle sème partout et l'insubordination difficile à réprimer quand elle se rattache à une personne aussi intelligente qu'opiniâtre dans ses déterminations, résumant l'orgueil, la vanité et l'envie, et que nous considérons, comme tous nos collègues,

---

[25] Hersilie Rouy's medical records are held at the Archives de l'Assistance publique in Paris. The original certificates do not tell us any more than Hersilie herself reveals in her memoirs.

[26] Berrios (1993: 14): 'Personality disorders are defined by DSM-III-R as clusters of "personality traits [that] are inflexible and maladaptive and cause either significant functional impairment or subjective distress".'

comme un type de folie incurable, qui doit être retenue dans un asile d'aliénés, que nous verrions avec plaisir n'être pas celui d'Orléans. (443)

Of a list of personality traits that reads like an inventory of feminine vices, Hersilie asks, 'où est la folie là-dedans?' (443).

Hersilie's behaviour and writing in the asylum could leave her open to a variety of modern psychiatric diagnoses. The clinical description of narcissistic personality fits many of the character traits exhibited by Hersilie, recorded by her doctors as ideas of grandeur:

People with this disorder have a grandiose sense of self-importance and are boastful and pretentious. They are preoccupied with fantasies of unlimited success, power, beauty, or intellectual brilliance. They think themselves special and expect others to admire them and offer special services and favours. They feel entitled to the best and seek to associate with people of high status. [...] They appear arrogant, disdainful, and haughty, and behave in a patronizing or condescending way.[27]

The French psychiatric textbooks reiterate some of these observations, but also attempt a psychodynamic explanation for what seems to occur, which closely corresponds to the observations to be made here about the narrative voice of 'Hersilie':

Ces manifestations contrastaient avec une sexualité perturbée par des échecs hétérosexuels, par une abstinence ou par une homosexualité. [...] Ces patients éprouvent un besoin constant de se mettre en avant, mais ils font preuve d'une profonde vulnérabilité avec déficit de l'estime de soi. [...] D'autre part, [ces personnes] échappent au clivage du soi et de l'objet; certaines qualités ou des dons spéciaux leur ont permis de se protéger par la constitution d'un soi grandiose.[28]

Matlock argues that Hersilie's 'doubling' of her personality through the adoption of multiple pseudonyms could be read as symptomatic of her mental illness, which resembles multiple personality disorder.[29] This disorder has now been re-labelled 'dissociative identity disorder', and appears relevant particularly in relation to the account given in Hersilie's *Mémoires* that she has been substituted for another, to be discussed in the next section of this chapter. The first diagnostic criterion for this disorder is 'The

---

[27] Gelder (2001: 170–1).
[28] Guelfi (2002: 407–8).
[29] Matlock (1991: 193): 'The psychiatric account of multiple personalities would require us to read Hersilie's doubling as another symptom of her mental illness' (in reference to Hawthorn 1983).

presence of two or more distinct identities or personality states (each with its own relatively enduring pattern of perceiving, relating to, and thinking about, the environment and self)'.[30] However, pegging so-called 'symptoms' to lists of diagnostic criteria is a potentially endless exercise, and it is sufficient at this point to note that as Hersilie Rouy was considered sick according to the diagnostic procedures in place in the nineteenth century, it seems that her pathology would be recognized today. The difference now, as recognized more fully in the French medical textbooks, is that the insights of psychoanalysis offer a more complex set of reasons why she might have been in the position she was. This in turn enables us to provide a more pertinent analysis of the sociological situation that gave rise to Hersilie's first committal.

Importantly, the psychiatrists never admitted that the error made in Hersilie's case was medical. She *had been* mad, and she was released because she was cured: her committal had always been 'motivée' (281). Sérieux and Capgras even suggest that she was only released because the doctors were too exasperated to continue treatment. So her victory was personal rather than ideological, but the fact that her sanity was never proved as having been constant in medical eyes makes her case more able to stand as a representative voice from the asylum. Because Hersilie was judged by all the doctors who examined her as being seriously ill, she was to their mind just like the other patients: the poor victim of her own sick imagination.

Hersilie was released twice, but lacking support and proof of her identity quickly found herself back in the asylum she was so desperate to leave. As early as 1855 Hersilie was released, let out in the clothes in which she had arrived: 'en robe de chambre à manches ouvertes, garnies de dentelles et de rubans cerise, tête nue, en pantoufles. Je n'avais ni argent, ni domicile, ni papiers... Il était six heures du soir' (113). The police sent her straight back to the public asylum. The second time she was released she lasted a few days, but a 'lettre délirante avec menaces au préfet de la Seine' soon had her recommitted (204). Sérieux and Capgras say that she was too wrapped up in her delusions of grandeur to accept the menial work they offered her, and argue that had she not found a protector in Le Normant des Varannes she would have ended up being recommitted even after her final release.[31]

---

[30] Gelder (2001: 265).
[31] Sérieux (1910: 221).

Their assessment is unwittingly pertinent. Had Hersilie been given the support that she needed, had her mental life been sustained rather than undermined, she might have been able to live a fuller life. We might view Hersilie's refusal to take unskilled, poorly paid work as a brave and honest decision, given that she was a highly qualified and competent professional. In many ways Hersilie was treated abominably by her family and by the authorities dealing with her case: no one sought to protect her identity, and there is not a word of compassion in the medical treatises about how she may have suffered. Psychiatrists were proud men, and the assumption that underpins their conclusions is that because Hersilie was an irritating and unappealing person who held delusional ideas, and because it could be demonstrated that she did, it was proper and right to incarcerate her.

As well as the politically tricky issue of 'personality disorder', there is also an important psychotic element to Hersilie's illness, and the other manifestation of 'folie raisonnante' outlined by Sérieux and Capgras, the 'délire d'interprétation', is present in Hersilie's delusions about being connected in some way to the Bourbon heir. Being admitted under her mother's maiden name may have been a humiliating and shattering experience, and one that led her to construct a new reality in line with her desires, as if to efface the horrifying shame of her illegitimacy. This recreating of one's family history was famously theorized by Freud in 1908 as a 'family romance' scenario, 'which finds expression in a phantasy in which both his parents are replaced by others of better birth. The technique used in developing phantasies like this [...] depends upon the ingenuity and the material which the child has at his disposal.'[32] In Hersilie's case, the evocation of the connection to a legend available in her cultural paradigm—that of the duchesse de Berry's miracle child—is a very extreme version of this, for one's parents could not conceivably be of higher birth. Here, the illegitimate, abandoned child of unremarkable parents is transformed into the legitimate sister of the heir to the throne of France, with the hope of being welcomed back into the heart of a family that she fantasized would be far better than her own.

To form an opinion on the justice or injustice of what happened to Hersilie Rouy is to adopt one of three possible positions in relation to her text: we can read her, as the psychiatrists so effectively did, as a deranged megalomaniac and a troublemaker; we could view her

---

[32] Freud (1909: 239).

as a casualty of the law of 1838, which locked away vulnerable women with such ease; or we can read her as the victim of a mysterious plot to make her disappear. There is more than a grain of truth in all these assessments: she was both a genuine victim and a dissenter, and some people do seem to have wanted her out of the way. However, this is a compelling text, written by a person viewed as insane by the medical establishment, and it provides evidence of the institution's lack of therapeutic rationale. The text therefore stands as an indictment of a whole orthodox means of managing mental illness, and of the supporting legal system that underwrote the existence of a network of asylums in France.[33]

The specific excerpts of the *Mémoires* to be analysed in this chapter have been selected in order to offer a representative range of pieces of writing from a very long text, and cover the following: a section of narrative recounting events leading up to Hersilie's committal; the account of her admission to Charenton and transfer to the Salpêtrière; a letter to the Impératrice Eugénie, in which the author claims to be the lost daughter of the duchesse de Berry; and a letter to the minister responsible for the management of insane asylums. We shall now turn to the close analysis of Hersilie's text, by first examining these memoirs as a voice in isolation, characterized by a folding in on the self and libidinal investment in the textual 'je', in compensation for the poverty of relationships experienced by the individual who appears to stand as their author. We shall then analyse the vitality—as opposed to the pathology—of the *Mémoires* as a voice in dialogue, and the way in which rhetorical energy is successfully deployed in order to subvert and undermine the hegemony of the authoritative discourse of psychiatry. Finally, the way in which 'asylum' is presented and upheld as a pathogenic space will be examined in detail. Through this reading of both medical treatises on the case and the text of the *Mémoires*, the asylum can be read as the monster of patriarchal society, reinforcing the social alienation that might drive an individual to delusion. I demonstrate that the rhetorical success of the text is not dependent on its story being convincingly 'true'. Rather, we can be persuaded through Hersilie's polemic that she was terribly wronged by a society that claimed to know her best interest.

---

[33] Hersilie's own condemnation of the asylum system is corroborated by accounts of its inefficacy given by historians such as Roudinesco (1982), Fauvel (2002), and Ripa (1983).

If we are to credit this text with being a representative voice from among those unwillingly constrained by the asylum, then our first task is to put to one side the claim to sanity. If civilized society believes that psychiatric illness exists, and entrusts those afflicted to the care of medical experts, then we cannot read Hersilie's verbal expression as she asks: as the utterances of a sane person committed by accident or as a result of the machinations of her family. If we are to assert with integrity that the voices of patients are worth listening to, then we must endorse as meaningful the verbal productions of individuals who, it would appear, were seriously mentally disturbed. The only assumption that can be called into question with any rigour is that anyone is 'sane' or 'insane' in the first place, and this is not a new problem. Szasz, writing from an anti-psychiatric perspective, has written: 'Obsession with false commitment obscured the fundamental issue of freedom and responsibility of the so-called mad person, and reinforced the belief that incarcerating the truly insane was in the best interests of both the patient and society.'[34] In the case of Hersilie Rouy, we can read her claim to sanity as a further feature of the double bind in which she is held: her indictment of the incarcerating system carries with it an endorsement of that same system. Her argument that she should not be there tacitly supports the supposition that people exist who should be locked away. In reading her text instead as a representative female voice from the man-made asylum, we shall first examine the issue of a voice in isolation.

A VOICE IN ISOLATION

The first-person narrator and protagonist in this text can be read on one level as a voice in dialogue with itself via a fantasy other, which seeks to ensure against her own destruction through the creation of a replica image of herself. In the second chapter of the *Mémoires*, entitled 'Ce qui a précédé mon enlèvement', Hersilie describes how in 1840 a mysterious lady in black, dubbed 'la *dame noire*', appears on her doorstep warning of imminent danger. She is told she is the goddaughter of a powerful and influential man named Petrucci, and as such is 'mêlée

---

[34] Szasz (1994: 114).

d'une affaire de succession énorme' (29), that she is in danger of being kidnapped and made to disappear.

Il me faut à présent remonter un peu haut dans mes souvenirs, pour rendre compte de faits assez bizarres dont l'importance ne me fut révélée que plus tard.

A mon retour des forges d'Alais, où j'avais passé six mois dans la famille de M. le vicomte Benoît d'Azy, buvant du lait de chèvre et me reposant de mes fatigues, je fus reçue par mes connaissances, par les professeurs du Conservatoire, par Mme Orfila, par Mme la duchesse Decazes, avec des compliments et des félicitations sur mes succès dans le nord.

Stupéfaite, je voulus m'expliquer, prouver par le témoignage de la famille Benoît d'Azy que j'étais dans le midi et que ma présence dans le nord était matériellement impossible, puisque je n'avais pas quitté les deux jeunes filles auxquelles je donnais des leçons de piano.

On me signifia que Mlle Hersilie Rouy avait eu de grands succès dans le nord, que la presse en avait parlé, et qu'on ne comprenait pas pourquoi je niais des faits aussi honorables que flatteurs. [...]

J'en conclus qu'on prenait pour moi quelque autre pianiste blonde aux cheveux bouclés, ou qu'une artiste prenait mon nom pour donner des concerts et aller dans le monde. [...]

Vers la fin de 1840, une dame de la plus haute distinction, aux façons bienveillantes, se présenta chez moi un dimanche matin, un peu avant huit heures, et demanda à me parler en particulier. Elle n'avait pas dit son nom à ma domestique.

Cette dame s'informa du prix de mes leçons, me parla d'une place fort lucrative à l'étranger, insista pour me la faire accepter; et sur mon refus, basé sur l'âge avancé de mon père que je ne voulais pas abandonner, me dit de réfléchir, qu'elle reviendrait; qu'elle m'engageait à me placer dans une famille, une jeune personne seule étant exposée, les leçons fatigantes, etc.

Elle revint ainsi trois fois à peu de distance, toujours sans se nommer. Ma sœur Dachinka, alors chez moi, pourrait au besoin en rendre témoignage.

Comme elle était invariablement vêtue de noir et la figure cachée par un voile épais qu'elle ne levait jamais, je l'avais surnommée la *dame noire*, ne sachant comment la désigner autrement.

Lors de sa dernière visite, me voyant toujours décidée à rester près de mon père, elle finit par me dire que je n'étais pas en sûreté en France, qu'on devait *m'enlever....* sans me donner aucune autre explication, ce qui, je l'avoue, me causa une certaine émotion. [...]

La *dame noire* revint en 1843, 1845 et 1848, de la même façon.

En 1849, cette dame (que j'ai su plus tard être la baronne del Lago) leva son voile et me donna des explications qui me firent comprendre, à ma grande stupéfaction, que le projet de mon elèvement, qu'on avait mis sur le compte d'un prince riche et amoureux ou d'un lord quelconque, était le résultat d'une étrange complication.

Elle me dit que j'avais pour parrain un Pierre, fils de Pierre, qui, tout en conservant cette dénomination constante, prenait plusieurs noms différents;

Que le nom le plus généralement adopté par lui était celui de *Joseph-Pierre Petrucci*, ce qui ne l'empêchait pas, comme on le voit dans nos actes, d'en prendre d'autres (Petracchi, Petroman, Petrowicht), mais toujours en conservant Pierre pour en former un nom de famille, ou répétant deux fois le nom de Pierre;

Que, comme filleule de Pierre, je me trouvais mêlée à une affaire de succession énorme; que personne ne pouvait hériter sans que les conditions du testament fussent toutes remplies, ce qui était très-malheureux pour moi.

Elle me confia que c'était elle qui, sous le nom d'Hersilie Rouy, avait donné des concerts et fait de la musique en plusieurs endroits, afin d'augmenter ma réputation et de me tirer de l'obscurité, qui pouvait m'être fatale en me laissant oublier, et qui permettrait de me faire disparaître à tout jamais.

Elle me montra un écrit, copié, me dit-elle, sur l'autographe de l'astronome Charles Rouy, déclarant "que la fille élevée par Charles Johnson, esquire, sous le nom de Charlotte Johnson, était la fille reconnue par lui, Charles Rouy, en 1814, sur les registres de Milan; que pour qu'elle fût riche, heureuse et héritât de Charles Johnson, qui n'avait pas d'enfant, il la lui avait abandonnée en toute propriété; mais que si Pierre, fils de Pierre, son parrain, la réclamait, elle était avant tout sienne, devait reprendre les noms des actes milanais et en subir les conséquences."

Il se trouvait donc, d'après cela, que c'était le porteur de cet écrit qui était Hersilie, et non pas moi, bien que j'eusse la possession d'état; qu'un changement d'enfant avait été effectué afin d'assurer à la fille de l'astronome une existence heureuse et tranquille, et la soustraire à Pierre.

Je restai confondue! Ceci m'arrivait au moment où M. Claude-Daniel m'écrivait de me déclarer *enfant adultérin....* où Désirée, sa femme, me disait que je n'avais pas droit au nom de Rouy.... Et voici que je n'étais même plus du tout la fille de l'astronome, mais une *inconnue* à tous et à moi-même, substituée pour dérober la trace d'une autre et tromper.... qui?

[La baronne del Lago] ajouta qu'en admettant que ce fût elle qui fût Hersilie, je n'en avais rien à craindre; [...] *qu'elle se chargeait de tout.* Elle me prevint que, grâce à ce double personnage, grâce à des choses que je saurais plus tard, on répandrait sur mon compte une masse de bruits contradictoires. Elle m'engageait à bien réfléchir, à mesurer mes forces, afin de savoir si j'acceptais l'étrange destinée qui m'était faite. Elle ne pouvait rien me dire au sujet de Pierre, fils de Pierre, auquel nous nous trouvions ainsi appartenir toutes deux, si ce n'est que sa puissance occulte était grande; qu'il avait besoin d'une Hersilie, et que si l'une manquait, l'autre devrait la remplacer. [. . .]

Rendez-vous fut donc pris à trois mois. Je devais, si je revenais, ne plus me tenir recluse comme je le faisais, me mettre en évidence, me lancer dans le monde, donner des concerts, publier un album avec mon portrait, ayant pour titre: *L'Etoile d'Or*, surnom qu'on m'avait donné étant enfant, à cause de mes cheveux blonds et bouclés qui faisaient comme une auréole autour de ma tête; enfin il me faudrait ajouter un tréma su l'*y* de Rouy, afin d'en faire un nom différent et de pouvoir, si celui sous lequel j'étais connue m'était contesté ou enlevé, conserver celui d'Hersilie Rouÿ comme un pseudonyme artistique auquel on ne pourrait plus toucher. Le secret le plus absolu me fut recommandé, quoi qu'il arrivât ou qu'on pût me dire.

Elle m'obligea à accepter une somme assez importante comme prix de mon mobilier, afin, me dit-elle gracieusement, d'avoir pour elle-même, si je venais à partir, un pied-à-terre où elle viendrait, en *notre* nom, s'occuper de *nos* affaires.

Comme je viens de le dire, nous prîmes rendez-vous à trois mois. La première arrivée devait attendre l'autre. Chacune de nous prit une clé.... Seule je suis venue au rendez-vous.

Le choix était fait. Ma destinée devait s'accomplir.

This piece of writing discloses the internal psychical mechanisms of a latency period, which holds the disparate pieces of a puzzle that will later construct a family romance scenario. It is characterized by extreme narcissism, of folding in on the self and the investment of narrative energy in the building up of the speaking 'moi'. The figure of 'Hersilie' is divided in two, for it transpires in these pages that this '*dame noire*' is in fact another 'Hersilie'. She bears 'un écrit' testifying that Charles Rouy had given up his daughter to be brought up by another man, leaving the woman who has grown up as Hersilie in doubt as to her true identity. If we can read the named personage—for we can hardly speak of a stable character—'Hersilie' as thus divided into the first-person speaker 'moi' and the mysterious impostor 'elle', it is arguably the 'other' Hersilie who is built up through the investment of narcissistic energy, at the expense of the Hersilie who really existed. This is not strictly speaking the splitting of one self into two, but rather the creation of a twin-like second self who has the life the existing person desires.

There is the 'me' who is here, suffering, and there is the 'me' who comes from somewhere else and who has a better life.[35]

This narcissistic energy is a creative defence, and can be read in terms diametrically opposed to the psychiatric assessment of 'monomanie ambitieuse' as reached through a process of reasoning.[36] Hersilie opens up a number of different options in relation to her own grasp of selfhood and succeeds in simultaneously doubting and believing all of them. We are introduced initially to the 'importance' of the events to follow, given such a status because they contribute to the creation of the fictional self, imagined as a desirable alternative. The period of psychic development displayed here is one of brooding over ideas, of uncertainty. Paragraphs are constructed according to a retrospective logic, as though the speaker is creating something of significance out of apparent banality. The opening line of this extract depicts the thinker travelling back through her own memories and ascribing meaning to them in terms of her present experience: 'Il me faut à présent **remonter** un peu haut dans mes souvenirs, pour **rendre compte** de faits assez bizarres dont l'importance ne me fut révélée que **plus tard**' (26). The enigmatic '*dame noire*' is in retrospect given a spurious identity, 'cette dame (que j'ai su **plus tard** être la baronne del Lago)' (29). The speaker situates herself as the indirect object of the verb 'révéler', and arbitrary events are presented as urgently requiring to be ascribed a meaning. This is articulated through expressions revealing a process of deduction, such as '**J'en conclus** qu'on prenait pour moi quelque autre pianiste' (27); 'des explications qui **me firent comprendre**' (29); 'Des faits **analogues** se reproduisirent à Paris même' (27). The placing of the self as the indirect object of verbs of enlightenment and

[35] My argument here draws on the concepts offered in Freud's essay 'On Narcissism' (Freud 1914: 67–102). Freud notes that 'megalomania' is characterized by a diversion of interest from the external world—the world of people and things. Object-libido, normally directed towards attaching to external 'objects', has been withdrawn and directed to the ego. Since Freud posits that there is a state of 'primary narcissism', in other words an original libidinal cathexis of the ego that is later directed to objects, this is a normal stage through which human infants pass on their way to adult object relations. This becomes a point of fixation in adult pathological states, such as megalomania. Narcissistic individuals are therefore 'plainly seeking *themselves* as a love-object' (88). Similarly, in this section I demonstrate that any stable sense of self experienced by the speaking subject is undermined by the investment of libidinal energy in the realm of fantasy and desire, rather than in the realm of reality. Freud writes that one of the things that the narcissistic type may love is 'what he himself would like to be' (90), which is, I contend, what occurs in this text through the creation of another version of the self according to what Hersilie desires she might be.

[36] See Chapter 5 on Camille Claudel for a more detailed investigation of ideas about paranoia and the role of the reasoning process within this psychopathology.

understanding, 'révéler' and 'comprendre', implies that these ideas do not simply emanate from the inside, but are stirred up by an external force.[37]

No convincing explanation is offered for the progress of events; concerts are held to have been given 'dans ces conditions **inexplicables**' (27), and Hersilie grows anxious about warnings regarding her safety, given 'sans me donner aucune autre **explication**' (28). The expression of this troubled feeling reveals a need arising to create one's own explanation. This is born of the anxiety caused by the threat to the self, conveyed in a previous sentence where the 'je' is undermined through the subtraction of the crucial noun of stability, 'sûreté': 'je n'étais pas en sûreté en France [...] on devait *m'enlever*' (28). This is compensated for through an artificial building up of the self where the ego comes under the sway of desire, which sweeps aside the threat that reality presents, and makes a story that it would like to be its own.

The need to see arbitrary, mundane, and apparently unexplainable events in terms of willed and causal connections, which are presented in direct relation to the textual 'je', is the first consequence of the need to defend the fragile self by making it bigger. Hersilie tells us: 'Le projet de mon enlèvement, qu'on avait mis sur le compte d'un prince riche et amoureux ou d'un lord quelconque, était le **résultat** d'une étrange complication' (29). The 'megalomania' of which Hersilie is accused literally means 'self-exaltation', and these words are ample evidence in medical terms of such a state of mind. Here, references to princes and lords are accompanied by the adjectival attributes 'riche' and 'amoureux', once again presenting the exalted personage in direct relation to the 'je' (for one cannot be 'amoureux' alone). If patriarchal society requires 'normal' female members to be modest and self-deprecating, and tolerates such self-elevation only in socially important or prodigious males, these details are somewhat embarrassing.

The irony of these references, for the reader who has access to psychiatric accounts and case-historical material, is, of course, that it represents a direct reversal of the speaker's own drama: Hersilie's own 'prince' may have cruelly abandoned her, and exhibited little interest in the progress of her life. The literal raising of the self's status here is so disproportionate as to painfully reveal its logical corollary: the desperately, pathologically

---

[37] Freud (1915: 270) writes of such interpretive strategies: 'This deferred use of impressions and this displacement of recollections often occur precisely in paranoia and are characteristic of it.'

destitute 'true' self, which must be mended through the creation of an artificial, textually inflated version of the same. The devices used in this are lexical, and proper names, nouns concrete and abstract, adjectives and adverbs, all serve to embellish the picture created.

The proper names deployed in this piece are given in full with preceding titles, and frame the story in a world of people of high social standing. This is particularly noticeable at the beginning, where in an introductory paragraph three names are given, two of them aristocratically titled: 'M. le vicomte Benoît d'Azy'; 'Mme Orfils'; 'Mme la duchesse Decazes' (26). These individuals are presented as Hersilie's 'connaissances', a reference through which she presents herself as socially affiliated to people of eminence. Their status is reinforced through the description 'les professeurs du Conservatoire'. The nouns 'compliments' and 'félicitations' and the adjectives 'honorables' and 'flatteurs' are selected to depict the judgement of Hersilie's career success. Following this pattern, it could not transpire that the *dame noire*, since she represents Hersilie's 'other' better self, turns out to be a woman humbler than Hersilie. Instead she is 'la baronne del Lago', with an aristocratic air and an exotic Italian twist to boot: in line with the notion of a 'family romance' the *moi* is necessarily replaced by one of higher birth. The diminished status of the real self is evidenced here in the fact that it is the fantasized *dame noire* who is being congratulated.

Other names that appear in a revealing context are those of family members, such as Hersilie's brother 'M. Claude-Daniel' and his wife 'Désirée' (30). These names are presented without social augmentation, and are held directly responsible for the depletion of Hersilie's status which elsewhere is bolstered through the evocation of proper names: '[Il] m'écrivait de me déclarer *enfant adultérin*.... où Désirée, sa femme, me disait que je n'avais pas droit au nom de Rouy' (30). The quarrel over the name of Rouy, over the right of an illegitimate child to bear the esteem that the father's name brings her, is evoked later in the excerpt where Hersilie creates her own version of this name where the 'y' is marked with a 'tréma': 'Rouÿ'. This name arises by analogy with the childhood nick-name, *Étoile d'Or*, given to Hersilie 'à cause de mes cheveux blonds et bouclés qui faisaient comme une auréole autour de ma tête' (32), for it is a name that only she has and therefore one that nobody can take from her. As 'L'Étoile d'Or' will be the name of her album of music, so 'Rouÿ' will be taken in order to protect the more vulnerable 'Rouy', which will be her 'pseudonyme artistique': an unstable name for a precarious profession.

The psychiatrists who examined Hersilie make much of the appro-priated name 'Étoile d'Or' as evidence of delusions of grandeur. This name, accompanied by references to her artistic achievements all amounts to a folding in on the self that produces a distorted picture of one person's importance in the shared external world. We can read a threat of annihilation in the sense of urgency with which she must project her 'self' forward: 'Je devais [. . .] me **mettre** en évidence, me **lancer** dans le monde, **donner** des concerts, publier mon **album** avec mon **portrait**, ayant pour titre: *L'Étoile d'Or.*' The significance of the use of the noun 'auréole' to describe a child's hair is that the simile itself, 'comme une auréole', projects that same child into a metaphysical realm where her name may be protected. 'Étoile d'Or' is like an angel, and Hersilie is nothing, not even deserving of an honourable family name.

This is the most frequently cited of many pseudonyms taken by Hersilie in the asylum, in protest against the institutional imposition of a new name. Other names adopted include 'Polichinelle', 'Sathan', 'L'Antéchrist', 'La Sylphide', 'La Sirène', 'La Saltimbanque', and 'Sœur du roi Henri V' (264–5). The partial adoption (for Rouy claims never to really believe she is any of these people) of these multiple identities seems to lend power to the weakened self, and to disrupt the administrative procedure of the asylum that has named her 'Chevalier'. These characters exercise power over those around them, whether supernatural spiritual potency (Satan and the Antichrist) or the fantasized political power of the royal family. To parallel her own experience to that of the French royal family at this time in history is to draw an unconscious comparison between the precariousness of an institution under mortal threat with the insult done to her own sense of self. The remaining characters she assumes are manipulators and tricksters: the seductive siren; the evasive and flitting sylphid; the playful Punchinello; and the acrobat. These traits reflect the strategies deployed by Rouy, whose use of multiple signatures and identities forms a counter-tactic aimed at outmanoeuvring the system that has named her 'Hersilie Chevalier-Rouy'; it is also subversive of the clinician's signature given on official statements. However, the multiple selves textually expressed are also indicative of the disintegration of the coherent sense of self that the process of attempted reparation called 'megalomania' produces. This results in the creation of a new 'me', constructed to mitigate the unbearable suffering of the real 'me'.[38]

---

[38] The psychoanalytical notion that 'megalomania' is the result of a sexual overvaluation of the ego, which occurs as a result of libidinal energy being withdrawn from external objects, and as the result of emotional disappointment, is outlined in Freud's 'Case History of Schreber' (1911: 65). Jung (1907: 145) puts forward an argument that

This extract plays out a psychical turning in on the self, the speaking 'je', and the predominant feeling here is one of reaching out to the external world to find meaning, but one where all meaning found is connected to the self. It is the textual representation of one voice in dialogue with itself, and the doubling of the self that occurs is worth examining in some detail.[39] Here the discussion that ensues between 'elle' and 'moi', the *'dame noire'* (the 'real' Hersilie) and Hersilie (an *'inconnue'*), is a devastating ontological interrogation that lies beneath a relatively banal surface narrative. The figure of 'moi' as a speaker is rooted in real experience, and that of 'elle' in the fantasy of a better reality. The speaking 'moi' is in this excerpt progressively effaced as if to reflect the author's own experience of humiliation and rejection. Meanwhile, the character of 'elle' is expanded and made into an appealing version of Hersilie, even being allowed to take her name.

The 'other' Hersilie is not introduced until the fourth paragraph, where the 'je' previously established as a stable speaking voice is thrown into doubt. The opening sentence reads: 'On **me** signifia que Mlle **Hersilie Rouy** avait eu de grands succès dans le Nord' (26–7). The appearance of 'moi' and 'Mlle Hersilie Rouy' as logically distinct individuals produces a tension between the speaker and the object of her reference, who shares this name. The suspense created at this point announces the later revelatory shock, where the character of Hersilie appears simultaneously in the first and third person: 'Il se trouvait donc [. . .] que c'était le porteur de cet écrit qui était **Hersilie**, et non pas **moi**' (30).

The idea of the creation of another is thematized through the use of the term 'autre', as both noun and adjective. The idea of the 'autre' is crucial in the appreciation of 'Hersilie' as the embodiment of self-estrangement. The use of the first and third person at once sets her apart uniquely in her distress: she is not at one with herself, and neither is she identical to herself. Hersilie as the speaking 'moi' is declared an *'enfant adultérin'*, and

---

resonates more closely with my own. In his 1907 analysis of the word associations of his patient Babette Staub, he observes that delusions of grandeur are compensatory: 'The conscious psychic activity of the patient, then, is limited to a systematic creation of wish-fulfilments as a substitute, so to speak, for a life of toil and privation and for the depressing experiences of a wretched family milieu.'

[39] The model of Diderot's *Le Neveu de Rameau* evinces a textual blurring of two characters, 'lui' and 'moi', of two voices that repeat in their own speeches the assertions of the previous speaker to the point that it is difficult to distinguish between the two voices. Here, similarly, is presented a paradoxical textual dynamic of symbiosis and strained attempted fission, where 'elle' and 'moi' struggle between the poverty of real experience and the vibrancy of fantasized experience.

as such is no longer anyone, but 'une *inconnue* à tous et à moi-même, substituée pour dérober la trace d'une **autre** et tromper . . . . qui?' (30). The tagged-on relative pronoun sums up her confusion, for this writer has lost the thread of her own narrative. 'I' am just a substitute for 'une autre', whose importance as an existing consciousness is raised above that of 'moi', who has been relegated to the status of a nobody.

The figure of the 'autre' reappears throughout the extract: 'on prenait pour moi quelque **autre** pianiste blonde' (27); 'je l'avais surnommé la *dame noire*, ne sachant comment la désigner **autrement**' (28); 'il avait besoin d'une **Hersilie**, et que si l'une manquait, l'**autre** devrait la remplacer' (31); 'La première arrivée devait attendre l'**autre**' (32). Particularly striking is the use of the adverb 'autrement' when trying to name the 'other' Hersilie: we can read not only the adverbial application of the term to the verb 'désigner'—'otherwise'—but also as applying to the very essence of the '*dame noire*', who is 'otherly' in nature. Hersilie names her 'autrement', as if in a moment of self-interrogation she asks: who is she to me? This alternative version of 'moi' is a better, lovelier, and stronger rendering of the person of Hersilie, who speaks 'gracieusement', promises '*qu'elle se chargeait de tout*' (32) and 'de veiller sur **moi** autant que cela sera en son pouvoir' (28).

The character that speaks as 'moi' is dogged by darkness and death, which threaten to plunge her into obscurity and oblivion. We are told that 'sous le nom d'Hersilie Rouy', 'elle' has demonstrated the strength to bring 'moi' into the limelight, 'afin d'augmenter **ma** réputation et de **me** tirer de l'obscurité, qui pouvait **m'**être fatale en **me** laissant oublier' (29). Personal pronouns here reinforce the sense that it is the speaking 'je', whose name is lent to another, who is the object of the verb 'oublier', and the obscurity with which she is threatened—that of the asylum—could kill her off at any time, being potentially 'fatale'. The evidence presented here of such an anxiety of annihilation pre-empts the fundamentally obliterating experience of the asylum, and throws light on the devastating fear of nothingness that prompts the creation and expansion of the new self.

The figures of 'elle' and 'moi' are finally elided in the last paragraphs of this extract: the '*dame noire*' is to come 'en *notre* nom, s'occuper de *nos* affaires' (32). The deliberate and explicit emphasis placed on these third-person-plural, possessive determiners underlines the paradoxical situation that these persons do not exist autonomously, but are nevertheless subsumed in the category 'nous'. The image of two voices doubling up, or overlapping, can be usefully compared to the imagery used to depict the '*dame noire*'. She is a dark figure—either a 'dark lady' or a 'lady in black'—and is portrayed as veiled, 'invariablement vêtue de noir et la figure cachée par un voile épais', as if Hersilie's shadow (28).

If this part of the text represents a psychical regression to the infantile stage of narcissism as described by psychoanalysis, then the '*dame noire*' is Echo to Hersilie's Narcissus. Juliet Mitchell discusses Echo's much-neglected role in the myth of Narcissus as that of 'the absolute *other* [...] who did no more than repeat the words of Narcissus' own self-fascination'. She adds that 'Narcissus is confined in intra-subjectivity', and Hersilie's account is here reduced to a depiction of a self that has two versions. The speaker specifies at a revelatory moment in the narra-tive, as the '*dame noire*' gives her explanations, 'cette dame [...] **leva son voile**', allowing Hersilie to deduce what she does from the information given (29).[40] Later in her *Mémoires* Hersilie will exclaim: 'Que je sois en personne Hersilie Rouy, que je sois son ombre, peu importe, mes bons amis! peu importe mon nom, mon identité. C'est *moi, moi*, l'être fatale-ment choisi pour marcher dans cette voie lugubre [...]' (511). This sense of simultaneously being Hersilie and her shadow self recalls the earlier stage in the text where the character is portrayed as two. In this later excerpt we learn explicitly that both 'Hersilie' and 'son ombre' are reduced to one in the category 'moi'.

This multiplication of selves occurs in relation to other individuals, also. Significantly, the portrayal of the paternal role is mediated through the figures of Charles Rouy and the godfather Petrucci. These figures, too, dissolve into a multiplicity of names: 'Pierre', 'Petrucci', 'Petracchi', 'Petromand', 'Petrowicht' for the godfather; and 'Charles Rouy' or 'Charles Johnson' for the father (29–30). The names adopted by Petrucci are Italian-, Russian-, and French-sounding in reflection of the places where Hersilie had lived with her real family, and her sister Dorothée's name is similarly rendered unstable through a reference to her via the nickname 'Dachinka' (28). Hersilie presents herself as being at the mercy of Pierre, 'auquel nous nous trouvions ainsi appartenir toutes deux': she is physically at the whim of a fictional godfather in a comparable way to being at the legal mercy of a real father. Both figures are conflated in the pronoun 'on', which stands as the giver of the childhood nickname 'Étoile d'Or', 'surnom qu'**on** m'avait donné étant enfant'. It is also the indistinct presence that threatens to take a name away, 'un pseudonyme artistique

[40] Mitchell (2000: 38–9).

auquel **on** ne pourrait plus toucher' (32). 'On' holds at once the poisonous effect of a real family and the nourishment of an imagined one.[41]

A key allusion in this extract represents a striking point of disintegration for these duplex figures. During the description of Hersilie's supposed adoption by Charles Johnson, it is revealed that the 'écrit' produced by the '*dame noire*' states: '**il la lui** avait abandonnée en toute propriété' (28). First, the voice of Hersilie or the '*dame noire*', or both, frames the quotation of a piece of writing that puts 'her' into the third person, as an object of exchange between two actors, 'la'. Early in the sentence the object pronoun 'lui' refers to Charles Rouy, but at this later point he is made the subject of the action 'il', and the indirect object pronoun 'lui' replaces Charles Johnson. Also, since 'la' refers to the abandoned infant 'Hersilie' who would grow up to be the '*dame noire*', but also implicitly to the child who grew up thinking she was Hersilie, now speaking, it is unclear who abandoned whom, and to whom. This intricate web of complicity reflects the complexity of the speaker's relation to her own father, who here appears as one man split in two. This father is rejecting and threatening, but also welcoming and nurturing, and these two attitudes are reflected in the evocation of two 'Hersilies': the nameless, suffering self and the legitimate, powerful, other self.

The title of Hersilie's first version of her memoirs, *Mémoires d'une feuille de papier*, calls to mind the scraps of paper used to write down her experiences in the verbally prohibitive asylum. However, reading the first version through the perspective of the later text, *Mémoires d'une aliénée*, is an extremely uncanny reading experience. The narrative point of view presented at the opening of *Mémoires d'une feuille de papier* is that of a piece of paper personified, which is the speaking 'je'. In the story this piece of paper is cut in half, and on its two halves are written the birth certificates of an unnamed 'moi' and her twin sister, who, like Echo, is described as voiceless: 'ma pauvre sœur était muette'.[42]

J'ai près de soixante ans; je suis bien vieille, bien usée; j'ai échappé jusqu'ici à tous les dangers; mais je vais en courir de si terribles que je n'y survivrai sans doute pas. J'ai été témoin, servante ou complice involontaire de tant de choses étranges, que je ne veux pas en laisser le souvenir périr avec moi. [...] moi, pauvre petite feuille de papier jaunie, prête à tomber en poussière. Je lègue à ces feuilles jeunes et vivaces sur lesquelles j'écris mon histoire, le soin d'achever ma tâche.[43]

---

[41] Falret (1890: 235) notes this as a textual commonplace in patients' writing: 'Ils s'imaginent être les victimes de leur entourage; ils accusent, la plupart du temps, le personnage anonyme ON.'

[42] Burton (1882: 4).

[43] Ibid. 1.

This metaphorical depiction of an original split, occurring at the very inception of identity, reveals the extent of the devastation caused by the anxiety provoked: from the naming process itself recorded on a birth certificate, Hersilie represents an 'I' irrevocably alienated from herself. Her life and writing form an attempt to reconcile these two aspects, through the appropriation of another's story as her own. The story narrated in *Mémoires d'une feuille de papier* reveals much that the later text conceals about the extent of Hersilie's beliefs, and regarding the motivation behind her incarceration.[44]

The tale opens with Petrucci giving a child to Georges Champigny (Charles Rouy) whom he must register under the name 'Eucharis' (Hersilie). This child is nicknamed 'Stella d'Oro' (Étoile d'Or), and grows up frequenting European high society. One evening at a ball, Petrucci introduces Stella d'Oro to another little girl, Lily, who looks like her and will be her little sister. The next morning Stella d'Oro is found dead in her bed. Petrucci takes the child's body away and gives Lily to Georges Champigny to replace the dead girl, who in turn is given the name Eucharis. Eucharis I (Stella d'Oro; the '*dame noire*') is not really dead, and reappears later in the story to Eucharis II (Lily; first-person voice of Hersilie).[45] The main narrative voice is therefore that of

---

[44] Here I am working on the assumption that Hersilie is the author of *Mémoires d'une feuille de papier*. Matlock argues that Hersilie's memoirs are unlikely to have been significantly altered by her editor because so many internal inconsistencies are left unresolved, which if ironed out might have made the text more convincing. Sérieux and Capgras (1910: 220), however, argue that given the fantastical nature of the first version of the *Mémoires* it is likely that Le Normant des Varannes tidied them up: 'C'est lui qui publiera et au besoin, sans doute, expurgera les mémoires de cette aliénée.' This is a curious assertion given that it was Varannes who published a far less sanitized version of the story under his own pseudonym, and that the saner sounding version was published under the name of Hersilie Rouy. I would argue, therefore, that it is more likely to have been Hersilie herself who made her story more palatable to the reading public in recognition of the fact that her secret version of events, if widely shared, would not be well received.

[45] These characters are split in the two texts as follows:

Eucharis I	Eucharis II
original child given by Petrucci	second child given by Petrucci
first child of Champigny/Rouy	second child of Champigny/Rouy
Stella d'Oro	Lily
dame noire ('elle')	main narrative voice ('je')
the original Eucharis/Hersilie	'inconnue' and substitute Eucharis/Hersilie
the original, stronger self	daughter of the duchesse de Berry
'énergique et fière'	'douce et timide'
free	incarcerated
takes place of Eucharis/Hersilie in the world	has taken the place of Eucharis/Hersilie in the asylum

The story of *Mémoires d'une feuille de papier* is summarized in Sérieux (1910: 206–8).

Eucharis II, who has been brought up believing she is Eucharis, but is herself the '*inconnue*'. This version of events corroborates in a more explicit way the state of affairs above-mentioned in *Mémoires d'une aliénée*. The relationship between the two versions of 'Hersilie' is one of sorority. The 'original' Hersilie (Eucharis I) is the stronger and better one: she is energetic and proud, and strong enough to take the place of the substitute Hersilie in order to bring prominence to her name. Most importantly, perhaps, she is free. The substitute Hersilie (Eucharis II) is timid and reticent when faced with her counterpart; she is the one controlled by a terrifying outside agent (Petrucci), the abducted daughter of the duchesse de Berry, possibly even the Antichrist; she is incarcerated and defeated and her name covered in shame.[46]

These excerpts produce the effect of mental isolation by drawing meaning out of external events that are arbitrarily connected. This part of the text is characterized by narcissism, where energy is deployed not in attaching to others in meaningful relationships, but in creating a new sense of 'me' to back up the one in peril. The result of this is textual alienation, where the speaking subject is split into a negative and a positive version of herself: one unknown and unknowing, weak and nameless, and another that holds the power of a name and is received into the arms of a welcoming family. Sérieux and Capgras argue that there never occurred in Hersilie's mind a true 'dédoublement de la personnalité', but revealingly concede that in creating her own 'double' in the figure of another who represents the 'real' Hersilie, leaving the speaking subject with only the status of an '*inconnue*', that 'elle a cherché par là, d'une manière subconsciente, à effacer une page lamentable de sa vie, voulant d'abord nier la présence d'une Hersilie dans les asiles d'aliénés et ensuite excuser sa conduite à l'égard de sa famille'.[47]

The doctors have flagged up a very important issue here, but the question of Hersilie's motivation is arguably a central and not a peripheral one. We recognize that Hersilie wanted to erase something

---

[46] Freud suggests that all human beings fancy themselves at the point of primary narcissism as 'His [or Her] Majesty the Baby' in his essay 'On Narcissism' (1914: 91). This grandiose desire translates very literally in this story into 'Her Majesty Hersilie' through the author's conception of her royal origins. In the second part of 'The Interpretation of Dreams' Freud (1900–1: 353) says the figures of the Emperor and Empress (or the King and Queen) represent the dreamer's parents. The psychotic experience is frequently compared to being analogous to dreaming, and is made manifest in Hersilie's consciousness through the translation/exaltation of parental figures into royalty.

[47] Sérieux (1910: 209).

*

desperately painful and replace it with something better, but the causal factors that lie behind this desire are only superficially alluded to in the psychiatric analysis. And yet the key to these reasons, both sociological and emotional, is situated in what the text itself reveals about the lonely, eccentric voice that lies behind its composition. However, the folding back on the self that occurs here is only one aspect of a complex text, and we shall now examine the dynamics of a voice not only in dialogue with itself, but also with clinicians. It is too simplistic to present the narrative point of view as being solely that of the weaker, 'substitute' Hersilie. It is also important to note the energy and vitality of the 'real' Hersilie that engages so effectively in polemical dialogue with her incarcerator.

A VOICE IN DIALOGUE

Mémoires d'une aliénée can be read as a form of philosophical challenge to the unquestioned assumptions that underwrote psychiatric medicine. The question as to how far the text can be viewed as rhetorically successful will be based on an appreciation of what the author does that is convincing and persuasive and which gives a sense of health and vitality, rather than what can be read as dubious, fantastical, or patholog-ical. Hersilie manages to subvert the authoritative discourse of psychiatry through the only technique, according to Lucy Irigaray, available to women:

> Il n'est, dans un premier temps, peut-être qu'un seul 'chemin', celui qui est historiquement assigné au féminin: *le mimétisme*. Il s'agit d'assumer, délibéré-ment, ce rôle. Ce qui est déjà retourner en affirmation une subordination, et, de ce fait, commencer à la déjouer. Alors que récuser cette condition revient, pour le féminin, à revendiquer de parler en 'sujet' (masculin), soit à postuler un rapport à l'intelligible qui maintient l'indifférence sexuelle.[48]

This is the essence of Hersilie's success as a manipulator of words, for she exploits a negative experience to gain a positive result, and succeeds. Where Hersilie is universally viewed as devious and dissimulatory by her incarcerators, we shall read her as resourceful and flexible in her mimicry of the 'masculine' position—the alienist discourse of reason—and successful in raising enough reasonable doubt in the minds of her readers to convince others that a mistake had been made.

[48] Irigaray (1977: 73–4).

The feminist philosopher Judith Butler draws on speech act theory when she argues that gender is performative. The idea of 'gender' is a notion that 'constitutes the very identity of woman which it purports to both analyse and politicize', and 'madness' can similarly be argued to be a concept that actually defines those it seeks to describe.[49] The parameters of sickness and health that psychiatry claims to establish are necessarily normative and exclusionary, but this process can be subverted by the dissenting voice of the 'aliénée'. If the medical appreciation of sickness constitutes the madwoman as much as she constitutes it, this memoir can be viewed as an arena where resistance to this process is played out. The description 'délire de revendication' can be viewed as being tailored to fit a set of impressions of Hersilie as a tireless complainer, but these character traits can also be read as indicative of a healthy, personal form of resistance to a misogynistic system that addressed individual suffering with contempt. The official documents diagnosing and committing Rouy to the Salpêtrière in 1854 read as follows:

Nous, soussigné, etc., certifions que Mlle Chevalier-Rouy est atteinte de délire partiel; qu'elle peut encore soutenir, dans certains moments, une conversation à moitié suivie, mais qu'elle est le reste du temps en proie aux idées les plus fausses, aux conceptions les plus déraisonnables; qu'elle s'abandonne aux actions les plus extravagantes; qu'il y aurait du danger à l'abandonner à l'entrainement de sa folie; qu'il est à désirer qu'elle soit maintenue séquestrée.

11 novembre 1854.

Signé: Calmeil

Paris, 30 novembre 1854

Je, soussigné, etc., déclare que la nommée Rouy-Chevalier, sortant de Charenton, où elle est en traitement depuis septembre 1854, est atteinte de délire partiel, actes incohérents, manque de direction dans sa conduite, forme chronique constatée par le docteur Calmeil, *et réclamant plus long examen.*

Signé: Lasègue (92)

The Calmeil report frames the notion of being able to maintain dialogue as a healthy sign in his first statement: 'elle peut encore soutenir, dans certains moments, une **conversation** à moitié suivie'. This ability to hold forth in conversation is set in direct opposition to Hersilie's beliefs, which are '[les] idées les plus fausses' and '[les] conceptions les plus déraisonnables', and to her behaviour, '[les] actions les plus

[49] Wright (1992: 82).

extravagantes'. Lasègue's assessment lacks the positive aspect of his colleague's report, and simply reiterates his words in more medicalized terminology: 'délire partiel' and 'actes incohérents' (92). Calmeil significantly proposes that Hersilie's state of mind is dangerous, and removes any sense of the freedom and responsibility of the patient from the equation when he states that she is '**en proie aux** idées les plus fausses'. Hersilie's freedom is absolutely curtailed, for she is physically a victim of those who restrain her, and is mentally prey to her own 'idées'. Her response to this assessment reads:

N'est-il pas effrayant de voir comment se font les certificats qui décident, cependant, du sort et de la liberté des gens *contre* lesquels ils sont dressés?

Ainsi donc, voilà le docteur Lasègue, qui a pourtant un air de supériorité, d'incontestable intelligence, de franchise et de bienveillance presque joviale... Il me trouve secourant, consolant, nourrissant mes compagnes... et il m'accuse d'*actes incohérents!* [...]

Il est vrai que M. le docteur Lasègue ajoute que mon état *réclame un plus long examen*.....Qu'on lui donne alors à lui-même les moyens et le temps de s'assurer personnellement de cet état, avant de prendre sur lui la responsibilité d'une séquestration aussi terrible, qui détruit tout une existence humaine! (93)

Where the medical assessment provokes a sense of fear through the allusion to potential danger, in the use of the conditional phrase 'il y aurait du danger', Hersilie responds with a question designed to arouse the reader's possible fear of 'séquestration arbitraire'—that any sane person could find themselves locked away—and asks, 'N'est-il pas effrayant de voir [...]?' She reclaims the notion of freedom and questions the validity of certificates such as these, 'qui décident [...] du sort et de la liberté des gens *contre* lesquels ils sont dressés' (93). The emphasis placed on the preposition 'contre' reinforces the adversarial relationship between diagnosing clinician and patient.

Hersilie's decision not to suppress any of the diagnostic statements about her mental illness is a source of rhetorical strength in the text, and it represents a remarkable exploitation of her position of subordination in order to achieve the affirmation of her reader. She re-quotes her psychiatrists' statements and allows them to stand as pointedly foolish conclusions. She appeals to the reader's sense of justice, and makes her own voice sound reasonable where that of the clinician sounds crazy. The manifest imprecision of vague notions such as 'délire multiforme'; 'actes incohérents'; 'délire partiel' are held up to the scrutiny of Hersilie's version of reality. She puts her reader in direct touch with the truth that statements made on the basis of hearsay have grave consequences for her: '[Lasègue] ne m'a vue qu'une minute ou deux [...] et il me condamne sur la foi du docteur Calmeil, qui m'a condamné sur la foi d'un médecin ne m'ayant jamais vue, lequel m'a enlevée, par complaisance, sur la foi d'autrui!' (93). The emphatic repetition of the construction 'sur la foi de' builds a chain of complicity and guilt linking all the doctors to a malevolent plot against one relatively defenceless woman.

At this point in the text, also, Hersilie interrogates the underlying state of mind of the doctor, and in doing so adopts a method uncannily similar to his own. She describes Lasègue as having 'un air de supériorité, d'incontestable intelligence, de franchise et de bienveillance presque joviale' (93). As the clinical appreciation of Hersilie is that she is haughty, intelligent, and confrontational, she reflects this assessment in her own written portrait. And just as the doctors emphasize the discontinuity between how Hersilie presents herself and what lurks beneath the surface, so she brings to light the contradiction between how doctors act towards the patient and the cruel implications of their diagnoses. The statement 'il m'accuse d'*actes incohérents*' stands in ironic contrast to the presentation of Hersilie's actions through the present participles 'secourant, consolant, nourrissant'. It also raises the question as to what or whom the epithet 'incohérent' should apply. As Hersilie's actions are depicted as being full of meaning, simultaneously scorn is poured on the validity of 'incoherent' medical opinion (93).

In comparison to the first excerpts examined, the presence of the figures 'je' and 'elle' is in these parts of the text diminished. In fact Hersilie as narrator only names herself 'je' at the end of these passages: 'J'étais *installée, pour le reste de ma vie, comme pensionnaire indigente du département de la Seine*' (99). The personal pronoun 'me' appears as the object of the actions of 'il', in reference to Lasègue and Trélat. Hersilie reiterates the issue of freedom and responsibility, of whom should ultimately be held to account for her misery, when she suggests that Lasègue should indeed have a proper look at her and decide for himself, 'avant de prendre **sur lui** la responsabilité d'une séquestration aussi terrible' (93).

The doctor's statements are held up as meaningless: 'Que **signifie** son certificat, après tout?' The absence of concrete, empirical evidence to support the statement made is highlighted through the use of the verb 'voir', for her claim is that Lasègue has not witnessed anything of significance: 'Témoigne-t-il de ce qu'il a **vu** lui-même? Non, certes!. ...' (93). The idea of seeing connects with the key concept of the asylum being a stage, a 'lieu du dévoilement', where the performance of madness could be played out and translated into diagnosis via the gaze of the alienist doctor.[50] What Hersilie so effectively challenges here is the legitimacy of the doctor to pass judgement on a patient he has barely observed. His point of view is exposed as being fundamentally flawed by the prejudice that every manifestation of human behaviour observed in the asylum is viewed as part of the spectacle of madness. Hersilie demonstrates that the words of her incarcerators can be exposed to similar scrutiny, and rendered meaningless. She reproduces the certificate given by the police to effect her 'placement d'office' in her *Mémoires*:

Paris, le 30 novembre 1854.

Nous, préfet de police,

Vu l'article 18 de la loi du 30 juin 1838;

Considérant que la N[ée] *Hersilie-Camille-Joséphine Chevalier-Rouy, maîtresse de piano, âgée de 40 ans, née à Milan, demeurant rue de Penthièvre, n 19, sortant de la maison de Charenton, où elle ne pouvait plus payer la pension,* est dans un état d'aliénation mentale qui compromet l'ordre public ou la sûreté des personnes, ainsi qu'il est constaté par un procès-verbal du commissaire de police de la section du Palais-de-Justice,

Et certifié par MM. les docteurs *Calmeil* et *Lasègue,*

Avons arrêté et arrêtons ce qui suit:

M. le directeur de l'*hospice de la vieillesse (femmes)* recevra du porteur du présent et placera dans ledit établissement:

Ladite *Chevalier-Rouy,*

pour y être traitée de la maladie dont elle est atteinte, laquelle s'est manifestée par des actes extavagants.

Le Préfet de police

Signe: PIÉTRI

Pour ampliation,

Le Secrétaire général,

Signé: (illisible).

In her discussion of the certificate the author highlights the vagueness of the terms of 'placement' in an asylum. She emphasizes the personal details added to the certificate, and allows the information given elsewhere to stand as evidence of a catch-all, imprecise, depersonalized, and

---

[50] Silvestre (1968: 5–6). This observer calls the asylum a 'lieu du dévoilement' where the 'spectacle de l'aliénation' could be played out.

depersonalizing assessment of mental illness. The key problem posed by such patients is that they disrupt the accepted order of things: they are prone to 'actes extravagants', the expression of excess in any form, and their state of alienation is serious enough to compromise 'l'ordre public' (94). This pro forma layout is challenged by Hersilie in a brilliantly simple rhetorical point, immediately following the official document: 'Tout ce qui n'est pas en italiques est imprimé sur le certificat. L'appréciation médicale est donc la même pour tous' (95). Here, once again, she appeals to the reader's sense of justice, and to her fear that anyone could fall foul of this system. The specificity of Hersilie's experience is reduced to a fill-the-blanks exercise. Similarly, Doctor Trélat is accused of simply copying the assessement previously made by his colleagues:

Certificat immédiat

1er décembre 1854

Je, soussigné, médecin, chef de service à l'asile de la Salpêtrière, certifie que la nommée CHEVALIER-ROUY, âgée de quarante ans, profession de maîtresse de piano, née à Milan, département de (Italie), entrée le 30 novembre 1854, au traitement des aliénées,

Est affectée de délire partiel.

Signé: Trélat.

Comme on le voit, M. Trélat n'a fait que prendre un mot, *délire partiel,* sur le certificat du docteur Calmeil pour constater mon entrée.

Son certificat de quinzaine ajoute:

Est affectée de délire multiforme en voie de démence; en cet état, est dangereuse pour elle-même et pour les autres.

Signé: Trélat (98–9)

Trélat's diagnosis of Hersilie grows from 'délire partiel' to 'délire multiforme' in a fortnight: a diagnosis that ironically becomes less, not more, specific. Hersilie raises the possibility that Trélat had simply reiterated the assessment of a colleague in the first instance, indicating a very literal—and not projected and paranoid—sense of fraternity between these men, and an attitude of solidarity in relation to decisions taken by colleagues.

After presenting these official documents, Hersilie offers a paragraph of provisional closure tense with narrative drama. The adversary 'on' reappears as a figure who has defeated Hersilie, and a series of past participles reinforce the sense of closure and defeat: 'On y était **parvenue,** c'était **entendu, fini**'. The remainder of the sentence is emphasized through the use of italics, 'J'étais *installée, pour le reste de ma vie, comme pensionnaire indigente du département de la Seine*', producing a breathtaking sense of dramatic irony for the reader, who knows that she will escape, and a clear instance of hiatus between the narrative point of view of the 'je' who is telling the story, having successfully escaped the asylum, and that of the 'je' who is in the moment of the story, who feels as if she will be imprisoned forever. The quotation following this statement is a terrifying, double-edged assertion:

les maisons de l'État, 'd'où on ne sortait jamais, (d'après ce que mon frère m'avait dit en 1848), où on ne manquait de rien, l'administration fournissant le nécessaire; où nul n'allait vous voir, défense étant fait de pénétrer dans l'intérieur et de déranger les malades quand on n'était pas de la famille'. (99)

On the one hand, it presents the reader with the uncomfortable truth of the sane person's justification for supporting or simply turning a blind eye to the horror of the asylum—that the insane are provided for, and it is best not to disturb the status quo. On the other hand, the quotation, attributed to Hersilie's brother, gives a devastating sense of the threat that this family posed to one of its members. If it had the power to truly ostracize and isolate her, then the possibility of being erased from the view of the outside world was a very real threat.

The rhetorical success of Hersilie's engagement in dialogue with those who justify her detention has been observed, for in overtly discussing the statements made about her that mark her out as mad, she highlights the real human consequences of the medical assessment of madness or sanity. Payen at the Orléans asylum, along with other clinicians, emphatically and without compassion labelled Hersilie as incurable, provocative, and insubordinate. He prescribed that she ought to be contained and prevented from infiltrating the sane and normal outside world. Hersilie provides her own ironic assessment of Payen, though: 'Vous êtes un parfait commissionnaire, un assez bon maître d'hôtel, mais surtout un excellent geôlier' (275). In the course of Hersilie's supposedly pathological attempt to constantly 'se mettre en avant', we bear witness to what was unquestionably a terrible human injustice. In the management of vast numbers of insane residents it is appreciable that Hersilie's adversarial behaviour was an impediment to the smooth running of the establishment. But without her constant annoying complaint, so bitterly disparaged by the medical profession and subsumed in a diagnosis of severe mental illness, we would not have such a valuable written record of how it actually felt to be a single, independent woman in France at this time, called sick and forced to undergo 'treatment' without her consent. It felt the same as being imprisoned for life without trial. Rouy was the victim of the insecure mood of the post-1848 era, during which hope in the 'moral treatment' had decreased among clinicians and patients were increasingly likely to be judged incurable. In practice, treatment for mental illness in an asylum had become far removed from Pinel's ideal of the progressive, therapeutic environment conceived with the aim of relieving mental distress. That asylums effectively became a repository for society's unwanted placed residents such as Rouy in a doubly desperate position: no hope for release, because deemed 'dangerous', but no hope for relief from mental distress, because deemed 'incurable'.

THE ASYLUM AS A PATHOGENIC SPACE

When discussing the narrative point of view of these memoirs, we discover that there is a constant tension between a story believed but concealed and a more plausibly 'sane' version of events presented to doctors and Hersilie's implied reader. Sérieux and Capgras write of Hersilie: 'La malade tente même des explications spécieuses pour donner le change et empêcher de prendre au sérieux ses conceptions ambitieuses que nous savons profondément ancrées dans son esprit.'[51] This cunning 'dissimulation', or should we say profound awareness that her ideas were invariably disbelieved, is seen by medical commentators as a widespread symptom of the rebellion of the patient. However, it may also be read as the failure of the asylum to help those it sought to cure. The manifest lack of compassion in the words of the clinicians, when discussing Hersilie's case, reflects the professional failure to recognize that the patriarchal society, of which the asylum formed an integral part, might have been a causal factor in the sickness of talented women whose life opportunities were severely restricted.

The pieces of writing to be examined next are highly compelling, for they reveal the true face—rather than that presented to clinicians—of an individual irrevocably damaged by the asylum experience. The first excerpt to be analysed is a piece of correspondence composed in the time between Rouy's final release from the asylum at Orléans, in 1868

---

[51] Sérieux (1910: 210).

and the settlement of her compensation claim in 1878. The second is a letter written to the Impératrice Eugénie in 1862, in which Hersilie details her suffering in the asylum, and tells of her spurious relationship to the duchesse de Berry. In the first, she effectively demonstrates that, irrespective of an individual's state of mind, treatment in a mental asylum is a humanly degrading experience. In the second, the asylum can be read as a reinforcement of the pathogenic experience of social isolation, which contributed to the onset of illness in the first place.[52] In short, the asylum makes people sick, not well, because it isolates, degrades, and disbelieves the patient in the same way that the outside world does, and consequently encourages her to seek refuge in fantasy. The first extract reads as follows:

Qu'ai-je à craindre maintenant? Qu'ai-je à perdre? Ne m'a-t-on pas tout pris, tout ôté? Quels torts ai-je eus? Celui de prendre *des sobriquets*, de répéter ce que chacun a dit? C'est une plaisanterie, n'est-ce pas, Monsieur l'inspecteur, que cette accusation? Ne m'a-t-on pas mise en position d'agir ainsi, de tout oser?

Que je publie les lettres que j'ai entre les mains; ma vie, que chacun connaît, en la faisant appuyer de nombreux témoins; mon journal, mes impressions, mes mémoires. . . . qu'y verra-t-on? Dévoûement, travail, honneur!

L'honneur, Monsieur l'inspecteur, à la place du *déshonneur officiel* dont on m'a abreuvée depuis quinze ans.

Et vous me dites de me taire, de rester dans mon coin, d'attendre les secours de la bienveillance qui m'entoure! . . .

De quelle bienveillance? Quelle est la bienveillance qui m'a secourue depuis six mois que je suis libre? Est-ce la bienveillance officielle, ministérielle? – Voulez-vous savoir ce qu'elle est? [. . .]

Vous me dites de me taire! Est-ce là votre justice, Monsieur? Accepter la honte, le déshonneur, un nom équivoque, une réputation flétrie. . . . faible, misérable, malade, traîner une vie de mendicité, de mépris. . . . Pourquoi? Pour qui? – Que dois-je à personne? Qui donc m'a tendu la main avec courage, bonté, justice? . . . .

En admettant que je me taise, le terrible *on* se taira-t-il? (317–18)

---

[52] The aim of the asylum was to ease mental suffering through the creation of a healing environment:

Je suis intimement persuadé [. . .] qu'il y a plusieurs fous qui le sont devenus pour toujours, parce qu'on les a *fermés* trop tôt; beaucoup, parce qu'on les y a trop longtemps *tenus*; et d'autres, parce qu'ils l'ont été pendant toute leur vie. Il n'est pas douteux qu'on réussirait certainement à en guérir un plus grand nombre, si, libres dans un clos vaste, spacieux et agréable [. . .] ils pouvaient aller, venir, se promener à leur gré, et jouir d'un air plus sain et moins infect que celui qu'ils respirent communément dans leurs cachots. (Daquin, quoted in Brierre de Boismont 1854: 3)

The patient's memoir tells us that, despite good intentions, little had changed by the latter half of the nineteenth century.

This extract can be set in the context of Hersilie having realized her initial objective of being released, and addressing the question of being fairly compensated for what she has suffered. The effectiveness of this piece is achieved through the manipulation of relationships between multiple 'destinataires', and through the shifting position of the narrative 'je' from subject to object and back again. Through the repeated questioning of the justifications of her treatment in the asylum, Hersilie succeeds in creating a heterodox point of view that stands as counterpoint to that of medical 'expertise'. Where previously Hersilie's critique of the asylum has endorsed the orthodox position, in that her claim to be sane must be based on the assumption that some people actually are insane, she here demonstrates how the treatment she has received might justify an individual having recourse to eccentric behaviour, if this gains the attention needed to make possible her release.

This excerpt presents a complex web of perceived relations among Hersilie, her implied reader, and her persecutors. At a superficial level, the letter format, with a named addressee and signatory, suggests a simpler set of relations. The direct addressee is 'M. Durangel' ('vous'), who is the first object of the numerous interrogative sentences in the letter; but the letter, cited as it is as part of a wider text with a larger potential readership, has multiple 'destinataires'. The process of aggressive questioning by one party in order to elicit a response from another is complicated by the fact that the letter is published in a book of memoirs, which makes a third party privy to the dispute. This third party could be the putatively sympathetic reader, or it could be the diagnosing psychiatrist seeking to demonstrate why Hersilie's behaviour is indicative of madness.

This passage has at least three potential addressees, and hints at three possible motivations for its composition: justice, the rousing of public sympathy, and the settling of old scores. The implicit addressees in this text—the sympathetic and the hostile reader—are, in addition, assembled in the pronoun 'on'. We have 'le terrible *on*' referred to in the final line of text, a conflation of all those responsible for locking Hersilie up, for her maltreatment, and for obstructing the course of justice. This is also the 'on' evoked in the repeated interrogative structure 'Ne m'a-t-**on** pas tout pris?'; 'Ne m'a-t-**on** pas mise en position d'agir ainsi?' It is again the 'terrible *on*' that has tarnished Hersilie's reputation through official shaming, the '*déshonneur officiel* dont **on** m'a abreuvée depuis quinze ans.'

The figure 'on' is also, however, the unspecified reader of the whole text, 'mon journal, mes impressions, mes mémoires', as opposed to the reader of the letter, who can perceive personal qualities rather than shame as a direct result of reading the whole memoir. 'Qu'y verra-t-on?' asks Hersilie, 'Dévouement, travail, honneur!' Three abstract nouns describing the positive attributes perceptible in the text parallel the emphatic listing of abstract virtues lacking in those who have dealt with Hersilie's case—'courage, bonté, justice'—and contrast with the negative adjectives that describe her present state: 'Faible, misérable, malade'. The use of suspension points at these positions in the text is notable, serving either to introduce a stark reminder of the tragic reality of the protagonist's situation or to allow the reader to pause to reflect on her virtues. The attention of this other 'on' is only possible via the publication of the letter as part of the text of the *Mémoires*, 'Que je publie les lettres que j'ai entre les mains; ma vie, que chacun connaît, en la faisant appuyer de nombreux témoins'. The various parties that could constitute the ever present 'on' are brought together in the indefinite pronoun 'chacun'; every reader, whether a supporter or an adversary, should be exposed to the other side of the story, and Hersilie should be able to plead her case.

The fluid use of the pronoun 'on' is linked to the effect created by the oscillation between the objectification and the subjectification of the 'je', the former reinforcing her victim status and the latter emphasizing the effect this victimization has had on the here and now of the speaker, and on her future. The first paragraph is formed of a series of seven short, interrogative sentences that alternate between 'moi' as subject and 'moi' as object. The constructions that place Hersilie as the object of the sentence (the third and the seventh questions) reinforce her status as victim: she has had everything taken away and has been forced into this position by others. Here, the placing of the 'je' in the position of object does not create an air of passivity; on the contrary, it serves to underline Hersilie's aggressive, proactive discursive position. Her attack is implicitly legitimated by the horror of the asylum experience: 'Ne m'a-t-on pas tout pris, tout ôté?'; 'Ne m'a-t-on pas mise en position [...] de tout oser?' When the 'je' is placed in the position of subject, however, the narrator describes the logical outcome of this past victimization, which has made the future hopeless: 'Qu'ai-je à craindre maintenant? qu'ai-je à perdre?'

As well as exclamations, suspension points, and interrogatives, extensive use is made of italics for rhetorical emphasis. The words italicized in this passage, '*des sobriquets*' and '*déshonneur officiel*', are both used ironically. The second example is an ironic reprise of the noun 'honneur'; the repetition of this term in the negative noun 'déshonneur' places the cruelty of the establishment in direct opposition to Hersilie's blamelessness. The italicization of the phrase '*des sobriquets*' places ironic emphasis on a notion felt to be of little consequence, and therefore holds up to ridicule the idea that Hersilie could be accused of madness for something so insignificant. However, a reverse twist of irony is that this emphasis also undermines Hersilie's argument. The issue of her shifting identity, demonstrated in part through her adoption of pseudonyms, is indeed of primordial importance: it is the founding evidence upon which doubts over Hersilie's sanity are based.

The speaker in the passage sets herself up as a victim of both the atrocities of the asylum and of a corrupt and negligent administration. She achieves this through varying emphatic devices: the use of numerous interrogatives, exclamatory punctuation and, frequent italicization of words. The 'je' of the text is engaged in a struggle for justice and is proactive as much as reactive. The experience of victimization provides the resources for this struggle, and it is this fighting spirit that creates and sustains the feeling of disharmony and strife in dialogue, which is presented and re-emphasized throughout the text.

The letter to the popular Empress and wife of Napoléon III, Eugénie, thematizes the question of the circumstances of Hersilie's birth, and therefore her own sense of her beginnings and a problematic sense of identity. The sense of threat to the validity of her existence communicated through this piece of writing indeed reflects the precarious position of the French nobility, with whom she aligns herself to some extent, finally ousted in the Revolution of 1848. It also indicates that the misery of asylum existence pushes the author of the letter to cling more tenaciously to her appropriated story. The asylum can therefore be read as pathogenic in that it reinforces the deepest desire for intimacy and acceptance that this narrative accommodates. This piece is constructed around a paradoxical anxiety, that of appearance and disappearance, the concern of belonging and the terror of being eradicated. This central and contradictory anxiety is brought to bear in this excerpt through the evocation of the dual themes of birth and belonging, and of exclusion and disappearance, which will be examined in turn:

Madame,

Avant d'en appeler à la noblesse française, avant d'instruire une famille infortunée du sort de l'une de ses enfants plus malheureuse encore que sa malheureuse famille, c'est à vous, à l'Empereur, votre auguste époux, que je m'adresse, Madame, et j'ose espérer, pour moi comme pour tous, que ce ne sera pas en vain.

Après l'assassinat du duc de Berry, la duchesse, sa femme, mit au monde un fils et une fille.

Il n'est pas nécessaire, Madame, de vous rappeler la position de la famille royale en ce moment, pour que vous compreniez la nécessité absolue de sacrifier la pauvre fille au repos de la France.

Elle fut donc enlevée du palais des rois et soustraite à la vue de la nation.

Cependant on avait vu *emporter* un enfant, et le secret n'en put être si bien gardé que le bruit d'une substitution ne prît la place de la triste vérité.

Cette enfant fut embarquée au Hâvre, pour la Russie, fut remise entre les mains du grand-maître de la police à Saint-Pétersbourg, et après avoir passé quelques années enfouie dans une campagne aux environs de Moscou, elle fut renvoyée en France avec une famille richment rémunérée.

Elle passait alors pour un membre de cette famille faisant partie de la bourgeoisie, et par conséquent ne pouvait attirer sur elle l'attention générale.

Malheuresement, *par une complication de circonstances,* l'aisance procurée à cette famille fit bientôt place à la gène, et comme elle ne connaissait pas les parents de l'enfant.... la pauvre petite subit toutes les cruelles vicissitudes de ses parents improvisés, à l'insu de sa royale famille.

Car *c'est en Russie* qu'on a remis l'enfant au sieur Charles Rouy, qui s'est engagé à la faire passer pour sa fille, et ce Français, en acceptant, ainsi que sa femme, ce dépôt fragile, crut obliger une grande dame russe ou portugaise.

Bientôt même, la croyant pour toujours abandonnée, et sans autres parents et amis que ceux que sa destinée lui avait donnés, il la regarda comme sienne.

Cependant l'enfant grandissait, Madame; sa ressemblance frappante avec la duchesse de Berry étonnait tout le monde, et rappelait malgré soi le souvenir des bruits fâcheux qui avaient circulé lors de sa naissance.

Sans la position honorable de la famille Rouy, sans *deux frères et une sœur* du même père, sans *l'éloignement surtout* de l'astronome au moment où ces événements s'étaient accomplis, on aurait eu des doutes....

Bientôt on fit *disparaître,* l'un après l'autre, les deux frères de la jeune fille; on maria sa sœur avec une reconnaissance d'enfant naturel, pour ne pas produire l'acte de naissance.

....Et lorsque l'astronome, seul protecteur de la jeune abandonnée, fut mort, n'osant pas proposer à celle qui était involontairement entrée dans sa famille de quitter le nom qu'elle avait reçu de *celui* qui l'avait élevée avec tendresse, on l'enleva; on la fit disparaître dans une de ces bastilles qui ont survécu au régime déchu; on l'enferma dans un asile d'aliénation mentale, en jetant à ceux qui en sont chargés le nom de *Chevalier, de parents inconnus.*

Instruite de son sort et de sa naissance par celui qui l'avait emmenée hors de France et qui avait suivi sa destinée, l'infortunée pria les magistrats français de lui venir en aide, de vouloir bien examiner ce qui la concernait, de la prendre sous leur protection et de lui donner un nom la mettant à l'abri de tout danger.

On traita ses réclamations de rêve d'orgueil, de *folie ambitieuse*; on la jeta brisée dans les lieux les plus infects, les plus bruyants, les plus horribles; on la priva de nourriture, de vêtements; on la traîna dans des bouges, dans des cachots, dans des donjons; on l'appela indigente avec mépris; on lui fit épuiser toutes les privations, toutes les douleurs, la privant même de linge pour se changer dans des sueurs glaciales et nerveuses, d'autant plus douloureuses que le froid est plus vif et qu'elle passe dans ce donjon son hiver sans feu et sans lumière.

Ne pouvant résister, dans l'état où elle est, à tant de cruautés, elle vous supplie, Madame, de lui venir en aide, en adoucissant son sort et en priant S. M. l'Empereur de donner des ordres à son sujet.

Elle n'a pas demandé à naître! Le malheur de sa naissance ne peut lui être reproché comme un crime, et elle espère, Madame, que votre bonté lui épargnera la douleur d'en appeler à ceux qui l'ont *reniée.* . . . peut-être même en la croyant *morte-né.* . . .

Inconnue elle a vécu, inconnue elle voudrait finir, si votre impériale bienveillance voulait la sauver d'en appeler à la publicité.

Daignez, Madame, agréer mes profonds respects.

HERSILIE

Sœur du roi Henri V

The letter is addressed 'A Sa Majesté', and is situated 'de mon donjon'. Hersilie immediately places herself in drastically inferior terms to her addressee, as if an imprisoned subject appealing to her sovereign for clemency. This might be viewed as analogous to the experience of the asylum as being imprisoned when innocent. This opening paragraph is the only part of the letter where Hersilie refers to herself in the first person, as a speaker directly addressing her 'destinataire'. It soon moves on to recount Hersilie's other story, that of a child substituted to take the place of another, told uniquely in the third person. The connection between the 'moi' of the opening lines and the 'elle' of the story told is posited in the signature, where the speaking 'je' names herself 'Hersilie' and, significantly, in the third person, as 'Sœur du roi Henri V': only at the end is the connection between the two revealed (170).

The first notions we have that this story is centred around the problem of Hersilie's birth—her appearance in the world—are the references to an unhappy family provided in the first paragraph: 'une famille infortunée' and a 'malheureuse famille'. Hersilie places herself in a position of subordination in relation to her addressee, through the deferential use of the verb 'oser' in the construction 'j'ose espérer'. She does, however, simultaneously place herself as a potential member of 'la noblesse fran-çaise', on a social level with the Empress. Hersilie indicates that she is at the bottom of the pile, in terms of the misery of the unenviable situation of the royal family, for she is 'plus malheureuse encore' than even they are. This suggests that her greatest unhappiness emanates from a sense of not knowing who she is, and of having been rejected by the family she knew as her own. This great unhappiness is reinforced, not alleviated, by the asylum experience. Hersilie hopes that her cries for help will not be 'en vain', just as every word from her position is uttered in futility.

The first line of the following paragraph introduces the theme of birth through the story of a little girl being born to the duchesse de Berry. She seeks to be welcomed into the arms of a family as a child found who was once lost, not to oust another member. The loss of this 'pauvre fille' is presented as an essential sacrifice, which gives Hersilie's cause the authentic stamp of nobility and necessity, just as the voice of the 'pauvre folle' (171), invoked at the end of the excerpt, asks to be heard as the genuine cry of a lost family member. Following the passage describing the fate of this child, made to disappear from public view, we are told that Hersilie nevertheless came to be noticed. 'L'enfant **grandissait**', and 'sa ressemblance frappante avec la duchesse de Berry étonnait tout le monde'; the striking use of the verb 'grandir', here used in a concrete sense, mirrors the metaphorical expansion and embellishment of a life story noted earlier in this chapter. The fact that a resemblance is posited between Hersilie and a duchess is noted by 'tout le monde', adding credibility to an unbelievable story (169).

The next paragraph explains that Hersilie's position within her family was not questioned. But crucially we are also told, through the enigmatic phrase 'on aurait eu des doutes....', that Hersilie's 'true' identity always threatened to slip out into the open. A sense of suspense here announces the later revelation that Hersilie would be: 'Instruite de son sort et de sa *naissance* par celui qui l'avait emmenée hors de France.' The themes of appearance and valid existence are brought to the fore in this paragraph through the reference to 'sa naissance', the fact that someone of impor-tance has 'suivi sa destinée'. In addition, the protagonist is concerned with

projecting herself into the public sphere, and the use of verbs denoting
authoritative action communicates this worry: 'l'infortunée **pria** les magistrats français'; officials are asked to 'lui **venir** en aide' and to '**examiner** ce
qui la concernait'. Although the individual 'elle' is presented as the object
of these actions, the narrator nevertheless succeeds in suggesting that she
could be brought to recognition and given the protection she seeks: 'la
prendre sous leur protection'; 'lui **donner** un nom la **mettant** à l'abri de
tout danger'. Ironically, what Hersilie seeks is 'asylum' in the true sense of
the word; the experience of the asylum is diametrically opposed to her most
basic desire for care (169).

Later, it is the Impératrice Eugénie herself who is presented as the
agent of Hersilie's recognition. She is the person who can bring her case
to light, and be instrumental in restoring her true identity. She can also
be a source of comfort and protection, 'en **adoucissant** son sort et en
priant S. M. l'Empereur de donner des ordres à son sujet' (170). The
theme of appearance in the world and the threat of disappearance that
the asylum presents are juxtaposed in the lines that follow: 'Elle n'a pas
demandé à **naître**! Le malheur de sa **naissance** ne peut lui être reproché
comme un crime.' It is hoped that the goodness of the addressee, 'votre
bonté', will spare Hersilie from having to fight against those who oppose
her: 'lui épagnera la douleur d'en appeler à ceux qui l'ont *reniée...*' (170).
This paragraph evinces an extreme tension between the parallel anxieties of appearance and disappearance, the term 'naissance' emerging
as the idea for which Hersilie is punished, 'comme un crime'. These
two central ideas are crucially brought together in the italicized adjectival use of the terme '*morte-né* [*sic*]'. Hersilie's existence is reduced to
the idea of being born dead, simultaneously appearing and disappear-
ing, having no name and being devoid of identity, like the living death
of the asylum experience.

This tension between the ideas of being given prominence and
importance, and being constrained and diminished as a person, are
repeated in the final paragraph in the excerpt that follows the conclusion
of the letter. Here, the figure of 'elle' is transformed once more into the
speaking character 'je':

Le docteur Léon Reber m'ayant appris, en 1857, qu'on me tenait enfermée
parce que j'étais sœur du roi Henri V, j'avais juré de m'en venger, et je lui tenais
parole en me servant de cette nouvelle version, comme je m'étais servie à la
Salpêtrière des suppositions du docteur Métivié, basées sur la ressemblance qu'il
me trouvait avec la duchesse de Berry et les bruits de substitution qui avaient

couru. Mes lettres aux ouvriers m'avaient valu ma mise en liberté comme *guérie*, bien que déclarées *délirantes*; il ne m'avait manqué que les moyens d'en profiter. Je n'avais plus qu'une chance de sortir de cet asile où on m'ensevelissait dans le silence le plus profond: c'était de faire parler de moi au dehors, fût-ce par des excentricités. Qui sait si ma lettre, qui certainement est parvenue à son adresse, ne serait pas remise à Sa Majesté à cause même de la bizarrerie de son contenue? On la disait légitimiste; cette façon de remettre en cause l'accouchement si discuté de la duchesse de Berry devait piquer sa curiosité. Elle voudrait peut-être savoir qui était cette pauvre folle implorant son secours.....et la moindre enquête m'eût sauvée. Mais il n'en devait pas être ainsi, et j'étais encore loin du port. (170–1)

In this paragraph assertions are made that emphasize Hersilie's lack of freedom and security: 'on me tenait **enfermée**'; her voice is reduced to silence: 'on m'ensevelissait dans le **silence** le plus profond'. The acknowledgment of identity and security sought are still precarious in the conclusion to this description: 'j'étais encore loin du port' (170–1). However, the sense of being positively identified and of defeating the asylum is put across with equal force in the same piece of writing. Mitivié, a reliable figure, is presented as recognizing the speculative link with the duchesse de Berry.[53] Hersilie's 'chance de sortir' lies in the exploitation of verbal devices, in order to inscribe her existence as real, and emphasis is laid on the necessity to '**faire parler** de moi au dehors'. Communication of her cause is presented as a source of empowerment, even if it appears strange: 'Qui sait si ma lettre [...] ne serait pas remise à Sa Majesté à cause même de la **bizarrerie** de son contenu?' The Impératrice is said to be on the side of the Légitimistes (those who supported the elder Bourbon line, ousted in 1830), and she offers the double advantage of potentially believing an unbelievable story, and of being able to warrant Hersilie's legitimate status through the endorsement of an alternative version of 'l'accouchement si discuté de la duchesse de Berry' (171).

In terms of the anxiety of disappearance, we can assert that the child presented in the first paragraph is from the outset placed in a position where she lacks agency in her own story. From birth separated from her mother, she is passed around locations as Hersilie is passed around the clinicians and asylums. 'Elle' is the passive subject of the verbs 'enlever',

[53] This doctor's name is variously (mis-)spelled as 'Métivié' in the *Mémoires*, as 'Métivier' in Sérieux and Capgras, and 'Mitivié' in Ripa (1986b: 114). On Rouy's 'certificat d'internement' the doctor himself signs as 'Mitivié', which is the spelling I therefore use.

'soustraire', 'embarquer', 'remettre' and 'renvoyer'. Since her life now is directed by the powers of medical authority, Hersilie reads the present experience into her past, in which she finds herself disempowered and her destiny absolutely controlled. Even when released Hersilie was not given a chance to try living on the outside, until she found a male protector who would shield her from the institution. Here, she seeks a female protector who might promise to give her a meaningful status as a member of a great family.

Hersilie passes unnoticed as a member of the bourgeoisie, '[elle] ne pouvait attirer sur elle l'attention générale', and is well concealed from the eyes of the nation. This ironically announces the later notoriety her case would gain in the press, because of what 'normal' people perceived her to have suffered at the hands of the medical profession. Hersilie then talks of suffering 'les cruelles vicissitudes de ses parents improvisés', which we can read on two additional levels here: first, the role of the alienist doctor is a paternal one, because the law of 1838 left patients with the status of a minor; second, the writer is here searching out a new set of 'parents improvisés' in a family of the very highest social standing, who, she fantasizes, might come to her rescue where her former 'adoptive' parents failed (168).

This spirited-away 'enfant' is given over to the protection of Charles Rouy, an adopted father, and is transformed into a reified object, passed from the hands of the aristocracy into those of the bourgeoisie: 'ce dépôt fragile'. The fragility of this person is made acute and immediate in the account of the brutality of the asylum that follows these introductory paragraphs. Hersilie's precarious position is highlighted through the adjective 'abandonnée', used to evoke her relationship to her surrogate family. The possessive pronoun in the phrase 'il la regarda comme **sienne**' re-emphasizes the sense of belonging that she is seeking to establish through adoption into what she believes might be her true family (169).

In the account preceding the part of the letter that deals with Hersilie's committal to the asylum, her own 'disappearance' is pre-empted by that of her brothers. In this and the three paragraphs that follow, a malignant agent in the narrative is the non-specific pronoun 'on'. The use of the emphasized verb 'disparaître' reinforces this sense of anxiety: 'Bientôt **on** fit *disparaître*, l'un après l'autre, les deux frères de la jeune fille.' The repetition of the construction 'faire disparaître' announces Hersilie's fate, recounted in the following paragraph: 'on l'enleva; on la **fit disparaître**'; 'on l'enferma'. The obscurity of the asylum is once again equated with being imprisoned, and the institution described as 'un de ces bastilles qui ont survécu au régime déchu'. Just as Hersilie pays homage to the Bourbon line as something that has, to some extent, survived the abolition of the monarchy, she draws our attention to the institutional brutality of the asylum that has outlived the Ancien Régime (169).

The treatment of the theme of disappearance and the insecurity of identity is evoked in this extract through the leitmotif of the 'inconnue' that recurs throughout the *Mémoires*. In reference to the conferral of the name 'Chevalier', Hersilie writes: 'on l'enferma dans un asile d'aliénation mentale, en jetant à ceux qui en sont chargés le nom de *Chevalier, de parents inconnus*' (169). Entry into the spaces of the asylum entails the total elimination of an individual's past, of the family history that she thought was her own, and inscribes her in a new system where she is made less than human. In this system she is made to inhabit places described as 'infects', 'bruyants', and 'horribles'; she is dragged through 'des bouges', 'des cachots', and 'des donjons'; she fails to have met her most basic human needs. The verb 'priver' and its derivative noun 'privation' appear three times in this paragraph alone, compounding the lack of basic sustenance and protection with the neglect of Hersilie's emotional state of mind.

Sérieux and Capgras emphatically argue that Hersilie exaggerated her complaints; they assert that she was very well treated, and that her doctors and the asylum administration did everything possible to make her life comfortable. Her complaints, they argue, form an integral part of her 'délire de revendication'. Several doctors are quoted in support of this point of view, including Dr Auzouy of the asylum at Fains. He writes:

C'est [...] la malade la plus insupportable que j'aie jamais connue..., il me faudrait plus d'une semaine pour relater les ennuis qu'elle me causa... Cette femme occupant, quoiqu'elle fût indigente, des chambres de pensionnaires, ne cessa de répandre dans la contrée où nous étions, les plaintes les mieux fondées en apparence, les plus fausses en réalité sur l'insalubrité des logements qu'elle occupait... [...] La femme d'un haut fonctionnaire arriva un jour chez moi, contenant à peine son indignation. Mlle C. R.... lui avait écrit une lettre portant pour épigraphe: 'De ma glacière', dans laquelle j'étais accusé de vouloir la faire mourir de froid.[54]

The article goes on to describe other occasions where Hersilie is argued to have greatly exaggerated her plight. The portrayal of Hersilie as an

[54] Sérieux (1910: 212).

ungrateful and immodest resident fundamentally ignores the most important aspect of her complaint, which was that she had been deprived of the freedom to live and care for herself as she pleased. And no amount of concessions could compensate for this loss.

In any case, there is much evidence to suggest that Hersilie's living conditions actually were substandard. Historians have painted a very different picture of asylum life. It is clear that the ideal of the spacious, clean, healing space of the 'asylum' was far from being the case in reality. Although some establishments were demonstrably better than others, for those unable to pay, the environment of the Salpêtrière and asylums such as Fains, Orléans, and Maréville were all that was available. Resources were stretched to the limit, and overcrowding resulted in squalid and insalubrious living conditions. Ripa paints a truly horrific picture: 'La capacité d'accueil est insuffisante [...] Les conditions hôtelières sont déplorables, qu'il s'agisse du réfectoire de 250 couverts, des deux ridicules salles de bains, ou des toilettes infectes.'[55] The asylum is demonstrated to have the very opposite of a curative effect:

La salle des admissions est donc déjà ancrée dans le monde asilaire. Regrettable localisation qui entretient aisément la confusion, déjà facile, entre l'affaiblissement nerveux et la folie. La mise en contact de maladies aussi dissemblables comporte des risques d'aggravation pour les moins atteintes; [...] Dans l'ensemble de l'hôpital, et principalement dans les dortoirs, le volume d'air est insuffisant par suite de l'encombrement.[56]

Elisabeth Roudinesco describes the institution in comparably dismal terms: 'Comme l'Hôtel-Dieu, gigantesque mouroir, la Salpêtrière témoigne de l'état du savoir médical où l'asile et l'hospice sont des cours des miracles habitées par la gangrène et la disette.'[57] Aude Fauvel has also found that as late as 1880, conditions in asylums had not improved and there were moves to debate and effect a change in the law because of public outcry at the widespread abuse of patients.[58] Life in the asylum,

---

[55] Ripa (1986b: 114).

[56] Ripa (ibid. 114–15) describes an asylum divided into five sections. The first for so-called 'paisibles' provided one cell for 40 women; the second section which housed 'agitées' and 'semi-agitées' had one for 14 women. The third section, the 'division Mitivié', in 1863 admitted double its capacity: 296 women for a facility designed for 150. Similarly, section five, which housed all recent admissions and mixed a range of different afflictions, accommodated 290 women in 39 cells.

[57] Roudinesco (1982: 23). This refers to these hospitals in the period following the cholera epidemic during the July Monarchy of 1830.

[58] Fauvel (2002). See Chap 1, n. 24.

for those who had to exist there day in, day out, was truly miserable. Even the asylum of Auxerre, praised by Hersilie for its superior aspect, disguises an ugly underside of squalor and human wretchedness. First impressions are good: 'Tout y brille, tout y est coquet, bien aéré; partout des galeries à colonnes: on reconnaît que le Baron Haussmann a passé par là' (178). But conditions are altogether different in the cells of the 'quartier des gâteuses':

Elles sont carrées, un peu plus longues que le lit en bois (lit de gâteuse) qu'elles contiennent. Un fauteuil percé est placé à côté. C'est tout le mobilier. [...] Elle est entourée de hauts murs, en sorte que la recluse ne peut absolument rien voir, ni être entendue de personne. Elle ne peut qu'entendre les cris de frénétique souffrance, de fureur indicible de ses malheureuses voisines. Rien n'est plus affreux [...] Il y a de quoi rendre furieuse la personne la plus douce et la plus calme ... De quoi pousser au suicide. (178)

The evidence regarding the conditions of the asylum shows that Hersilie's contentions about her poor treatment is corroborated by recent historical research. The juxtaposition of these convincing claims with a strange, delusional story connect conceptually the general sickness of the asylum with the aggravation of one individual's already susceptible state of mind. In short, the deathly kind of life one is forced to lead as an asylum resident gives impetus to the process of seeking psychological refuge, or 'asylum', in the story repeatedly quoted as the reason for her continued detention.

The doubt cast over her identity, in Hersilie's eyes, and the wish for her case to be made known is problematized in the final lines of the letter: 'Inconnue elle a vécu, inconnue elle voudrait finir, si votre impériale bienveillance voulait la sauver d'en appeler à la publicité' (170). Ironically, here Hersilie is already raising publicity in favour of her case. The claim to remain 'inconnue' is at once a call for recognition from her real family, from a fantasized perfect mother figure, and the expression of a desire to be protected and hidden from the cruel vicissitudes of the world.

The physical and psychological context of the asylum, which was designed to be one where the healing of mental distress could be facilitated, as an integral part of a pathogenic society—which created, upheld, and perpetuated the structures that prevented women (and indeed many men) from achieving their human potential—was likely to make the women it treated more sick than they were before being introduced into that space. In the two excerpts of writing we have examined, Hersilie first demonstrates how the degrading and demoralizing experience of medical treatment might drive the individual to desperate measures. The invention of stories and stirring up trouble, however, has the counterproductive effect of corroborating the accusations of insanity that represent the cause of her present suffering. The second excerpt shows how this experience translated into a direct rejection of reality, and how the asylum failed to re-integrate in Hersilie a sense of being able to partake of the shared truth of the external world. Instead, it drove her further into the realm of delusion that she chose in preference to what reality had to offer.

This analysis has taken as its principal themes three aspects of Hersilie Rouy's *Mémoires*: the feeling of extreme social and psychological isolation appearing as a major causal factor in mental illness; the sense that a mentally disturbed individual could understand that what was happening to her was unjust, and could respond with equal vigour to statements made by clinicians condemning her to a life of incarceration; and the way in which the 'asylum', far from achieving its aim of alleviating mental distress, in fact appears to have made Hersilie all the more intransigent in protest against a system that had ruined her life. As the feminist *mal du siècle* novels of the first half of the nineteenth century expressed the deep-seated melancholia of frustrated female protagonists, so Hersilie's text reflects the mental distress caused by the mighty combination of a misogynistic legal system with the unchecked power of the mad doctors. Her memoir shows that the treatment imposed on women deemed unmanageably different of mind caused considerable pain and frustration, and her inadequate or unreliable perspective does succeed in revealing something of the exasperating experience of being disbelieved. The remnants of reason, when refracted through a system of ideas considered to be false, cannot be heard in the asylum, and what we have read as signs of health, vitality, and resistance are those same aspects of her verbal output that had Hersilie labelled unsound of mind. If she was a danger to society and to herself, the attitude of disbelief inherent in psychiatric treatment did not encourage her to abandon her fantasies: on the contrary, it made her pore furtively over ideas that only exacerbated her problems. Hersilie was doubly disempowered, once by her family and once by the asylum, and was twice the victim of man-made laws that left her with no status. She was illegitimate, and so forewent the security of an inheritance; she was thought mad, and was readily integrated into a system invented by men to manage women who could not be controlled.

If the aim of 'moral treatment' was to gently persuade the patient of the error of her beliefs, and to re-mould her into a shape that would fit the norms of the outside world, the intended humanity of this procedure was entirely undermined by the fact that the asylum oppressed women in the same way that society did. If she found it difficult to fit this role on the outside, she would find it even more difficult on the inside where discomfort and a manifest lack of human intimacy and compassion meant there was little chance of strengthening a foundering ego's relation to external reality. If reality was refused, it was not without reason, and we must conclude this discussion on the positive note that even though Hersilie was wrong, she was right. The question of her really being the lost child of a Bourbon antecedent was and is an irrelevancy, because she was who she claimed to be: the victim of someone or something that sought to annihilate her. Self-delusion was in her case a legitimate strategy, because her fictions of empowerment clearly represent a metaphorical reversal of the experience of absolute disempowerment. Hersilie Rouy's writing stands as a remarkable testament to the strength of the human spirit in adversity, and despite there never being any recognition on the part of the medical profession that her wishes were valid, even after her release, we can conclude that on this subject she knew herself better than they, and that in an important way her insight was greater than theirs.

3

Marie Esquiron

'Ma triste et injuste séquestration'

Madame Esquiron's *Mémoire* carries a protracted title which sums up the author's case, and her complaint: *Mémoire adressé à Monsieur le Ministre de la Justice par Madame Esquiron, née de Gasté, Séquestrée dans la Maison de santé de M. le docteur Goujon, 90, rue de Picpus, à Paris, Où elle réfute elle-même l'imputation d'aliénation mentale et le Rapport de MM. les aliénistes Mottet, Magnan et Voisin.* The woman in question is Marie Esquiron, an individual of considerable wealth and keen intellectual insight, who in the latter half of the nineteenth century twice found herself incarcerated, at the request of her father, in private Parisian asylums.[1]

Esquiron had from January 1866, aged just 21, already spent over a year and a half as a 'placement volontaire' at the asylum run by the famous alienist pioneer Émile Blanche. In this text she deals with her second admission, this time as a 'placement d'office', to the clinic run by Dr Goujon at 90, rue de Picpus, in Paris. The circumstances surrounding her committal are woven into two opposing narratives, sustained by two textual voices: her own story, in which she accuses her father and her husband of conspiring to have her incapacitated in order to lay hands on her not insignificant personal fortune, and the account given by the doctors who assessed her case. This is given in a report reproduced in its entirety within the body of the text, alongside Esquiron's refutation of it, summarizing the version of events created as a result of interviews and consultations with these and various other men.

---

[1] The whole text is reproduced in the Appendix to this chapter. The reader is directed to read the short memoir in its entirety before proceeding to the analysis that follows here.

Esquiron's account tells us that in August 1891—now married, with no children—in the grip of a terrible bout of nausea, she suspected that she was being poisoned and went to the local police station in order to have the matter investigated. This, according to historian Laure Murat, was considered a 'démarche courante à l'époque', and taken as an event in isolation the doctors agree that her complaint was no more than 'la manifestation d'inquiétudes non justifiées [...] mais pas nécessaire-ment déraisonnables' (8).[2] Esquiron's father, Monsieur de Gasté, 'dé-puté du Finistère', was called, and duly arrived at the police station and declared that his daughter was insane (4). She was immediately taken to the special infirmary at the Préfecture de Police, where she stayed three days before being 'placée d'office' at the clinic of Dr Goujon.

In the intervening days, Esquiron's husband had visited the Préfec-ture de police in order to corroborate his father-in-law's opinion that his wife was mad. The testimony of these two men was enough to convince doctors Garnier and Blanche, both attached to the Préfecture, that her enforced committal was warranted. The decision to enact a 'placement d'office' was, Esquiron suggests, 'une perfidie bien calculée pour mettre mes adversaires à l'abri d'une responsabilité légale de ma part' (5). At this time Esquiron was taking steps to divorce her husband, whom she presents in the text as a penniless good-for-nothing living solely on her income. Upon admission to the infirmary, she requested that seals be placed on the doors of her apartment in Paris, in order to prevent her husband from gaining access to the dossiers she had assembled in support of her case for divorce. Her request was not carried out for nineteen days: in the mean time, claims Esquiron, her husband would obtain and destroy all the incriminating evidence against him (4).

From the date of composition we know that Esquiron was still in the asylum in January 1893, and therefore that her second committal lasted at least another eighteen months. Esquiron was incarcerated on 27 August 1891, and between this date and December of the same year she challenged the decision of her 'placement d'office' in a hearing of the 'première chambre' of the Tribunal civil de la Seine. In response to her appeal, three well-respected doctors, Magnan, Mottet, and Voisin, were

---

[2] Murat (2001: 189). This anxiety seems somewhat removed from our modern sense of reality, but at this time poisoning was not as uncommon a phenomenon as it is today. Extensive bibliographical searches have revealed Laure Murat to be the only historian to have commented on the case of Marie Esquiron, and she makes no mention of what this woman's fate might have been.

called upon to examine Esquiron's case and to recommend a decision concerning her detention. The exact date of the hearing is not cited, but given that the doctors were urged to come to a decision '*avant la fin de décembre 1891*' (4), we know that it must have been before this date. Esquiron tells us that the doctors' report was submitted on 28 June 1892. But according to the records of the Tribunal civil de la Seine, held at the Archives de Paris, this information is incorrect. No record of this case was made on this day or in the surrounding weeks. Even if the records of these hearings could be easily accessed, it would not throw any more light on the subject: when the report was finally submitted, the court must have rejected Esquiron's appeal, motivating her to take the case to the higher authority of the 'Ministre de la Justice'.

The question remains, however, as to what happened next. My own research at the Archives de Paris has unfortunately not thrown any light upon the subject. Esquiron's name does not feature in the registers of deaths of all the Paris arrondissements between 1893 and 1902. In addition, the registers held by the 1st and 12th arrondissements, the locations of Esquiron's home and the Maison de Santé in rue de Picpus respectively, have no record of Esquiron's death between 1902 and 1922. We can infer from this that Esquiron did not die in this particular asylum, but we cannot know at this stage whether she, like Camille Claudel and countless other 'aliénées', may have been transferred and left to languish in a provincial asylum.[3] Esquiron is likely, of course, to have died somewhere else in Paris after 1902, but to find this out would involve searching the registers of the individual arrondissements of the entire city. And this would not tell us when or where she died if outside of Paris, and whether she was ever released, and if so how soon after her appeal.[4]

---

[3] Ripa (1986b: 188) has demonstrated that women transferred to provincial asylums—because of the pressures of increasing numbers—were less likely to be released at the request of their families: 'Quelle que soit leur condition, les transférées abandonnées de tous ne bénéficient que très rarement des demandes de retrait: elles concernent 1 malade sur 54,25 en province contre 1 sur 11,16 à Paris de 1844 à 1858.' These statistics reflect findings in public asylums at an earlier point in the nineteenth century, but the fate of Camille Claudel, who was transferred by her family to an asylum in the south of France at the outbreak of the First World War, suggests that this may still be a plausible outcome to the story.

[4] See the bibliography for information concerning the documentation researched at the Archives de Paris.

The archives of the Préfecture de police hold some registers relating to nineteenth-century private asylums in Paris. However, with the exception of those institutions that accommodated famous patients, these registers were unfortunately all destroyed in 1961. The last records we have of Esquiron, until it is possible to carry out far more extensive researches into her family history, dates from 1893, when she remained incarcerated. This lack of conclusion, in terms of the status of available historical information, corroborates the tension created by a narrative that begs a response being left without closure. This is an assessment that was as relevant at the moment of composition as it is to the reading process now.[5]

As this book goes to press, however, the very recent digitization of some key historical French texts is beginning to reveal some potential new leads on the case of Marie Esquiron. It seems that Esquiron was an active campaigner in the women's movement and that her text written from the asylum is a natural continuation of her feminist activism. Esquiron gave a speech at the *Congrès français et international du droit des femmes* entitled 'Sur la violation de la loi au détriment des femmes', two years prior to her incarceration.[6] She also appears in a list of feminist activists in Richer's coverage of the campaign for women to be able to initiate divorce proceedings, and the case is mentioned in the 1893 *Mémoires* of the Préfet de la Seine. We can only infer from this new information that Esquiron probably did have some important supporters, and may therefore have stood some chance of being released as a result of her brilliant campaign, although this is still questionable if her case had already been rejected by the Civil Tribunal, despite a strong defence.[7]

By the time Esquiron was writing, the most significant change in the status of women that had occurred was the reinstating of the divorce law

---

[5] Given the types of documents held in these archives, we can almost certainly infer that the registers of this asylum no longer exist. The registers of the Maison de Santé at 6, rue de Picpus, where Nerval was first interned are retained, but no records remain of the clinic at 90, rue de Picpus. The loss of records relating to such institutions is confirmed in Ripa (1983: cxiii).

[6] *Congrès français et international du droit des femmes* (Paris: E. Dentu, 1889), 247–8.

[7] Google Books has recently digitized much obscure material from some US universities, notably the University of Michigan and Harvard. At the time of going to press, only very limited access to the references was available. Esquiron is mentioned in the following texts: *Mémoires de M. le préfet de la Seine & de M. le préfet de police et procès-verbaux des délibérations* (Imprimerie municipale, 1893); Bidelman (1975: 254); Curinier (1905: 138). According to Curinier, Esquiron had a 'brilliant' lawyer in Louis Duval-Arnould and her case caused some scandal in society, but does not state the outcome of the case.

in 1884, previously established after the Revolution and abolished under the Restoration. Esquiron's vociferous criticism of marriage and her explicit desire to divorce follows in the context of a significant debate over these issues by women writers in the period preceding her incarceration. Texts such as Louise Gagneur's *Le Divorce* (1872) and *Les Forçats du mariage* (1870), as well as Gyp's *Autour du divorce* (1886), contributed strong female voices to this debate. Feminism was gaining momentum at the end of the nineteenth century, with key women such as Louise Michel founding the *Association pour le droit des femmes*. The 1880s and 1890s continued to be a misogynistic era, however, concomitant with the anti-Semitism caused by the widespread anxieties provoked by the Dreyfus affair.[8] Despite these tensions, there is general agreement that women's writing was on the rise at this time and that the *fin de siècle* mood was one of the anticipation of change for the better.[9]

The Belle Époque, although primarily marked by the relative stability of the Third Republic, was also inflected with a renewed expression of the masculine *mal du siècle* in Decadent literature. Waller calls male writers of this movement 'latter-day avatars of the mal du siècle' and argues that authors such as Baudelaire and Huysmans use fictions of impotence in order to bolster the masculine authorial identity.[10] The decadent myth of woman as a natural but abominable creature is taken up by Rachilde in her presentation of a sadistic heroine's 'merciless destruction of a young male lover' in *Monsieur Vénus* (1884).[11] Rachilde rejected the label 'feminist' and declared herself 'homme de lettres'.[12] The decadent vision of woman as perverse and potentially dangerous is, as we shall see, an idea reflected in the discourse of the psychiatrists concerned with the case of Marie Esquiron: an illustration of how such ideas came to inhabit the popular imagination. This dark vision of humanity was also present in psychiatric thinking. Clinicians and theorists such as Morel and Valentin Magnan, one of the authors of the report on Esquiron, gave prominence to ideas of degeneration and the hereditary nature of illness and moral weakness. This perhaps gave

---

[8] See Rosemary Lloyd, 'The Nineteenth Century: Shaping Women', in Stephens (2000: 120–6).

[9] On sources to illustrate this rise, see Dudovitz (1990: 77).

[10] Waller (1993: 183) argues: '[T]hese decadent male writers, who mark the beginning of "our" modernity, are latter-day avatars of the mal du siècle, who make disabled subjectivity an integral part of an empowering (authorial) male identity.'

[11] Holmes (1996: 64).

[12] Rachilde (1886: xiv).

Esquiron less hope of release than patients of the earlier era during which belief was placed in the efficacy of the 'moral treatment'. Because of the time in which she was diagnosed, Esquiron was unlikely to be thought to be curable or indeed ever cured.

Published in 1893 under the authorship of 'Madame Esquiron', this memoir embodies the voice of protest of a woman of considerable financial means. She found herself at the mercy of a system that allowed decisions of the utmost importance concerning her well-being to be made by her closest male relations. The text has been produced in the form of a pamphlet, conceivably printed privately by the author, and is addressed to 'Monsieur le Ministre de la Justice'. It does not appear to be aimed at any category of general readership, and as far as we know the only copy is held at the Bibliothèque nationale de France (BNF). The text was printed by the Imprimerie Hénon, which according to the BNF catalogue also published documents concerning the administration of the Assistance publique, legal documents, and political and sociological tracts.[13] The manuscript is reasonably short, and runs to sixteen pages of written text. It comprises a title page, an epigraph, an introductory section reproducing a letter sent to 'Monsieur le Ministre' on 17 December 1892, and five sections entitled 'Ma réfutation'; 'Mon père'; 'Mon mari'; 'Réfutation du rapport'; and 'Ma conclusion'. The most lengthy and energetic part of the text is the section dealing with the 'Réfutation du rapport', in which Esquiron presents the complete text of the psychiatric report in a column on the left-hand side of the page, and her own refutation of their assessment in a parallel column. What is produced is an extraordinary piece of writing where the voice of the patient, the individual transformed into an object of clinical observation in the report, enters the realm of public discourse on madness through a rhetorical performance that surpasses that of the 'experts'. Esquiron emphatically insists, 'Je me connais moi-même, mieux que Messieurs les aliénistes ne me connaissent' (6), and for many readers the power of her claim will be convincing: she was wronged by a system that refused her the freedom to lead the life she desired.

Esquiron's involvement with the asylum system began with her committal to the private clinic run by Émile Blanche in 1866. Blanche admitted her as a 'placement volontaire' on the grounds of 'excitation maniaque hystérique'. At this time, Esquiron's problems centred upon

---

[13] According to the library catalogue this publisher was active between the 1870s and the late 1940s.

an extremely problematic relationship with her father. Blanche notes in his records:

Elle est sujette à des emportements extraordinaires [...] pendant lesquels elle méconnaît tout à fait l'autorité paternelle, pousse des cris, des sanglots qui mettent toute la maison en émoi; se livre à des voies de fait sur des personnes qui l'entourent et menace de se jeter par la fenêtre, lorsqu'on met la moindre opposition à ses volontés. Depuis quelque temps, Mlle de Gasté a pris M^r son père en aversion et prétend qu'il est cause de ses accès de violence et de fureur.[14]

The relevance of this assessment is that Esquiron's perceived 'passé pathologique', noted in the report, importantly influenced the decision to effect a 'placement d'office' the second time around, in 1891. As Murat asserts, the basis of the diagnosis of mental illness in this case was the judgement that the patient was considered to be in some way morally deficient and insubordinate. Her behaviour was pathologized because she sought energetically to escape the confines of the gender role that society had assigned her: 'Mme Esquiron n'était pas, à leurs yeux, mentalement malade, mais moralement malsaine.'[15]

Indeed, evidence of acute mental illness is not established in their report. What is certified is that she had already suffered problems in the past, 'un trouble d'ancienne date', and had recently been the subject of a delusional incident, a 'crise de délire de persécution' (7–8). Esquiron's suspicions about being poisoned did not persist beyond her consultation with the Préfecture de police, and the question of delusions of persecution does not preoccupy the reporting doctors as much as Esquiron's bizarre behaviour, her 'excentricités' and 'conceptions délirantes' (8). In particular, the rebellion against her father is seen as grossly improper and indicative of serious mental disturbance. It is barely necessary for the twenty-first-century researcher to read between the lines here to ascertain that what the text euphemistically veils are what appear to be—but of course which cannot be substantiated—allegations of sexual abuse by her father. What follows is part of the Magnan report and Esquiron's response:

Elle insiste sur son enfance, sur l'éducation qu'elle a reçue, ne cherchant, dans un prolixe exposé, que l'occasion de médire de son père, qu'elle accuse d'avoir perverti son imagination, de l'avoir initiée de bonne heure aux mystères de la fécondation des animaux. (9)

---

[14] All the information on Esquiron's first committal is taken from Murat (2001).

[15] Murat (2001: 194).

Si j'ai parlé de mon enfance, c'est parce que j'ai été interrogée sur mon enfance. [. . .] Il est bien vrai que mon père a perverti mon imagination, je ne médis pas, je constate un fait qui a nui à toute mon existence; je ne dissimule rien. (9)

This devastating attack on her father, clearly understood in the medical assessment as emanating from some deep-seated disturbance in Esquiron herself, rather than as an understandable response to abusive behaviour, forms one of three elements of their diagnosis of mental illness: her insubordinate attitude; impulsive decision making leading to bad investments; and 'la perversion de ses sentiments' (11).

Following her first committal, Esquiron sold a family property and lost a large amount of money, judged in the report to be evidence of mental instability: 'Mme Esquiron, en aliénant ses propriétés d'Ille-et-Vilaine, a certainement obéi à une *conception délirante*' (10). Esquiron, however, tells us that she sold the property following bad financial advice, and because she felt ostracized by the local community following her first committal. She in fact managed to secure damages of 400,000 francs against an 'échangiste frauduleux', suggesting that she might not have been to blame for this financial disaster (10).

Esquiron's preoccupation with gynaecological problems is also judged here as a cause for concern:

Un des côtés curieux de son trouble mental, c'est l'importance qu'elle donne à tout ce qui se rattache à l'appareil génital. Elle nous entretient, avec une visible satisfaction, du traitement qu'elle a suivi; elle désirerait que son médecin ordinaire lui continuât ses soins; elle nous montre les ordonnances. Elle insiste sur l'importance que devait avoir pour elle les douches vaginales par la lance du large qui lui avaient été prescrites. (12)

The tone of disgust and horror adopted in this description of the patient indeed reflects the Decadent myth of woman as inherently monstrous and degenerate. As for Esquiron, she is offended by their lack of discretion: 'Ceci prouve le peu de délicatesse du rapport, oubliant que les médecins respectent ordinairement le secret professionnel. Si j'ai suivi un traitement, ce n'est pas pour la tête' (12). This disagreement is representative of the general tone of the memoir, which plays out a power struggle between Esquiron, who is striving to take control over her own medical treatment, and an overbearing clinical presence.

The issue of the extent to which the clinician and other male figures have the insight and authority to make decisions about the patient's 'best interest' calls to mind Freud's famous analysis of the case of 'Dora', published under the title 'Fragment of an Analysis of a Case of Hysteria' in 1905.[16] This young woman was brought to Freud for treatment for *'tussi nervosa*, aphonia, depression and *tedium vitae'*,[17] and in the analysis was uncovered a complex web of unconscious attachments between Dora, her father, his mistress, and her husband ('Herr K.'), who attempted to 'seduce' Dora. Dora repeatedly rejected Freud's interpretations of her relationship with the K. family, in particular her analyst's assertion that she loved Herr K. and her insistence that this attempted 'seduction' was distasteful was a hysterical reaction. Eventually, Freud writes, Dora came to accept some of his interpretations as being correct.[18] However, this did not prevent his patient from cutting short the analysis before it was deemed complete.

Several important parallels can be drawn between this case and that of Marie Esquiron. Although Dora first met Freud in 1898, many of the events described in this case history are exactly contemporaneous with Esquiron's incarceration. In the case of the latter, the hysteria diagnosis is sidelined at the time of her second committal, with which this text is concerned. However, many of the symptoms identified in Esquiron's case fit with the clinical picture of hysteria as being characterized by behavioural disturbance. This may be linked to 'abnormal' sexual activity, including abstinence and a repudiation of sexuality, and these disruptions being metaphorically inscribed on the body via the physical symptom. Both sets of symptoms are relatively minor, voice loss and nervous cough compared to 'hysterical' vomiting, the important factor being that they coincide with a rebellion against patriarchal authority. Further parallels between the two cases are the presentation of a constellation of hateful patriarchal figures; the referral of both women for medical treatment by their fathers; the marked absence of a maternal figure in either text; the sense of lack of closure through the Dora case being a fragment, and Esquiron's memoir having no knowable outcome; a repudiation of sexual desire accompanied by the vitriolic expression of disgust towards male authority figures; and a sense of revulsion towards the body. The main difference between the two cases is in the attitude of the clinician: Esquiron's diagnosis can be placed firmly in the context of a certain *fin de siècle* anxiety about the

[16] Freud (1905: 1–122).

[17] Ibid. 27: *'tussi nervosa'*: nervous cough; *'aphonia'*: loss of voice.

[18] Freud (1905: 104) says to Dora: ' "So you see that your love for Herr K. did not come to an end with the scene, but that (as I maintained) it has persisted down to the present day—though it is true that you are unconscious of it."—And Dora disputed the fact no longer.'

degeneracy of society; Freud's analysis is rooted in the firm belief in the possibility of a cure.

The patient's sense of revulsion towards her own body is evidenced in the presence of another symptom in both patients: the problem of vaginal discharges or 'catarrh', and the accompanying preoccupation with cures and douching. The clues given in Dora's case to this problem may also provide the key to Esquiron's suffering. Freud thinks it plausible that Dora's father infected his wife and daughter with syphilis:

Her [Dora's] mother was suffering from abdominal pains and from a discharge (a catarrh) which necessitated a cure at Franzensbad. It was Dora's view—and here again she was probably right—that this illness was due to her father, who had thus handed on his venereal disease to her mother. [...] The persistence with which she held to this identification with her mother almost forced me to ask her whether she too was suffering from a venereal disease; and then I learnt that she was afflicted with a catarrh (leucorrhoea) whose beginning, she said, she could not remember.[19]

The horrifying possibility that Esquiron's father may, too, have passed on such an affliction to his daughter is an abuse made all the more gruesome by a second violation through medical examination, and the making public of intimate health problems through such a report. This parallels the metaphorical probing of Dora's unconscious desires by Freud, represented by some critics as a violation of sorts:

The Freud who is so certain of the pathology of her response is the Freud whose psychoanalytic knowledge is a violation of her psychosexual privacy, the Freud whose interpretations are like erect, violating members requiring her assent, even if it comes in a form which he, at least, regards as satisfactory, that of her vigorous *dissent*.[20]

The case of Dora has in recent years been the subject of great critical interest. In 1975, Hélène Cixous proposed the idea that Dora could be read as a proto-feminist figure, whose silent bodily protest represented a revolt against patriarchy.

Dora m'est apparue comme celle qui résiste au système, celle qui ne peut pas supporter que la Famille et la société soient fondées sur le corps des femmes, sur des corps méprisés, rejetés, humiliés une fois employés. Et cette fille qui, comme toutes les hystériques, était privée de la possibilité de dire ce qu'elle percevait en

---

[19] Ibid. 75–6.
[20] Forrester (2000: 150–1).

direct, d'avoir la parole en face à face ou au téléphone comme le père B ou le père K, Freud, etc. Elle a eu quand même la force de le faire savoir. C'est l'exemple nucléaire de la force contestataire des femmes. Ça s'est passé en 1899, ça se passe aujourd'hui là où les femmes n'ont pas pu parler autrement que comme Dora, mais ça a une efficacité telle que ça fait voler la famille en éclats.[21]

The critical discussion that followed, which will be examined in greater detail in the next section of this chapter, gave many interesting insights into the case of Dora and Freud's handling of it, and these are extremely useful in the unprecedented analysis of the case of Marie Esquiron.

Before moving on to the close analysis of the text, we must consider a second important dimension in the case-historical and clinical material under consideration here. In addition to the observations made regarding the hysterical nature of Esquiron's protest, the idea of pathological personality—a reflection once again of the contemporary concern with moral weakness—is given great import in the psychiatrists' report. They are, for example, alarmed by Esquiron's 'appétit des boissons très développé', adding 'On l'a surprise essayant de boire le vin qui restait dans les bouteilles. On nous signale, au dehors, ces tendances anciennes.' Esquiron denies these accusations outright: 'On m'a surprise essayant de boire le vin resté dans les bouteilles. C'est bien peu dire, quand mon père disait que j'avais l'habitude de boire un litre d'eau-de-vie par jour, quand j'étais en Belgique, ne buvant que de la bière. Est-ce sérieux?' (13). Magnan's readiness to point up this alleged behaviour might be due to the fact that he was an expert on the subject of alcoholism, and one of the forming minds behind nineteenth-century versions of the clinical category of personality disorder.[22]

If we return for a moment to Murat's suggestion that Esquiron was not really considered mentally ill but morally sick, here the diagnostic process enters the theoretical realm of what in English was termed 'moral insanity'. Murat is correct to suggest that Esquiron's doctors found no trace of psychosis, but we must not neglect the fact that moral sickness was considered a form of mental illness, and descriptions of moral shortcomings frequently fit into diagnostic pictures of states of partial insanity such as 'la folie lucide'. However, the fact that the clearly 'psychotic' Hersilie Rouy's delusions were included as case material in the 'folie lucide' treatise is evidence of how all-encompassing and potentially difficult to challenge such a diagnosis could be.

---

[21] Cixous (1975: 282–3).
[22] Magnan (1871, 1874, 1893).

In 1835 in England, basing the notion on Pinel's concept of 'manie sans délire', J. C. Prichard proffered the term 'moral insanity' to describe such symptoms: 'Morbid perversions of the natural feelings, affections, inclinations, temper, habits, moral dispositions [...] without any insane delusion or hallucination.'[23] These ideas grew into modern conceptions of what is termed personality disorder, or psychopathic personality. In France, Prichard's ideas were mirrored by Morel in 1857, whose writings on 'dégénérescence' in the physical, intellectual and moral realms described a number of pathological personality types.[24] Most interestingly for this analysis, it was Magnan himself who fine-tuned these ideas into systematic categories:

Magnan a systématisé en 1895 ces conceptions en distinguant des dégénérés, soit de l'intelligence, soit de la sensibilité, soit de la volonté; dans ces deux dernières catégories sont classés les égoïstes pathologiques, les obsédés, les altruistes, les hypocondriaques, les passionnels et les impulsifs. Il s'agit incontestablement d'une première différenciation de types particuliers de personnalités pathologiques.[25]

The particular type of 'pathological personality' described in the Magnan report, because of its ostensibly contradictory assessment of serious mental disturbance coexisting with a certain stability of the intellectual faculties, resonates strongly with current clinical descriptions of borderline personality disorder (BPD). This disorder is frequently described as being characterized by 'stable instability', and, although we should exercise caution in the use of retrospective diagnosis, reflects Esquiron's quite accurate observation that the assessment of her state of mind was actually inherently paradoxical and, to some extent, illogical. BPD comprises:

intense but unstable personal relationships; self-destructiveness; constant efforts to avoid real or imagined abandonment; chronic dysphoria such as anger or boredom; transient psychotic episodes or cognitive distortions; impulsivity; poor social adaptation; and identity disturbance.[26]

This description is used to characterize states of mind which cannot be diagnosed as psychotic, but which evince 'psychotic mechanisms' as

---

[23] Prichard (1835: 6).
[24] Morel (1857).
[25] Guelfi (2002: 357), referring to Magnan (1895).
[26] Bateman (1995: 223). 'Dysphoria' is defined in the Chambers dictionary as 'impatience under affliction; morbid restlessness; uneasiness; absence of feeling of well-being'.

described in Kleinian psychoanalytical theory.[27] The major characteristic of such patients is the deployment of so-called 'primitive' defence mechanisms: splitting, projective identification, idealization, denial, omnipotence, and devaluation. Rey describes these individuals as existing 'on the borderline between Oedipal and pre-Oedipal, between psychosis and neurosis, between male and female, between paranoid–schizoid and depressive positions, between fear of the object and need for the object, between inner and outer, between body and mind'.[28] The model of BPD as outlined above entails a conflation of earlier ideas about 'moral insanity' and some aspects of the hysteria diagnosis. Whilst the process of splitting is evident in Esquiron's depiction of a group of 'bad' male characters, further analysis will reveal these mechanisms to be widely present in all discourse, including clinical.

Esquiron's 'problems' may not have been mere fabrication, as she sometimes appears to suggest, and there does seem to have been a very real sense in which, because she refused to accept her subordinate position, she was unable to function 'normally' in the world. The pertinence of her criticism, however, lies in her demonstration of the fact that she was not the only one who should be made to take responsibility for these difficulties, even though she was the only one punished for them. Indeed, the patient's proposed self-knowledge, as offered in the author's statement, 'je me connais moi-même', is in fact an issue of great complexity that renders an apparently uncomplicated text profoundly problematic.

'JE ME CONNAIS MOI-MÊME': THE REASONING HYSTERIC

An effective close reading of this memoir must be based on problematizing what is ostensibly a text that lacks complexity. The reader is faced with a piece of protest writing in which one person's word is pitted against another's. Esquiron's critique of the psychiatric report overtly

---

[27] These so-called 'psychotic' defence mechanisms relate to the period of development theorized in object–relations psychoanalytical theory by Melanie Klein: the 'paranoid–schizoid position'. It is characterized as follows: 'The aggressive instincts exist from the start side by side with the libidinal ones and are especially strong; the object is partial (chiefly the mother's breast) and split in two: the 'good' and the 'bad' object; the predominant mental processes are introjection and projection; anxiety, which is intense, is of a persecutory type (destruction by the 'bad' object)' (Laplanche 1988: 298).

[28] Rey (1994), paraphrased in Bateman (1995: 223).

seeks to reverse the power dynamic at the centre of the clinical relationship by making positive assertions based on the refutation of doctors'
statements. However, the complexity of the text reveals itself in the
apparent fact that the presenter of this text must align herself with its
'destinataire': the putative male authority figure embodied in the addressee, 'Monsieur le Ministre'. In order to effect this alignment, the
voice of dissent must necessarily draw on the rhetorical strategies of
reason. This is the belief system of those with the power to save her, but
it is also that of her oppressors. By contrast, close analysis of both first-
person voices in this text, Esquiron's 'je' and the psychiatrists' 'nous',
reveals that strategies of reason are not the exclusive preserve of male
doctors, and that irrationality is not exclusive to the speech of the female
'hysteric'.[29] In this chapter, I reject the suggestion that the protest of
the female hysteric is a silent one, as suggested by Cixous, and instead
argue that in this text, as in the case of Dora, the patient's protest is
discursive as much as it is bodily.

With these issues in mind, after a brief excursus on the insights raised
by the critical appreciation of the case of Freud's Dora, Esquiron's text
will be examined in three parts. First, an analysis of Esquiron's claim 'je
me connais moi-même' will look at the question of the patient's textual
projection of the impression of insight into her own mental state,
through the coming together of body and mind: a dialectic and a bodily
protest. We shall here examine the way in which Esquiron's writing can
be read as that of a 'reasoning hysteric', by considering what appears to
be occurring textually on a conscious level. As Rouy mimicked the
discourse of her incarcerators, Esquiron here assumes what is traditionally viewed as a 'masculine' stance, exploiting arguments that appear
conscious, rational, and judicious and adopting an adversarial, proactive
stance.[30] In the next section we shall see that there is much that is, by
contrast, irrational in psychiatric discourse, enabling us to observe the

---

[29] My argument here acknowledges Derrida's critique of Foucault, which identifies
the problem of arguing against a concept from within the system that has constructed it.
Derrida (1967: 51–97) argues that Foucault's attempt to write an 'archaeology of
silence', that of the mad in the age of reason, is flawed because the writing of history is
itself a product of that same age. See also Wordsworth (1987).

[30] This section will analyse the opening section of the text, including the letter to
'Monsieur le Ministre' and the sections entitled 'Ma réfutation', 'Mon père', 'Mon mari',
and 'Réfutation du rapport'. The next section will look at the part subtitled 'Texte du
rapport—Mes réponses', which reproduces the psychiatric report side by side with
Esquiron's response. The final section will consider the theme of interminability
throughout the text, and will look specifically at the section entitled 'Ma conclusion'.

institutional 'hysteria' of the medical profession. This section considers the textual unconscious, and the extent to which the literal textual splitting of the two voices, into two columns on the page, is mirrored in the process of splitting the world of objects into good and bad: the use by all the authors of 'psychotic' defence mechanisms as previously outlined. The psychiatric voice here reveals itself to be contradictory and irrational, and Esquiron disrupts the authoritative–subordinate positions imposed by the text of the report. This is achieved by blurring these voices through the process of mimicry, via ironic and subversive citation. The final section addresses the idea of the interminable narrative: two opposing accounts produced from the same source 'facts' result in a sense of narrative stasis and inertia. In this section we shall see that the final piece of text offered, 'Ma conclusion', represents a false closure to a text that lacks a sense of finality or resolution, and only offers yet more deferral and potentially endless hermeneutic possibilities.

The critical discussion surrounding the case of 'Dora' has resulted in, among other assertions, Cixous's argument that the symptoms of the hysteric represent a proto-feminist, silent protest against patriarchal authority. Whilst this assertion is valid and thought-provoking, in focusing on the symptom it neglects the fact that an important part of Dora's protest was discursive: she was conscious of the fact that she was being used as a pawn in a game of exchange between several men, and she articulated her objection to this in words, which are recorded in Freud's analysis of the case. In Esquiron's memoir, the physical symptom, as much as it forms part of a clinical picture of rebellion, is of less importance than her vocal and written protest. This aspect of her self-expression is compelling and convincing, where her 'bodily' protest is murky and ambiguous.

The arguments put forward by Toril Moi on the subject of Dora offer greater analytical mileage in this case. Moi argues that hysteria is not a positive symbolic act, but rather an admission that there is no other way of a woman inscribing her protest:

Hysteria is not, *pace* Hélène Cixous, the incarnation of the revolt of women forced to silence but rather a declaration of defeat, the realization that there is no other way out. Hysteria is [. . .] a cry for help when defeat becomes real, when the woman sees that she is efficiently gagged and chained to her feminine role.

Now if the hysterical woman is gagged and chained, Freud posits himself as her liberator. And if the emancipatory project of psychoanalysis fails in the case of Dora, it is because Freud the liberator happens also to be, objectively, on the side of oppression. He is a male in patriarchal society, and moreover not just any male but an educated bourgeois male, incarnating *malgré lui* patriarchal values. His own emancipatory project profoundly conflicts with his political and social role as oppressor of women.[31]

Just as Dora's self-positioned 'liberator' incarnates patriarchal values, so do Esquiron's incarcerators. However, their project is arguably less than emancipatory. In her memoir, Esquiron attacks from within the system that oppresses her: rather than protesting via the symptom, showing up the injustice of a series of decisions made by men, she addresses them on their own terms. In doing so, Esquiron shows us that reasoning processes are not and have never been the sole preserve of the patriarchal order. Esquiron's counter-attack is resourced by the weapons proposed by Moi:

> The attack upon phallocentrism must come from within, since there can be no 'outside,' no space where true femininity, untainted by patriarchy, can be kept intact for us to discover. We can only destroy the mythical and mystifying constructions of patriarchy by using its own weapons. We have no others.[32]

Esquiron uses these strategies in her own struggles. Examining approximately the first third of the text, we shall now address the questions raised by the statement 'Je me connais moi-même'. This assertion is apparently straightforward because it is an outright denial of others' assessment of the author's state of mind, but it is also hugely problematic because it embraces the position of reason, the 'cogito', and the belief system of her adversaries. Like Rouy, Esquiron places herself unwittingly in the double bind that tacitly endorses the reasoning processes of her captors, and by extension the validity of psychiatric practice. It projects the impression of self-awareness through the deliberate assumption of what is traditionally viewed as a 'masculine' position of argument, which relies upon and validates the conscious and the rational. This is achieved through the endorsement of some parts of the psychiatric report, and through the embracing of the concept of 'raisonnable' as the hegemonic signifier.

In line with the view that authoritative male figures do not hold the monopoly on reasoning strategies, Simone de Beauvoir's objection to psychoanalysis in *Le Deuxième sexe* centres upon a rejection of the way in which the experience of the female is always reduced to a comparison with that of the male. Criticizing Adler in particular, she argues that

---

[31] Moi (1985: 192–3).
[32] Ibid. 198.

activities carried out by females can be viewed as ends in themselves: 'Il appelle "protestation virile" tout projet où s'incarne la transcendance; quand une fillette grimpe aux arbres c'est selon lui pour s'égaler aux garçons: il n'imagine pas que grimper aux arbres lui plaît.'[33] Similarly, if Esquiron here succeeds in projecting an impression, on a conscious level, of insight into her own state of mind and ability to make decisions, it is because her reasoning faculties are intact. In these terms 'reason' can be viewed as a basic human faculty, and Esquiron can be said to succeed in arguing her way out of the conclusions posited by the report as outlined in her letter to 'Monsieur le Ministre'.

One major question posed in this opening section of text is that of the extent to which we know ourselves, and the issue of whether the word of the 'aliénée', who is defined in psychiatric discourse as estranged from herself, can and should be taken seriously. An issue that follows on from this is that of who, if anyone, has the power and expertise to act in another's interest. Esquiron quotes the text of the report: 'Dans son **intérêt**, cette dame doit être maintenue dans une maison de santé spéciale.' She responds with the exclamation: 'C'est un comble d'iniquité!' (3), refusing their monopoly of knowledge in relation to what is in her interest. She demonstrates that she knows herself, and that her 'best interest' cannot be defined by a third party with only a superficial knowledge of her mind. The alignment of her self-knowledge with the professional knowledge of 'Messieurs les aliénistes' is mirrored in the parallelling of small, private matters with affairs of state in the opening lines of the letter to 'Monsieur le Ministre': 'Si l'on peut comparer les **petites** choses aux **grandes**, je viens vous parler de ma triste et injuste séquestration chez M. le docteur Goujon' (3). This alignment brings the private, female sphere of Esquiron into the same realm as the public, male sphere of the statesmen with the power to make an impact on decisions at a local level.

The assumption of the masculine, rational position in relation to the assertion of self-knowledge here is also reflected in the simplistic division of positively and negatively connoted signifiers in relation to the textual 'moi' presented. Language suggesting moral or mental weakness is distanced from the image created of the speaker, and from references to her freedom and well being: the adjectives used to describe her detention are 'triste' and 'injuste', and the emphatic use of the negative

---

[33] Beauvoir (1976: 94).

conjunction 'ni' in the fifth point listed distances the figure of 'elle' from nouns associated with mental degeneration: 'Chez elle il n'y a **ni** démence, **ni** imbécillité, **ni** fureur.' Esquiron seizes upon the report's affirmation that her decision to consult the police was not 'déraisonnable', thus distancing her activity from anything detracting from behaviour considered 'raisonnable'. By contrast, the speaker is associated closely with nouns denoting clarity, intelligence, and moral strength through their apposition with first-person possessive pronouns: '**ma** parfaite **lucidité d'esprit**'; 'la **douceur** de **mon** caractère et **ma moralité**'. 'Je' is in addition placed as the subject of the verb 'employer' to place the speaker on the side of reason: 'j'ai employé tous les arguments que la **raison** et le **bon sens** peuvent invoquer, *en vain*' (3).

In addition to these examples, intelligence and sharpness of intellect are deployed as positive ideas, and are also posited as attributes of the speaker via the assumption of an 'objective' stance through the use of the third-person pronoun: '**elle** est très **intelligente**'; 'son **intelligence** n'est point amoindrie'; and '**elle** a au contraire une **acuité d'esprit** très grande' (3). These arguments are put forward as self-evident assertions of a person's sanity, but in fact miss the crux of the diagnosis in the report, which asserts that the patient's intelligence is deployed in the pursuit of what are deemed to be morally insane activities. Particularly problematic here is Esquiron's claim, 'j'entreprends de réfuter le rapport de Messieurs les aliénistes' (4), whilst drawing heavily on statements made within the text—statements with which she is in agreement—to discredit it. Consequently, the report is both 'favorable et contraire' as far as the patient is concerned, and her own refutation risks the same problems. Since it is based on the hegemony of reason, her protest must necessarily also be to some extent 'contradictoire et caduc' (4). What her acceptance of the negative–positive dichotomy does not question is the validity of the process that decides that an adjective such as 'contradictoire' is assumed to be negative.

This said, Esquiron sets her own predicament apart from that of others by positioning herself at the opening of a paragraph as 'victime', and by drawing attention to the unique importance of her case: '**Victime** d'une **très grande** injustice' (4). Her adoption of a 'masculine' stance is understandable, and arguably the only path open to her. Working with the system is surely the only way to evade it. However, the problems associated with reasoning from a position where you are accused of unreason are also highlighted. Even at the text's opening 'raison' and 'bon sens' are dismissed as being '*en vain*' (3). The technique used in the remainder of the text is for the author to place her own voice in proximity to the putative point of view of her interlocutors on the reason–madness continuum, through the adoption of an adversarial style. Esquiron sweeps aside the weaker arguments of her more powerful 'adversaires' through the posing of questions relating to the conduct of the latter, and through answering these with a damning adverb. For example: 'Comment mon arrestation a-t-elle eu lieu? Est-ce à l'occasion d'un cas de délire comme ils l'affirment? **Nullement**' (4); 'Où est-il ce bon mari? Est-ce de mon côté? **Aucunement**' (6). The use of adverbs as a whole clause, or to open a sentence, dramatizes the text by powerfully rejecting the notion that the answer to these questions could be in the affirmative. It also suggests that what seems obvious to the author should be obvious to the reader too, thus placing her voice once again in close proximity to a 'sane' implied reader: '**Evidemment**, ma séquestration ne peut se prolonger sans forfaiture' (3).

Esquiron's determination to succeed matches the energy expended by her father and husband in order to keep her incarcerated. In the closing section of the letter, she asserts confidently that she will provide the evidence required to prove her soundness of mind through the use of the definite, concrete, and unambiguous future tense: 'lorsque je **serai** libre' (3). She also allows her reader to wonder what might have been, though, and invokes once again a sense of injustice—traditionally constructed as a masculine sensibility—through references to the level of freedom and responsibility that money affords people. She shows herself to be a woman who knew the privilege of possession like a man, and whose rights were taken from her: 'Si j'avais été sans **fortune** j'aurais vécu en paix' (6). This might arouse a sense of indignation in her male reader, perhaps a man of privilege who understands the threat posed by others envious of one's own freedom and security, and lays bare motivations other than the writer's 'best interest' for keeping her from managing her own affairs. It also reflects a peculiarly *fin de siècle* misogynistic attitude, which views woman as inherently dangerous, unpredictable, and unreliable.

According to psychoanalytical theory, in particular the thinking of Jacques Lacan, the assumption of the masculine position when symbolizing one's own experience in language is the only option open to human beings. First proposed in 1953, the concept of the 'nom du père' denotes the prohibitive role of the father as the figure establishing the incest taboo in the Oedipus complex. 'C'est dans le *nom du père* qu'il nous faut reconnaître le support de la fonction symbolique qui, depuis

l'orée des temps historiques, identifie sa personne à la figure de la loi.'[34]
Later, in Lacan's seminar on the psychoses, the term is capitalized and
hyphenated to become the 'Nom-du-Père', the fundamental signifier
presiding over the realm of language, the Symbolic, making the very
process of symbolization of ideas in language possible.[35]

Since it is the 'Nom-du-Père' that is posited as the agency that makes
symbolization, or the expression in words of experience, possible at all,
Lacan's view has been widely criticized for its unapologetic denial of the
possibility of symbolizing the feminine. Since from a psychoanalytical
point of view the assertion 'Je me connais moi-même' is always to some
extent illusory, because a vital aspect of our mental life is unconscious,
the impossibility of representing the feminine in language—impossible
because the feminine is defined by its inability to be symbolized—
means that Esquiron only has recourse to conscious, rational modes of
argument if she is to effect any change in reality.

Placing herself within the masculine Symbolic is doubly problematic,
then, because Esquiron's word is twice removed from the essence of her
experience: once because she can only draw on what is conscious
material, and once again because the only possibility for symbolization
is in the masculine realm. Added to this necessary alienation in language
of the mental processes occurring here, what we are presented with in
the introductory section of text is a series of demonized, authoritative
male figures: 'mon père', 'mon mari', and 'Messieurs les aliénistes'.
Esquiron's complaint positions itself within the Symbolic, but entails
a refusal of that very same order of meaning, which according to Lacan
is the basis of psychosis: '[The Name-of-the-Father] was the inaugurat-
ing agent of Law, but also gave birth to the mobility and the supple
interconnectedness of the signifying chain. Once this fundamental signifier was expelled the entire process of signification was thrown into
disarray.'[36] Now, we shall examine how it is that Esquiron convincingly
constructs the impression of clear insight into her own case through the
rejection of the 'Nom-du-Père'.

In the sections entitled 'Mon père' and 'Mon mari', these characters
are placed firmly in a context of male authority, invoking the law,
professional status, and traditional gender roles within marriage. However, these roles are assumed in an abusive manner, and the actions of

---

[34] Lacan (1966: 157–8).
[35] Lacan (1981).
[36] Bowie (1991: 108).

these two men are demonstrated to be calculated and inhumane. The position in which Esquiron finds herself, that of accusing the two most significant men in her life, is presented as a last resort, a 'nécessité'. They are in the first lines of this section invoked as the controlling forces behind her suffering: 'les **auteurs** de ma séquestration actuelle'. The private, paternal authority of the father is aligned with the public, paternalistic institution of the 'Chambre des députés', through the reference to him as '**député** du Finistère'. Other indicators of generational authority are the references to her father's status, his 'prestige' as 'président d'âge', brought into play alongside the verb 'user' to denote the corrupt abuse of such authority: 'Mon père [...] a **usé** de son prestige' (5).

The repeated use in these paragraphs of the construction 'faire' plus the infinitive verb form links conceptually the ability to act, through the semi-auxiliary verb 'faire', and decisions that have resulted in the current state of affairs: 'me **faire envoyer** d'office au dépôt'; 'à défaut de pouvoir la **faire prononcer** par le Tribunal'; 'un certificat d'aliénation mentale qu'il me **fit donner**'; 'je te le **ferai donner**'. The capacity to act upon his wishes is reflected in the use of the verb 'vouloir' in relation to the figure of the father as subject: 'Il a la *manie* de **vouloir** mon interdiction'; 'mon père a toujours **voulu** me gouverner à sa fantaisie'; 'le jour où je le **voudrai**' (5). So it is the will of the father that translates into action, not the will of the disempowered narrator–protagonist here. The selection of the nouns 'manie' and 'fantaisie' is interesting, also, because as terms that distance the person described from the idea of reason they turn the discourse of the 'aliéniste' on to those Esquiron holds responsible for her suffering. The term 'manie' is repeated later in the excerpt: 'Aujourd'-hui, par la même *manie* de mon père, je subis une nouvelle séquestra-tion'. This is juxtaposed with the statement 'Je n'étais nullement **folle** alors' (5), and the author effectively shows that the accusation of unreasonable behaviour works just as well for men of responsibility.

A further feature of the 'Nom-du-Père', as a metaphor representing all the forces of prohibition and legislation, that is undermined in this piece is the demonstration of the way in which the law is used to keep women such as Esquiron from exercising their civil liberties. Within one paragraph are mentioned the 'Tribunal', the 'article 489 du Code civil', and the 'loi de 1838'; all are deployed with the following aim: 'de priver de leur **liberté** des gens sains d'esprit'.[37] Official documentation is

---

[37] Article 489 of the Code civil states: 'Le majeur qui est dans un état habituel d'imbecillité, de démence ou de fureur, doit être interdit, même lorsque cet état présente

presented as being put to the same use, for example in the repeated use of the phrase 'au moyen d'un certificat d'aliénation mentale' (5), leading first to her committal to Blanche's clinic and later to her current predicament.

Esquiron aligns herself with the concerns of the contemporary women's movement when she describes the process of being infantilized by her father. The whole system of 'aliénisme' is portrayed as a force in league with him working to deprive women of the right to live as adults in the world: 'Depuis ma **majorité**, mon père a toujours voulu me gouverner à sa fantaisie, comme il le faisait dans mon **enfance**. En ceci, Messieurs les aliénistes lui ont prêté la main pour lui complaire' (5). The author turns this process of infantilization around in the following section on 'Mon mari', where she presents her husband as a weak-willed, dependent, and powerless figure. It is initially suggested that the husband's role should be to 'protéger', but we quickly discover him to be a man whose weakness is such that this promise is quickly broken when he comes under the influence of one stronger than him: 'mon père'. The negatively connoted actions associated with the verbs 's'empresser', 'trahir', 'se rallier', and 'perdre' noticeably contradict the verb 'protéger' (6).

The pitiful feebleness of this husband figure is such that he does not emerge as a complex individual in the text. He functions only as the negative subject of verbs of positive action, and is helplessly guided by the dominant figure of the father. He is 'incapable d'**administrer**' and merely a passive pawn in the father's game: 'Il **reçoit** l'argent de mon père pour payer ma séquestration.' In addition, as the wife is traditionally defined by her relationship to a dominant male, his entire function is characterized in relation to his dependency on—and therefore his attempt to oppress—his wife: 'il n'a d'autre occupation que celle de s'opposer à toutes mes volontés, à toutes mes dispositions, en vertu de son *droit marital*' (6). The repeated use of the adjective 'toutes' here rounds off this impression of absolute antagonism between husband and wife.

In the paragraphs that follow, the section entitled 'Réfutation du rapport', the adjective 'toutes' once again aligns the three male forces present in the text: the father, responsible for (mis)informing the doctors, the husband, and the psychiatrists: 'Aussi se trompent-ils dans **toutes** leurs appréciations de mon caractère, de mes sentiments, de mes actes passés ou présents, de mes idées, de mes affaires, de **toute**

des intervalles lucides' (*Code civil*, Les codes annotés de Sirey, 2 vols (Paris: Marchal et Billard, 1882–6), i.article 489).

ma vie.' Their oppression of her is complete, as is her demonization of them, and her statement here lacks the complexity of her previous assertions. Here, arguably, Esquiron contradicts herself, having already based her argument on the fact that the observations made in the report are in some way favourable to her cause. The doctors are ranged in the same category as her other 'adversaires', and the picture painted is all bad. Esquiron's claim to know herself is based on her judgment that everything any of these other characters have to say about her is wrong, and that she is the only one who can act in her own best interest, as opposed to the husband who has compromised '**tous** mes intérêts' (6).

The author's insight is at once sharp and revelatory, but is also somewhat problematic and disingenuous. As Freud claimed eventually to have managed to convince Dora that there was another element to her mental life than that which she experienced consciously, so there is an element of activity that remains latent in this text. From this perspective, the assertion 'je me connais moi-même' is deceptive, for the speaker cannot know herself fully. But neither can the doctors assessing her case have full insight into the motivations behind their actions, and those of Esquiron's family. In this sense, Esquiron also highlights the irrational agenda inherent in the psychiatric report.

THE INSTITUTIONAL 'HYSTERIA' OF THE PSYCHIATRIC PROFESSION

In the middle part of the text, entitled 'Texte du rapport—Mes réponses', the process of splitting is manifested on a superficial level through the division of two textual voices, two first-person presences, 'je' and 'nous', into two columns on the page. However, the necessity of splitting in order to make sense of the world is not limited to the discourse of the 'aliénée', but can be extended to the analysis of psychiatric discourse. This results in the paradoxical process of the blurring of two ostensibly distinct voices, which casts doubt on anyone's claim to knowledge. This is necessary because Esquiron needs to draw the medical discourse into her own textual voice in order to have her assertions sanctioned.

Arguably, the unconscious process of splitting is present in both Esquiron's account and in the psychiatric report. But where in the former this functions as a rhetorical strength, in the latter it emerges as a rhetorical weakness. This splitting of objects into good and bad, on the part of both speakers, sets up an aggressive object relation from the point of view of Esquiron, and the negation of any object relation from that of her doctors.[38] Her voice, in their report, is silenced and sidelined; but the patient engages with their assertions and finds a means of positively symbolizing her own experience in language. The medical report results in a character assassination, whereas Esquiron's response is a coherently argued counter-attack, which reflects the unbalanced power dynamic at the centre of this debate: the concerns of one individual patient are subordinate to the greater good of the stability of society and the perpetuation of its structures. For the individual in question, however, the outcome of the case is of the utmost importance.

If we can assert that splitting occurs in the text of the psychiatric report, it is because all observations of Esquiron's modes of behaviour are made to fit a simplistic picture that can be summed up as 'patholog-ical'. In one of the opening paragraphs it is emphasized that Esquiron has a 'passé pathologique', and the rest of the report serves to demon-strate that current medical concerns can be placed in the context of a '*trouble d'ancienne date*' (7), carrying a past judgement into the present. Even observations that the doctors cannot view, in isolation, as evidence of mental disturbance are subsumed into the category 'pathologique' through the insistence that they form part of a larger picture.

Actions not essentially viewed as resulting from mental disturbance, '*pas nécessairement déraisonnables*', are nevertheless cause for concern when looked upon in terms of Esquiron's psychiatric history. They have 'des racines profondes', the notion of the interconnectedness of roots contrasting sharply with that of an 'acte isolé'. The process of conflation here clearly shows the medical concern to split off all the patient's behaviour into the category of sickness: 'Ce n'était pas seulement un **acte isolé**, c'était un épisode à **ajouter** à beaucoup **d'autres** dans une existence où la bizarrerie, les excentricités, les conceptions délirantes ne sont plus à compter' (8). The result of this is that even behaviour and statements that might not be viewed as delusional in a different context, such as Esquiron's quite understandable anxiety regarding the motiva-tions of her father and husband, are here identified as evidence of mental instability.

Magnan goes on to elucidate some of the clinical difficulty in this case, which is that Esquiron's intelligence is deployed in the service of

[38] See n. 26.

Marie Esquiron

her 'conceptions délirantes', with the result that 'il est quelquefois difficile de démêler ce qui est **vrai** de ce qui est **faux**' (9). According to Esquiron, no attempt is made to investigate what could be said to be the truth. The result is that no unravelling actually occurs, because all is ranged in the category 'faux'. It is a widespread textual commonplace in psychiatric literature of this period, particularly in relation to different forms of partial or lucid insanity, to assert that the afflicted patient's intelligence is not diminished in such mental disturbances; rather, it serves to exacerbate the problem. Despite the common acknowledgement of this state of affairs, the diagnostic process, as evidenced in this analysis, is ultimately a reductive one. The doctors accuse the patient of distorting the 'facts' of the case, but the medical voice reveals itself to be equally capable of manipulation of source material.

The psychiatric report descends into an extended value judgement at this point, and expresses disapproval of Esquiron's general attitude, as if to bolster the picture of sickness of mind initially evoked. The construction 'avec' + noun + adjective is used on several occasions to achieve this effect, such as: '**Avec** une **vaniteuse satisfaction**, Mme Esquiron se livre à des digressions interminables'; '**Avec** une **complaisance égoïste**, elle insiste sur son enfance' (9); 'Elle nous entretient, **avec** une **visible satisfaction**, du traitement qu'elle a suivi' (12). The suggestion is that the subject of their enquiry ascribes herself a position of superiority, an attitude that clearly riles Magnan: 'Vis-à-vis de nous, elle a pris une attitude de **supériorité dédaigneuse**' (11). The patient is chastised for wanting to speak for herself, with authority and personal conviction, and for daring to step outside the prescribed roles of the clinical relationship.[39]

Further evidence of overgeneralization in the appreciation of this case is found in an earlier paragraph, where we learn that Esquiron will seize any opportunity to 'médire de son père'. Just a few lines previously, the report notes that 'Mme Esquiron se livre à des digressions interminables [...] **dissimulant** avec une certaine habileté ce qu'elle ne tient pas à nous dire; elle **insiste** sur son enfance' (9). The totality of Esquiron's utterance is pathologized in very contradictory terms, where she is

---

[39] This apparent alarm at Esquiron's self-satisfied attitude is mirrored in Henry Maudsley's restricted meaning of the term 'moral insanity', which from 1885 was used to describe patients with 'no capacity for true moral feeling—all his impulses and desires, to which he yields without check, are egoistic, his conduct appears to be governed by immoral motives, which are cherished and obeyed without any evident desire to resist them' (Gelder 2001: 163).

accused simultaneously of frankness and dissimulation in regard to her revelations about her father, showing the diagnostic process itself to be, in a significant way, fraught with contradictions and irrational agendas.

Those characters constructed as 'good', being placed unproblematically on the other end of the reliable–unreliable spectrum, are male figures that hold official public office of some variety. Here the doctors are themselves dissimulatory in their systematic suppression of detail throughout the report, and instead insidiously undermine the credibility of Esquiron's claims through their choice of vocabulary: 'M. Le Brisoys, son conseil, M. Messelet, son avoué, M. Saint-Aubin, son avocat, ont bien voulu, à plusieurs reprises, nous exposer une situation compliquée' (10). We are spared the details of these testimonies.

Rather than offering convincing concrete examples, the reporting doctors undermine Esquiron's subjective beliefs through the use of constructions such as 'se croire', which echoes in French the possible distinction between the verbs 'imaginer' and 's'imaginer', where the latter denotes error on the part of the thinker.[40] We are told: 'Elle s'est crue l'objet de la haine, du mépris de tout le monde dans le pays'; 'elle s'est crue persécutée' (10); 'elle s'est livrée à des recherches sur les auteurs d'une tentative d'empoisonnement dont elle s'est crue victime' (11). In addition, it is Esquiron's general demeanour that is given as the cause of her social alienation in the community, which 'n'avait pas d'autre cause que l'excentricité de ses allures et de son langage' (10). Judgement is passed without listening to the content of what this woman had to say, because their decision about her state of mind was predetermined: 'Sa tenue, ses discours dans la maison de santé ne laissent pas de doute sur le trouble de son intelligence, sur la perversion de ses sentiments' (11). Esquiron identifies here a clear discrepancy between what the reporting psychiatrists deem to be adequate contact to form a fair assessment, and the patient's own sense that she is not known to these men, and ultimately not heard.[41]

What is predecided is stated in the middle of the report: 'Elle appartient à cette catégorie de malades qui n'acceptent pas les questions

---

[40] One of the definitions given for the verb 's'imaginer' in *Le Petit Robert* is 'croire à tort'.

[41] Contrary to her own impression, Esquiron actually elicited a great deal more attention from psychiatrists than the average asylum resident. Although patients in private asylums fared better, apparently Leuret, médecin–chef at Bicêtre, calculated that he could devote only eighteen minutes per year to each patient. It is disheartening to find that even those patients who were given the most attention still felt fundamentally misunderstood (Murat 2001: 366).

et qui poursuivent avec une ténacité invincible le thème invariable qu'elles ont la prétention d'imposer.' The choice of the verb 'appartenir' is noteworthy, because Esquiron's 'ténacité invincible' links her to Rouy, Claudel, and Lamotte in terms of the writing tradition of which she forms a part. The doctors even go so far as to state: '*Nous ne voulons pas dire que ses affirmations sont absolument mensongères*' (12), as if in admission of the injustice of this case. But because of their inability to grasp the complexity of the situation, and their dismissal of the totality of Esquiron's verbal output, her words have no power and no meaning, and their decision holds sway.

Far from being an '*appréciation impartiale*', as the reporting doctors assert, under the disingenuous guise of impartiality they silence the voice of protest through the indisputably dubious decision to uphold the 'placement d'office'. It is quickly decided that it would be dangerous to leave Esquiron to her own devices, particularly in the handling of her financial affairs. The report reveals much that is fundamentally irrational in the attitude taken towards women such as these, and a significant level of anxiety about what might be the unknown and unknowable consequences of giving women freedom. The only option available, it seems to them, is the incapacitation of possibly dangerous and potent women who threaten to wreak havoc on men's affairs. Hence the urgent need to construct a clinical picture of a person who is 'incapable', a 'maniaque chronique', victim of her own 'excitation intellectuelle permanente' and 'perversion de la sensibilité morale affective' (13). This image of complete excess, of lack of moderation in the moral and intellectual faculties, kept Esquiron incarcerated where she may well have fared better on the outside.

This splitting of the world of objects into good and bad, capable and incapable, contained and excessive, has very real consequences for Esquiron. We have seen evidence of the same splitting process in the first section of this discussion, where all the male characters in the text are conflated into a 'bad' paternal figure. This continues to some extent in the 'réfutation' part of the text. Esquiron evokes malevolent male groups through frequent references to figures such as 'Ces Messieurs', 'mon père et mon mari', 'la Préfecture de police', and 'M. le docteur Goujon', collecting them together repeatedly through the term 'mes adversaires'. However, what makes the part of the text penned by Esquiron more interesting, and more complex, is the variety of different textual processes at play. Arguably, her integration of the report through the repeated process of quotation and subversion is evidence of the paradoxical process of simultaneous splitting, of people and statements, into good and bad, and of rendering the 'bad' unstable by blurring it with her own voice, putting it to the service of her own argument.

The textual process occurring here is that of mirroring and introjecting the first textual voice in a second one. In Esquiron's part of the text, the process of splitting, of partitioning off medical statements and all malevolent male figures as 'bad', actually functions as an important aspect of her rhetoric. The first section of this chapter examined the extent to which her argument might be seen to be limited, because ostensibly based on the same philosophical premises as her adversaries. However, Esquiron also exploits her position of relative powerlessness in relation to the authority of these doctors, and exposes the institutional insanity of the report. Both sets of arguments are constructed from a position of putative sanity, but one of them emerges as the more convincing. Esquiron succeeds in showing medical discourse, regarding her own case, to be flawed and irrational where it claims only to be rational. This is achieved through the technique of quotation and subversion, and through the extensive use of irony and hyperbole to emphasize the extent of the injustice of the case. The result is that we bear witness to a double 'mise en abyme' of this psychiatric report, once reproduced verbatim and contained within a wider text with the aim of discrediting it, and once mimicked through ironic citation.

Esquiron does not challenge overtly the assumed 'raisonnable–déraisonnable' dichotomy. However, she also demonstrates that an action judged 'déraisonnable' in a different context could be viewed as perfectly rational. She shows that pinning actions to a diagnosis is merely a rhetorical exercise that can be easily reversed, and is one that does not necessarily stand up to scrutiny. The very notion of supporting evidence is problematized through the appropriation of the term 'preuve', and the turning of the verb 'prouver' into a rhetorical weapon. This casts doubt on the idea that anything in this case can be proved to the extent that such drastic actions are warranted: 'Où est la **preuve** de ce délire?' (8); 'Chez M. le docteur Goujon, la **preuve** qu'il ne me croit pas folle, c'est qu'il ne me soumet à aucun traitement médical mental. Pourquoi m'y retient-on? Voilà encore une **preuve** du crime dont je suis victime' (12). The term appears twice more in this short extract. Additionally, the repetition of the construction 'cela ne **prouve** pas', with terminology repeated from the original report, undermines the assumption that behaviour of which some men disapprove is evidence of madness: 'Cela ne **prouve** pas ma *folie*, ni mes *conceptions délirantes*' (10). This is used also to deny the inappropriateness of Esquiron's actions in relation to her financial affairs: 'Cela ne **prouve** pas ma folie, pas plus que la nécessité de mon envoi au dépôt, *d'office*' (11).

The confusion between the discourse of the clinician and that of the patient, with the effect that the dominance of the former is challenged, occurs in relation to the frequent evocation of terms denoting lucidity and consciousness. Esquiron tells us: 'Ma **raison**, ma **conscience**, ma **clairvoyance** n'ont jamais failli.' This forms part of a strategy that imposes proximity between the position of the patient and that of the doctors and the men responsible for her care: just as their decisions are apparently reasoned, but are in fact based on irrational fear, so Esquiron's protest is informed by an enhanced level of insight into the functioning of medical discourse. Other examples of this strategy are found in those parts of the text where the narrator appropriates psychiatric terminology and demonstrates that it can be logically applied to the behaviour of the sane: 'Mes deux séquestrations n'ont eu d'autre cause que la *manie* de mon père avec laquelle il a persisté à me déclarer **folle**' (7). The ironic application of the noun 'manie' and the epithet 'folle', applied respectively to the father and the speaker, demonstrates that these concepts are fluid enough to contain any inconvenient behaviour, including that which is bothersome for Esquiron.

Esquiron also draws the idea of what 'reality' can be said to be, by bringing these parts of language into her own speech. This successfully refutes the claim that Esquiron does not have an adequate grasp of what is relevant to this matter, of what reality really is: 'Mais [ses affirmations] n'ont que peu de chose à voir à la situation présente, et nous ne pouvons le faire comprendre à Madame Esquiron' (10). What exactly the patient does not understand is unclear, perhaps because she understands only too well. Indeed, she affirms the concrete and literal truth of her story: her sickness was 'une réalité', her symptoms 'très réels', and her reaction to this 'logique'. The author here perceives the tendency in medical observation to categorize types of behaviour and individuals into subsets of pathologies: 'ils devaient se borner à établir ma folie **pathologiquement**' (13); 'MM. Les aliénistes voient des fous partout' (8); and she declares the evacuation of meaning in their reasoning processes: 'Ce sont des mots **vides de sens**. C'est évident' (8). Esquiron here simultaneously endorses and rejects psychiatric categories: she uses psychiatric terminology such as 'manie' and 'folie' and applies them to the discourse of the clinician. However, in suggesting that her doctors 'voient des fous partout' she is highlighting the double bind in which she and perhaps all patients find themselves: their every utterance, including the claim to be sane, can be ranged into some form of pathological category.

Esquiron also turns to question the evidence basis of their assessment. Selecting the verb 'raisonner' once again, she turns it back on her interlocutors and challenges their notion of source facts: 'Ils **raisonnent**, non *de visu*, mais par suppositions.' Her financial decisions are contrasted with these groundless assumptions, being 'au contraire très **raisonnables**' (10). As she demonstrates that terminology denoting irrationality can be logically applied to those characters presented in the report as sane figures, so she makes clear the possibility of her own decisions being informed by reason.

In addition to reclaiming the notion of reason, which is systematically pitted against her in the unfavourable report, Esquiron employs the notions of 'fantaisie' and 'imagination' against the figures of her adversaries. She thus distances her own thought processes from the realm of unreality and the unconscious. She writes: 'Quant à dire que ma tenue, mes discours dans la maison ne laissent pas de doute sur le trouble de mon intelligence, sur la perversion de mes sentiments, c'est absolument **fantaisiste**' (11). Similarly, the concept of 'imagination' is negatively connoted later in the text: 'L'aventure rappelée ici, c'est une affaire Pacault, intrigue **imaginée** par mon père et mon mari, [...] Ce sont, en effet, des *infamies imaginaires*' (12). This process is also used to denounce the thought processes that lie behind the composition of the medical report, and the term is here placed in juxtaposition with the similarly accusatory concept of insanity: 'ils rassemblent toutes les **insanités imaginées** par mes adversaires' (13). As Esquiron claims sanity and reason for herself, she must distance the official discourse of reason from her own voice by hurling at it descriptions that place its basis in the realm of the imagination, the intangible, the irrational, and ultimately the unreal.

The presence of hyperbole in Esquiron's part of the text is indicative of the flow of excess in the information she presents: she does not suppress information, as the exercise of restraint forces the doctors to do, but rather allows shocking facts and accusations to stream through the narrative. For example, rather than passing over the accusation of alcoholism, the speaker takes this statement and competes with it, undermining its credibility through ironic exaggeration: 'C'est bien **peu** dire, quand mon père disait que j'avais l'habitude de boire un litre d'eau-de-vie par jour, quand j'étais en Belgique, ne buvant que de la bière' (13). The expression of such excess is extended to descriptions of her sufferings as a result of her first period of internment, where everything is evoked in the extreme: '**tout le monde** me fuyait'; 'on ne me recevait **nulle part**' (10).

Having poured scorn on their conclusions, a final ironic twist is found in the use of the capital letter 'E' in the following statement: 'si Messieurs les **Experts** savaient lire dans mon entendement, ils verraient que mon intelligence n'a rien de désordonné' (13). She mimics and subtly mocks their repeated use of the construction 'avec' + noun + adjective, in the first instance used to express general disapproval of Esquiron's habits and general demeanour, to call into question the integrity of the report: 'MM. les aliénistes, **avec** une **désinvolture éton-nante**, disent que tous les actes de ma vie ont été déraisonnables' (10).

The insertion of the conjunction 'si' at the opening of clauses in Esquiron's part of the text is an important tool, which is used to place emphasis on a positive idea regarding the patient, first outlined in the report, and here re-evoked in order to introduce a request for action or a denunciation of the proposition. It is used on seven distinct occasions, and merits further attention here:

Si je ne suis pas aliénée, **si** on ne peut pas m'interdire en vertu de l'article 489 du code civil, il faut ma mise en liberté immediate. (9)

Si j'ai parlé de mon enfance, c'est parce que j'ai été interrogée sur mon enfance. (9)

Si j'ai quitté mon pays, c'est que [...] mon père m'avait fait une telle réputa-tion que tout le monde me fuyait. (10)

Si j'étais ridicule, c'était l'œuvre de mon père et de ma famille. (10)

Si j'ai voulu rompre par le divorce, c'était mon droit. (11)

Si j'énonce des banalités, c'est qu'on me soutient des banalités contraires et contre la vérité. (12)

Si j'ai suivi un traitement, ce n'est pas pour la tête. (12)

The repeated use of this construction, on all but one occasion using the formula 'si [...] c'est', shows Esquiron continually engaging with the text of her incarcerators and picking their claims apart point by point. She cites an aspect of the case against her using the conjunction 'si', centring herself overtly at the heart of the problem by immediately following each occurrence of this term with the personal pronoun 'je', and sweeps aside the reasons compounded into a case against her with an equally plausible explanation.

The psychiatric report, upon close examination, reveals much that is unconscious and motivated by deep-seated and irrational fear of the emancipation of women such as Esquiron. Esquiron extends her command of sharp, critical faculties by holding up a mirror to the justifications given for her indefinite imprisonment, and shows them to be dubious. We shall now turn to examine the issue of closure, for both patient and clinician, because the text before us defers the possibility of resolution on to a decision, the outcome of which we do not know.

THE INTERMINABLE NARRATIVE: 'MON INTERNEMENT À PERPÉTUITÉ'

The interminable nature of this narrative is evidenced most clearly in the lack of conclusion to the story. The theme of interminability is one that needs to be addressed before moving on from the analysis of Esquiron's memoir, because it is one that recurs regularly in the psychiatric report, in her refutation of it, and in the context of the general state of information on the outcome of the case. In the light of the significant presence of the theme of interminability in the main body of the text, the final section entitled 'Ma conclusion' can be read as an ironic closure, which falsely concludes a matter that had already been decided. The fact that we do not currently know what the outcome of the dispute might have been, and how long Esquiron was made to endure this ordeal, makes the notion of 'conclusion' especially poignant. The effect created is narrative stasis and inertia, the reader being left deserted, wondering whether the writing of this memoir achieved anything, or whether it ended up being, for its author, a futile exercise.

The idea of unending discourse, interminable speech, writing and complaint, is initially one evoked repeatedly in the clinical description of the patient's communication strategies. The theme of the contrast between the clinician's pithy style and the patient's inability to stem the flow of discourse is commonly identifiable in psychiatric literature. It is also evident in the presentation of this text, in which Esquiron's narrative takes up a third more space in the middle part.[42] This brings to

---

[42] See for example Parant (1888: 74–5):

Quand ils sont enfermés dans les asiles d'aliénés, ils écrivent lettres sur lettres, réclamations sur réclamations; ils formulent de longues plaintes, rédigent des mémoires justificatifs **interminables**, adressés principalement aux magistrats, aux autorités dont ils se sont en droit de réclamer l'intervention. Dans bien des cas, tout ce qu'ils disent est si vraisemblable, si parfaitement empreint d'intelligence et de raison, que les magistrats ou

mind once again the nineteenth-century concept that some forms of madness were something normal—intelligence, reason, or verbal utterance—manifested in a hypertrophied form. It is a rich accusation to make, on behalf of a profession whose treatises line the stores of the BNF and which frequently exceeded five hundred pages of observation and classification. When supposedly being listened to by these doctors, we are told that Esquiron 'se livre à des digressions **interminables**', and that her accusations against her father are worked into a '**prolixe** exposé' (9). As the pro forma certificate used to effect a 'placement d'office' defines mental alienation in part as being characterized by 'actes extravagants', all the descriptions pertaining to Esquiron's verbal production infer the idea of excess and superfluity.

Magnan continues on the theme of prolixity, even going as far as to suggest that this interminable protest is experienced as an insufferable intrusion into the smooth running of psychiatric practice: 'Avec une **prolixité** que nous devons subir, elle reprend sans cesse les mêmes récriminations. [...] Elle finit par se perdre au milieu de banalités **sententieuses** [*sic*] qui se déroulent **imperturbablement** pendant des heures' (12). The evocation of this feeling of torturous tedium, involved in actually listening to the patient, reveals that Esquiron is right when she claims not to be taken seriously.

Esquiron identifies the idea of verbosity as being a mark of guilt and pathology early in her refutation. As she is paradoxically accused of dissimulation and 'digressions interminables', she argues that it is rather the lack of openness inherent in psychiatric practice that is the mark of guilt: 'Je pourrais dire que c'est là une dissimulation plus **coupable** que celle qu'ils me reprochent, tout en m'attribuant des digressions interminables' (9). The author here overtly distances herself from the reproach of interminable discourse. Covertly, however, and perhaps unconsciously, she positively symbolizes the act of self-expression and speech by rebuking her interlocutors for their refusal to name those who

---

d'autres personnes ne peuvent manquer, tout d'abord, d'en être émus. Mais une enquête se fait, les allégations sont contrôlées, et la folie des plaignants devient alors facile à reconnaître. Les archives des tribunaux sont riches en documents de ce genre, qui fourniraient matière à une volumineuse publication.

Séglas (1892: 217, 230) calls such writers 'quérulants' and 'graphomanes', and mentions as a characteristic of their written production the fact that they produce '**interminables** paraphrases' of the same ideas.

have testified against her. The notion of interminability for Esquiron will become a far more serious matter, for the reasons outlined in the psychiatric report will come to represent the very essence of her incarceration and denial of freedom, 'ce qui équivaut à une interdiction **perpétuelle**' (14).

The debate as to whether this story will have an end is also left open at the closure of the middle part of the text, preceding Esquiron's conclusion. Here she ends with two rhetorical questions, to which she has, in a display of linguistic aptitude, already provided the answers: 'Qu'en savent-ils? Ont-ils le droit de juger l'avenir de mon existence?' (14). However, these closing words are loaded with a sense of futility. Despite her ability to show that she is lucid and intelligent and knows her own mind, the reality is that the law gave men—husbands, fathers, and doctors—the right to decide what was best for women, according to what ultimately was in the interest of men.

The notion of an incarceration 'à perpétuité' renders the last part of the text, 'Ma conclusion', very problematic. If the story is to end in indefinite, unending, painful imprisonment, then this is not a conclusion at all, but an ominous beginning. It is a plea for a conclusion to the story, but the sense that the requested decision will not be made hangs tragically over the text. The use of the future tense in the opening paragraph reveals a last investment of faith in the system of justice, but also appears as an ironic statement in its definitiveness, given that it refers to unfinished business which may never be resolved: 'Mon internement **à perpétuité**, qui comblerait de joie ma triste famille, ne leur sera pas accordé, sans un appel de ma part à la justice de mon pays qui me **protégera**' (15). The report made by these doctors is interestingly referred to as a 'plaidoyer', implying that their testimony involves both the endorsement of a decision and the emotional investment of a defence of the underlying ideas of alienist medicine. It is this unswerving belief in the premises of a school of thought, which sustains the cultural construct of what femininity ought to be and punishes those that deviate from this model, that is identified by Esquiron and so effectively taken apart.[43]

What the author's attempted conclusion also emphasizes is the irony of one individual's situation, which is a reflection of the central paradox

---

[43] *Le Petit Robert* defines the noun 'plaidoyer' in two ways. First, as a 'discours prononcé à l'audience pour défendre le droit d'une partie'; second, as a 'défense passionnée (d'une ou plusieurs personnes, d'une idée), dans une grave affaire publique'.

at the heart of diagnostic procedure in psychiatric medicine at this time: that madness is not about a lack of intelligence, but abnormally deployed intelligence. And the assessment that overactive intellectual engagement with one's situation is abnormal is determined by culturally constructed ideas about 'normal' gender roles. Esquiron's personal irony is that, although it is recommended that she receive medical treatment, she is not treated for mental illness: a reflection of the pessimistic attitude of the time regarding curability. In addition, she does not receive the medical attention she actually does need, and her request for this is added to the list of behaviours that have her marked out as 'mad': 'chez M. le docteur Goujon, je n'ai été soumise à aucun traitement médical mental [...] j'y suis privée de tous les soins que je puis me procurer chez moi, sans peine, ma fortune était suffisante!' (15). So Esquiron is doubly disempowered, and her freedom twice infringed, by being unnecessarily detained and by having relief withheld.

In the fourth paragraph we learn that the prescription that Esquiron be 'séquestrée à perpétuité' is more to do with control and 'surveillance' than genuine concern. The wider issue here seems to be that women should be subject to the surveillance of men, and therefore to perpetual control. Esquiron therefore represents a highly problematic case, because her personal wealth potentially gave her the freedom to escape the confines imposed by her father and husband. Since the structure of the family could not contain her actions, the pseudo-familial structure of the asylum is called upon to step in and to keep her 'extravagance' in check.

The ultimate possibility for closure lies in two places: in the hands of the higher male authority of 'Monsieur le Ministre', and in the eyes of the rest of society. The first is ascribed official authority through the choice of the verb 'ordonner', implying agency and the power to effect action: 'je viens insister auprès de vous pour **ordonner** la fin de mon supplice en me mettant en liberté immédiate' (16). The second is the appeal to a wider shared reality that departs from the introspective psychiatric view, that of 'le plus vulgaire jugement' (15). The author aligns herself with the vulgar, that which is defined by *Le Nouveau Petit Robert* as 'très répandu; admis, mis en usage par le commun des hommes', in other words with the judgement of ordinary people whose perspective may be more merciful than that of the blinded 'experts'. Although we cannot know at this stage whether the desired conclusion was reached, the survival of this unique document has made accessible the patient's voice to the modern reader. The doctors' conclusion is reached through the twisting of evidence to fit a pathological model of female behaviour of which the patriarchal order disapproved; ours is reached through the acknowledgment of the fact that Esquiron's assertion that she knew herself, and was competent enough to make her own decisions, is more compelling than the psychiatric assessment.

Esquiron had as much insight as anybody else into the complex and shadowy workings of her family, and her claim to be the victim of people who wanted to divest her of power and status should have been believed, or at least heard. Her reasoning capacity was as adequate as any man's, and she was able to show that the decisions made concerning her fundamental freedoms were based on irrational fear and prejudice. Contrary to the idea of the female hysteric subverting the 'masculine' realm of reason, discourse, and knowledge through writing the body, we should assert that she challenges them effectively on their own ground. Similarly, men also unconsciously write their own bodily protest in ostensibly reasoned reports, such as that critiqued here, through the inscription of their primitive anxieties about moral decline. What occurs, therefore, on a textual level, is dissolution of difference between male and female speakers. However, in terms of the political consequences, we are left with the problem that the system of law and authority remained a patriarchal one: it could not hear 'reason', or different levels of truth, when emanating from a source that the system has irrationally constructed as a threat. The result is a testament to the experience of being repeatedly silenced and disbelieved, which amounts to a heightened sense of pain, isolation, and disempowerment. Although Esquiron acted in isolation, her text, in its frequent deployment of the future tense, reflects the feminist mood of the times of hope for improvement. The issue of incurability and the lack of investment in treatment perhaps also means that Esquiron's struggle was frustrated in a similar way to that of *fin de siècle* feminism. And ultimately, too, our conclusion is open-ended, because the outcome of the case remains unknown and, at present, unknowable. Perhaps we can only conclude by attributing success to a compelling piece of writing, whether or not it was deemed to be successful by its author, and by suggesting that further primary research into this case could produce results of great interest. If the outcome of the case ever came to be known, it might reveal that women patients like Hersilie Rouy and Marie Esquiron were more self-empowering than history has recognized, and that their memoirs represent a form of rhetorical victory—despite the double bind imposed on them by psychiatric observation—over oppressive diagnostic procedures.

Appendix

Full text of Madame Esquiron's memoir

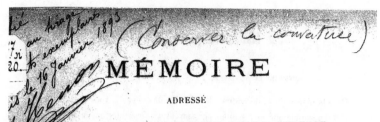

(Conserver la couverture)

MÉMOIRE

ADRESSÉ

A MONSIEUR LE MINISTRE DE LA JUSTICE

PAR

MADAME ESQUIRON, NÉE DE GASTÉ

Séquestrée dans la Maison de santé de M. le docteur Goujon,
90, rue de Picpus, à Paris,

*Où elle réfute elle-même l'imputation d'aliénation mentale et le Rapport
de MM. les aliénistes Mottet, Magnan et Voisin.*

ÉPIGRAPHE

En novembre 1865, avant ma première séquestration, chez M. le docteur Blanche, je disais à M. de Gasté :

« Mais, mon père, vous ne pouvez pas me mettre dans une maison de fous, puisque je ne suis pas folle !

— Il suffit pour cela d'un certificat d'aliénation mentale et je te le ferai donner le jour où je le voudrai. »

Telle était sa réponse.

Janvier 1893.

Lettre du 17 décembre 1892, adressée à M. le Ministre de la Justice, par Madame Esquiron, née de Gasté.

MONSIEUR LE MINISTRE,

Dans la séance du 15 décembre à la Chambre des députés, vous avez dit :

« Il me semble que mes paroles ne peuvent laisser douter un instant de ma ferme « volonté d'arriver à la vérité et à la justice. »   *(Question du* PANAMA).

Si l'on peut comparer les petites choses aux grandes, je viens vous parler de ma triste et injuste séquestration chez M. le docteur Goujon, rue de Picpus, n° 90, où je suis depuis le 27 août 1891.

Tous mes amis ont protesté et affirmé ma parfaite lucidité d'esprit, la douceur de mon caractère et ma moralité.

Moi-même, j'ai employé tous les arguments que la raison et le bon sens peuvent invoquer, *en vain*.

Sur mes instances, la première chambre du Tribunal civil de la Seine a nommé trois docteurs pour m'examiner. Ces Messieurs ont déposé leur rapport au greffe du Tribunal où l'on peut en prendre communication; j'en ai eu le texte sous les yeux et j'y ai lu les phrases suivantes :

1° Mme Esquiron n'est pas aliénée ;

2° Elle est très intelligente ;

3° Son intelligence n'est point amoindrie ;

4° Elle a au contraire une acuité d'esprit très grande ;

5° Chez elle il n'y a ni démence, ni imbécillité, ni fureur. Il serait impossible de justifié son interdiction en se basant sur les termes de l'article 489 du Code civil.

Puis ces Messieurs ajoutent : Dans son intérêt, cette dame doit être maintenue dans une maison de santé spéciale.

C'est un comble d'iniquité !

Evidemment, ma séquestration ne peut se prolonger sans forfaiture.

Un mot de vous, Monsieur le Ministre, suffira pour me rendre à la liberté et à mes affaires, en grande souffrance.

Je me ferais un devoir, lorsque je serai libre, de fournir tous les documents que je possède pour prouver mon bon droit.

J'attends avec bon espoir, Monsieur le Ministre, l'ordre de ma mise en liberté.

Votre très humble et très respectueuse,

MARIE ESQUIRON, née DE GASTÉ,

séquestrée, 90, *rue de Picpus.*

MA RÉFUTATION

Du rapport de Messieurs les aliénistes, en ce qui me concerne.

Victime d'une grande injustice, j'entreprends de réfuter le rapport de Messieurs les aliénistes, chargés par le Tribunal civil de la Seine de constater mon état mental actuel.

J'ai à dire, tout d'abord, que ce rapport m'est favorable et contraire, tout à la fois ; que par conséquent il est contradictoire et caduc ; de plus, il est entaché d'affirmations hasardées, de faits articulés sans preuves, notamment en ce qui concerne un prétendu *délire* de persécution, un *état d'aliénation mentale* dont les *actes* remontent à *différentes époques* : époques dont ces Messieurs n'ont pas pu être et n'ont pas été les témoins.

Le Tribunal avait compris que ma séquestration, peu motivée, devait prendre fin à bref délai. Dans ce but, il dispensa Messieurs les aliénistes du serment ordinaire, *vu l'urgence*, et décida que leur rapport serait déposé le plus tôt possible, avant la *fin de décembre* 1891. Il ne l'a été *que le 28 juin 1892*.

Je constate que ces Messieurs ne m'ont interrogée que trois fois au début et qu'ils se sont adressés, en dehors de moi, à tous ceux qui ont intérêt à ma séquestration ; ils le disent eux-mêmes dans leur rapport. Donc, leurs informations sont suspectes.

J'ai, en vain, offert à ces Messieurs de faire lever les scellés apposés sur mon appartement, rue des Bons-Enfants, n° 20, afin d'aller avec eux chercher les documents écrits qui pouvaient leur prouver ma lucidité d'esprit, la douceur de mon caractère, ma prudence dans la conduite de mes affaires, et montrer combien est mal fondée la réputation d'aliénation mentale qui m'est faite par mes adversaires. Ils ont résisté à mes instances, sans égard pour ma personne et mes affaires qui exigeaient ma mise en liberté, sans égard pour l'urgence indiquée par le Tribunal.

J'avais fait remarquer aussi à ces Messieurs qu'ayant été envoyée d'office au dépôt de la Préfecture de police, sans qu'on eût apposé les scellés sur mon appartement, scellés qui n'ont été mis que 19 jours après, mon mari avait pu s'introduire chez moi et disposer de tous mes dossiers contre lui, dans mon instance en divorce. Ils n'en tinrent aucun compte.

Comment mon arrestation a-t-elle eu lieu ? Est-ce à l'occasion d'un cas de délire comme ils l'affirment ? Nullement.

Le 24 août 1891, ayant eu des vomissements extraordinaires, je me rendis chez M. le Commissaire de mon quartier qui est à côté de mon domicile, 21, rue des Bons-Enfants. Je croyais avoir été empoisonnée et je voulais en informer M. le Commissaire de police. Cette démarche n'avait rien de déraisonnable, les experts le disent.

M. Delalonde, le Commissaire en fonction ce jour-là, fit écrire à M. de Gasté, mon père, demeurant rue Saint-Roch, n° 19, qui vint pour affirmer que *j'étais folle*, ce qu'il répétait pour la millième fois.

Il n'en fallut pas d'avantage : je fus empoignée et transportée d'office au dépôt de la Préfecture de police, malgré mes protestations et sans que les scellés fussent mis sur mon appartement.

Je restai trois jours au dépôt, pendant lesquels mon mari vint répéter aussi que j'étais folle ; ce dire de mon père et de mon mari fut considéré comme vérité certaine, par MM. Garnier et Blanche, aliénistes, attachés à la Préfecture de police, lesquels conclurent dans un rapport que j'étais *aliénée*.

Mon mari insista pour que je fusse envoyée d'*office* dans la Maison de Santé de M. le docteur Goujon, 90, rue Picpus, avec recommandation expresse de me garder à vue, de ne me laisser communiquer avec personne du dehors par lettre.

L'envoi d'*office* était une perfidie bien calculée pour mettre mes adversaires à l'abri d'une responsabilité légale de ma part. C'est mon père qui donne l'argent à mon mari pour payer ma pension.

MON PÈRE

On voit que je suis dans la nécessité d'accuser mon père et mon mari, comme étant les auteurs de ma séquestration actuelle.

Mon père, député du Finistère, a usé de son prestige, comme président d'âge de la Chambre, pour affirmer la prétendue aliénation mentale qu'il m'attribue depuis longtemps, et me faire envoyer d'office au dépôt. Il a la *manie* de vouloir mon interdiction et, à défaut de pouvoir la faire prononcer par le Tribunal, en vertu de l'article 489 du Code civil, il a recours à la loi de 1838, sur le régime des aliénés, qui permet, au moyen d'un certificat d'aliénation mentale, affirmé par deux médecins, de priver de leur liberté des gens sains d'esprit.

Depuis ma majorité, mon père a toujours voulu me gouverner à sa fantaisie, comme il le faisait dans mon enfance. En ceci, Messieurs les aliénistes lui ont prêté la main pour lui complaire.

Dès 1866, à l'âge de 21 ans, j'ai été séquestrée par mon père chez M. le docteur Blanche où je suis restée pendant vingt mois, au moyen d'un certificat d'aliénation mentale qu'il me fit donner après m'en avoir souvent menacée. Il en était souvent question et je lui disais :

« Mais, mon père, vous ne pouvez me mettre dans une maison de fous, puisque je ne ... .is pas folle !

— Il suffit pour cela d'un certificat d'aliénation mentale et je te le ferai donner le jour où je le voudrai. » C'était là sa réponse.

Je n'étais nullement folle alors, pas plus qu'aujourd'hui. Aujourd'hui, par la même *manie* de mon père, je subis une nouvelle séquestration.

Si j'avais été sans fortune, j'aurais vécu en paix, mais je possédais au contraire une grande fortune, par ma mère, décédée prématurément. Cette fortune a été administrée par mon père jusqu'à ma majorité. J'ai gracieusement signé son compte de tutelle. On a peur que cette fortune échappe à la famille de mon père, puisque je suis fille unique et mariée sans enfants. On prétend m'empêcher d'en jouir en me faisant une réputation de folie imméritée, mais qui cause mon chagrin et ma ruine.

MON MARI

Mon mari m'a épousée en promettant de me protéger, puis il s'est empressé de me trahir, se ralliant aux idées de mon père, par intérêt, pour me perdre. Voilà le délire de persécution justifié. Où est-il ce bon mari? Est-ce de mon côté? Aucunement. Il reçoit l'argent de mon père pour payer ma séquestration chez M. le docteur Goujon; c'est un fait reconnu. Incapable d'administrer mes biens dotaux, ne possédant rien par lui-même, il n'a d'autre occupation que celle de s'opposer à toutes mes volontés, à toutes mes dispositions, en vertu de son *droit marital*. Il entrave de même M. Le Brisoys, mon conseil judiciaire, par des oppositions et des procédures de façon à compromettre tous mes intérêts; sans moyens d'existence, il ne peut m'assurer ni domicile, ni l'alimentation, et j'ai dû former contre lui une demande en divorce pour d'autres raisons; c'est pour s'en venger qu'il veut ma séquestration à perpétuité. Cela coûte cher, il a déjà versé 3,500 fr. à M. le docteur Goujon et redoit 5,000 francs. Que lui importe? C'est mon père qui paye.

RÉFUTATION DU RAPPORT

Je me connais moi-même, mieux que Messieurs les aliénistes ne me connaissent, surtout après m'avoir interrogée en trois séances, ainsi que je le dis plus haut. Aussi se trompent-ils dans toutes leurs appréciations de mon caractère, de mes sentiments, de mes actes passés ou présents, de mes idées, de mes affaires, de toute ma vie. La tâche ne m'est pas difficile, et je n'ai pas besoin d'avocat pour dire la vérité simplement.

Pour être claire, dans ce modeste travail je placerai, sur deux colonnes et par paragraphes, le texte du rapport et mes réponses, en regard, afin de mieux faire ressortir les contradictions dont j'ai le droit de me prévaloir; constatant aussi les affirmations qui m'autorisent à réclamer une mise en *liberté immédiate*, attendu que je ne suis pas *aliénée*, ainsi qu'ils le disent.

TEXTE DU RAPPORT	MES RÉPONSES

Nous, soussignés . . . .

1° Après avoir examiné Mme Esquiron à plusieurs reprises et avoir recueilli les renseignements de nature à nous éclairer, avons consigné dans le présent rapport, les résultats de notre examen.

2° Le passé pathologique de Mme Esquiron est connu. Il importe moins de le reprendre aujourd'hui que de déterminer les conditions de l'état mental actuel, de mettre en relief les caractères d'un *trouble d'ancienne date* et de préciser les causes qui, dans ces derniers temps, en ont rendu la manifestation plus évidente.

3° Mme Esquiron a été placée *d'office* dans la maison de santé de M. le docteur Goujon, le 27 août 1891.

1° Ces Messieurs m'ont interrogée trois fois au début. Chaque fois j'ai répondu que je ne suis pas folle, qu'ils peuvent s'en convaincre par mes réponses qui révèlent mon état mental actuel ; quant aux informations prises en dehors de moi, je les ai déclarées *suspectes*, et j'ai fait mes réserves, attendu qu'elles émanent de mes adversaires, et j'ai ajouté que la justice ne doit pas en tenir compte pour maintenir ma séquestration.

2° Un *trouble d'ancienne date*. Ces Messieurs n'ont pas pu le constater ; ce trouble est purement et simplement chimérique dans le passé et dans le présent. Mon passé pathologique a été une calomnie de folie, comme mon état actuel. Mes deux séquestrations n'ont eu d'autre cause que la *manie* de mon père avec laquelle il a persisté à me déclarer folle. Ma raison, ma conscience, mon esprit, ma clairvoyance, n'ont jamais failli. Je suis victime de la mauvaise réputation que mon père m'a faite dans le passé et dans le présent ; c'est évident.

3° L'envoi *d'office* au dépôt, puis à la Maison de santé, était prémédité, afin d'épargner à mon père et à mon mari la lourde responsabilité de ma séquestration. C'est une lâcheté impardonnable de leur part. Mon père était satisfait de se venger — de ce que le jugement du 8 août 1891, m'autorisant à emprunter, en dehors de lui, 15,000 francs, par délégation, sur mes futurs fermages, afin de lever personnellement un arrêt du 22 juillet 1891, condamnant Barroux à me payer quatre cent mille francs de dommages-intérêts — de l'échec de sa demande en interdiction contre moi; et mon mari pour se venger de l'instance en divorce que j'ai soulevée contre lui. Aussi m'ont-ils fait surveiller et garder à vue dans cet établissement, me privant de toute correspondance.

4° A ce moment elle était au plein d'une *crise de délire de persécution* et, à la suite d'un malaise de vomissements, elle s'était crue empoisonnée.

Elle s'adressa au commissaire de police de son quartier, à un pharmacien ; elle demandait une analyse des matières vomies et elle allait jusqu'à désigner les personnes qu'elle supposait capables d'avoir voulu attenter à ses jours.

Si tout s'était borné à cette recherche, on eût pu n'y trouver rien de plus que la manifestation d'inquiétudes non justifiées « peut-être » *mais pas nécessairement déraisonnables.*

4° Ici, ces Messieurs sont en contradiction avec eux-mêmes ; ils affirment *une crise de délire de persécution.* Où est la preuve de ce délire ? Ce n'est pas la démarche au commissariat qu'ils déclarent *n'être pas déraisonnable.*

Mes vomissements étaient une réalité ; j'avais eu des symptômes d'empoisonnement très réels. Il était logique de demander l'analyse des matières que j'avais vomies. Donc ici, il n'y avait ni folie, ni délire, et c'était un acte révoltant de m'envoyer au dépôt de la Préfecture de police, à cette occasion.

5° Mais les préoccupations avaient dans le passé des racines profondes. Ce n'était pas seulement un acte isolé, c'était un épisode à ajouter à beaucoup d'autres dans une existence où la bizarrerie, les excentricités, les conceptions délirantes ne sont plus à compter.

5° Ici encore, Messieurs les aliénistes donnent libre carrière à leur imagination féconde : sans m'avoir connue autrefois, sans m'avoir vue, ils affirment des *épisodes en nombre,* de la *bizarrerie* de ma part, des *excentricités,* des *conceptions délirantes.* C'est bientôt dit.

On sait que MM. les aliénistes voient des fous partout. C'est leur moindre péché d'habitude.

Je nie tous les cas qui ne sont pas prouvés et je constate que toutes ces affirmations suggestives sont bien peu charitables.

De quelles conceptions délirantes veut-on parler ? Ce sont des mots vides de sens. C'est évident.

6° Si, en effet, nous voulons reprendre la vie de Mme Esquiron, nous y trouvons les plus *étranges anomalies.*

Ce serait se faire une idée très fausse de cette

6° Le présent paragraphe est l'aveu involontaire du crime commis contre moi sous le prétexte de *folie,* d'*anomalies,* de *conceptions délirantes.*

*dame, que de la considérer comme une aliénée
dont l'intelligence est amoindrie ; elle a au contraire, une acuité d'esprit très grande.* Elle la
met au service de ses conceptions délirantes,
si bien, qu'il est quelquefois difficile de démêler ce qui est vrai de ce qui est faux, dans
les récits où elle se pose en victime, où elle
présente les faits avec assez d'habileté pour
se réserver le beau rôle.

Avec elle, l'observation doit être prolongée, patiente, et dès nos premières entrevues
nous avons pu nous assurer qu'elle seule ne
nous éclairerait pas sur sa situation.

Il nous fut presque impossible d'obtenir
d'elle des réponses précises, à des questions
simples.

Avec une vaniteuse satisfaction, Mme Esquiron se livre à des digressions interminables et toujours en scène, dissimulant avec
une certaine habileté ce qu'elle ne tient pas
à nous dire ; elle insiste sur son enfance.

En effet, j'y trouve ceci :

« *Ce serait se faire une idée très fausse de
cette dame que de la considérer comme une aliénée
dont l'intelligence est amoindrie ; elle a au contraire une acuité d'esprit très grande.* »

Après cette affirmation, ma cause est gagnée. Si je ne suis pas aliénée, si on ne peut
pas m'interdire en vertu de l'article 489 du
code civil, il faut ma mise en liberté immédiate. De quel droit M. le docteur Goujon
me retient-il chez lui, puisque je ne suis pas
aliénée ?

MM. les aliénistes avouent une observation prolongée, patiente. En réalité, ils ne
m'ont visitée et interrogée que trois fois au
début des 8 mois qu'ils ont mis à faire leur
rapport. Ce n'est qu'à force de réflexions
qu'ils ont imaginé des anomalies et des
conceptions délirantes. Ils les ont rencontrées
toutes faites chez mes adversaires, ils le
disent eux-mêmes ; mais ils ne les nomment
pas. Je pourrais dire que c'est là une dissimulation plus coupable que celle qu'ils me
reprochent, tout en m'attribuant des digressions interminables.

Si j'ai parlé de mon enfance, c'est parce que
j'ai été interrogée sur mon enfance.

7° Avec une complaisance égoïste, elle insiste sur son enfance, sur l'éducation qu'elle
a reçue, ne cherchant, dans un prolixe exposé,
que l'occasion de médire de son père, qu'elle
accuse d'avoir perverti son imagination, de
l'avoir initiée de bonne heure aux mystères
de la fécondation des animaux.

Ce grief, *vrai ou faux*, est le premier
qu'elle ait à lui reprocher ; une foule d'autres
sont venus ensuite s'accumuler et dont nous
avons eu à entendre la monotone et diffuse
énumération.

Nous avons dû, pour nous retrouver au
milieu de véritables divagations, nous mettre
en rapport avec les hommes qui, au milieu

7° Il est bien vrai que mon père a perverti mon imagination, je ne médis pas, je
constate un fait qui a nui à toute mon existence ; je ne dissimule rien. Mais ces faits
anciens ne prouvent pas ma folie actuelle.
Mes griefs contre mon père ne sont que trop
réels. Il a sur la conscience mes deux séquestrations illégitimes, surtout d'avoir com-
promis ma réputation, ma vie et mes affaires ;
ma fortune est attaquée avec fureur pendant
que mon père et mon mari se font un plaisir
de me séquestrer et de paralyser tous mes
moyens de me défendre.

Mes défenseurs ont bien fait d'exposer
les difficultés sans nombre où je me débats,

de difficultés sans nombre où elle se débat, lui ont prêté le concours le plus dévoué, le plus désintéressé. M. Le Brisoys, son conseil, M. Messelet, son avoué, M. Saint-Aubin, son avocat, ont bien voulu, à plusieurs reprises, nous exposer une situation singulièrement compliquée.

8° Nous ne saurions les suivre dans les appréciations qui portent, surtout, sur la désastreuse opération qu'a faite Mme Esquiron, en achetant le domaine de Mercoire. Nous n'en voulons retenir que ceci : c'est que Mme Esquiror, en aliénant ses propriétés d'Ille-et-Vilaine, a certainement obéi à une *conception délirante*.

Elle s'est crue l'objet de la haine, du mépris de tout le monde dans le pays où elle avait tous ses biens, et sans se rendre compte que les avanies qu'elle a eu à subir n'avaient pas d'autre cause que l'excentricité de ses allures et de son langage, elle s'est crue persécutée.

Elle a décidé, sans autre motif plus sérieux, de s'éloigner pour toujours de ces lieux où elle supposait que sa sécurité était compromise.

Qu'elle se soit trompée, ou qu'elle ait été trompée, nous ne pouvons lui en faire un reproche, une spéculation malheureusement conduite n'est pas en soi la caractéristique d'un état d'aliénation mentale.

9° Mais les mobiles déterminants de cette spéculation relèvent de notre jugement et nous ne saurions hésiter à les retenir *comme déraisonnables*.

Il en est de même de tous les actes importants de la vie de Mme Esquiron.

Nous ne voulons pas insister sur les conditions dans lesquelles elle s'est mariée. Ce qu'elle nous en a dit, non moins que l'expression nettement formulée de l'intention de qui exigent ma mise en liberté. MM. les docteurs auraient dû s'en convaincre et me rendre justice en constatant que je n'ai pas perdu la tête.

8° Si j'ai quitté mon pays, c'est que, après ma séquestration en 1866, chez le docteur Blanche, mon père m'avait fait une telle réputation que tout le monde me fuyait. On me montrait au doigt ; on ne me recevait nulle part ; je ne pouvais me marier avantageusement là, malgré ma fortune personnelle.

Quant à l'acquisition de Mercoire, l'affaire eût été bonne si je n'avais mis ma confiance dans un notaire peu scrupuleux. Cela ne prouve pas ma *folie*, ni mes *conceptions délirantes*. J'ai su, depuis, obtenir de la Cour de Paris, par un arrêt du 22 juillet 1891, 400,000 francs de dommages-intérêts contre mon échangiste frauduleux.

Si j'étais ridicule, c'était l'œuvre de mon père et de ma famille. Il est bien inutile de dire que j'ai obéi à une conception délirante.

9° MM. les aliénistes, avec une désinvolture étonnante, disent que tous les actes de ma vie ont été déraisonnables.

Ils raisonnent, non *de visu*, mais par suppositions. C'est très commode, en vérité. Mais ils ne prouvent rien et je dis qu'ils se trompent du tout au tout. Les deux exemples qu'ils évoquent, mon mariage et l'acquisition de Mercoire, sont au contraire très raisonnables.

rompre cette union qui lui était à charge, nous a prouvé la mobilité de ses sentiments et la persistance, aussi, de ses idées de persécution.

Ce sont ces idées, dont l'acuité est devenue plus grande quand les difficultés créées par l'acquisition de Mercoire ont été plus pressantes, qui la dominaient au mois d'août 1891. C'est sous la pression de *son délire* qu'elle s'est livrée à des recherches sur les auteurs d'une tentative d'empoisonnement dont elle s'est crue victime.

Si j'ai voulu rompre par le divorce, c'était mon droit, après avoir constaté la trahison de mon mari, se concertant avec mon père, pour obtenir mon interdiction, afin de s'emparer de mes biens ; lui qui ne possédait rien, ne pouvait ni me protéger, ni me nourrir, ni payer la location d'un logement, ni administrer mes propriétés

Ma demande en divorce, pour d'autres causes encore, était des plus raisonnables et ne prouve nullement la mobilité de mes sentiments, ni la persistance de mes idées de persécution, mais le malheur d'une grande déception.

Quant à Mercoire, il existe sur ma propriété une forêt, dont la superficie exploitable en ce moment est de 262 hectares en taillis de 45 ans d'âge, évaluée à 150,000 fr. réalisables. Au mois d'août 1891, j'étais en train de faire la coupe de ces bois, afin de payer tous mes créanciers. Cela ne prouve pas ma folie, pas plus que la nécessité de mon envoi au dépôt, *d'office*.

10ᵃ Aujourd'hui Madame Esquiron proteste contre la mesure qui a été prise vis-à-vis d'elle et dont tout ce qui s'est passé justifie l'opportunité.

Sa tenue, ses discours dans la maison de santé ne laissent pas de doute sur le trouble de son intelligence, sur la perversion de ses sentiments.

Vis-à-vis de nous, elle a pris une attitude de supériorité dédaigneuse.

10ᵒ Je proteste, en effet, et surtout contre l'*inopportunité* de ma séquestration qui cause *ma ruine*, puisque ma détention m'a empêché de faire mes affaires et de réaliser mes coupes de bois pour payer mes créanciers, d'autant plus que mon domaine de Mercoire, estimé à 586,000 francs, a été vendu au prix dérisoire de 155,000 francs et que je suis obligée encore d'entrer dans un nouveau procès.

MM. les aliénistes auraient pu me l'éviter en se hâtant de déposer un rapport plus favorable.

Au lieu de cela, ils ont attendu huit mois pour le déposer, sans souci de ma ruine.

Quant à dire que ma tenue, mes discours dans la maison ne laissent pas de doute sur le trouble de mon intelligence, sur la perversion de mes sentiments, c'est absolument fantaisiste, ainsi que de dire que, vis-à-vis des docteurs, j'ai pris une attitude de supériorité dédaigneuse.

J'ai pu m'étonner dans ma conscience du faux jugement porté contre moi ; mais je n'en ai rien fait connaître aux experts, et tout cela ne prouve pas ma folie.

11° Elle appartient à cette catégorie de malades qui n'acceptent pas les questions et qui poursuivent avec une ténacité invincible le thème invariable qu'elles ont la prétention d'imposer.

Avec une prolixité que nous devons subir, elle reprend sans cesse les mêmes récriminations. Elle a dans l'esprit des faits, des dates, des épisodes, et scandant les mots, les phrases, elle finit par se perdre au milieu de banalités sentencieuses qui se déroulent imperturbablement pendant des heures.

Nous ne voulons pas dire que ses affirmations sont absolument mensongères. Mais, elles n'ont que peu de chose à voir à la situation présente, et nous ne pouvons le faire comprendre à Madame Esquiron.

12° Un des côtés curieux de son trouble mental, c'est l'importance qu'elle donne à tout ce qui se rattache à l'appareil génital. Elle nous entretient, avec une visible satisfaction, du traitement qu'elle a suivi ; elle désirerait que son médecin ordinaire lui continuât ses soins ; elle nous montre les ordonnances. Elle insiste sur l'importance que devait avoir pour elle les douches vaginales par la lance du large qui lui avaient été prescrites.

13° Nous comprenons mieux, à la suite de ces confidences qui révèlent un état d'esprit particulier, les *aventures* où Madame Esquiron aurait joué un rôle actif : certaine plainte portée contre elle et dont elle dit que ce sont des *infamies*.

A la Maison de Santé on a pu faire des remarques sur lesquelles nous n'insisterons pas ; cependant certaines particularités ont

11° Si j'énonce des banalités, c'est qu'on me soutient des banalités contraires et contre la vérité.

Mais, puisque mes affirmations ne sont pas tout à fait mensongères, MM. les Docteurs ne peuvent s'étonner que je ne comprenne pas que ces choses ne sont pas étrangères à ma situation présente. Cela prouve ma raison et non ma folie. Je comprends tout le préjudice qui m'est causé.

12° Ceci prouve le peu de délicatesse du rapport, oubliant que les médecins respectent ordinairement le secret professionnel. Si j'ai suivi un traitement, ce n'est pas pour la tête.

Chez M. le docteur Goujon, la preuve qu'il ne me croit pas folle, c'est qu'il ne me soumet à aucun traitement médical mental.

Pourquoi m'y retient-on ? Voilà encore une preuve du crime dont je suis victime.

13° L'aventure rappelée ici, c'est une affaire Pacault, intrigue imaginée par mon père et mon mari, afin de pouvoir m'accuser de *folie lubrique* et de répondre ainsi à ma demande en divorce. MM. les Docteurs auraient dû le savoir. Ce sont, en effet, des *infamies imaginaires*.

Voici qui est encore plus grave. On m'a surprise essayant de boire le vin resté dans

leur importance. Madame Esquiron a un appétit des boissons très développé. On l'a surprise essayant de boire le vin qui restait dans les bouteilles. On nous signale, au dehors, ces tendances anciennes.

Quant à nous, quelque condescendance que nous ayons montrée, nous sommes les instruments de ceux qui veulent la perdre.

14° Nous ne pouvons nous défendre d'un sentiment de pitié pour Madame Esquiron ; mais nous avons le *devoir de chercher ailleurs les éléments d'une appréciation impartiale.*

Nous ne faisons pas difficulté de reconnaître que Madame Esquiron ne manque pas d'intelligence, mais cette intelligence est absolument désordonnée. Elle n'a ni jugement, ni esprit de conduite ; elle est incapable de se diriger, non pas comme une démente dont l'intelligence, la mémoire sont affaiblies et qui arrive à l'incohérence, mais comme une maniaque chronique, avec une excitation intellectuelle permanente, doublée de perversion de la sensibilité morale affective.

les bouteilles. C'est bien peu dire, quand mon père disait que j'avais l'habitude de boire un litre d'eau-de-vie par jour, quand j'étais en Belgique, ne buvant que de la bière.

Et puis, je suis bien folle puisque je connais une foule de termes de procédure et que j'indique à mes Conseils les moyens de mener à bien mes affaires.

Est-ce sérieux?

MM. les Docteurs se fâchent à la pensée que je les crois être les instruments de ceux qui veulent me perdre.

Le présent rapport me donne raison sur ce point, à défaut d'autres preuves ; ils devaient se borner à établir ma folie pathologiquement, et, comme cela ne leur est pas possible, ils rassemblent toutes les insanités imaginées par mes adversaires.

C'est bien peu concluant.

14° Je repousse ce sentiment de pitié dont je n'ai pas besoin ; si Messieurs les Experts savaient lire dans mon entendement, ils verraient que mon intelligence n'a rien de désordonné.

Ils ne se sont pas aperçus de la contradiction qu'ils commettent en reconnaissant d'une part que j'ai de l'intelligence, d'autre part que je manque de jugement. Comme si le jugement et l'intelligence pouvaient se séparer dans mon entendement. Enfin, selon eux, je n'aurais ni jugement, ni esprit de conduite et je serais incapable de me diriger.

Tout cela veut dire que je suis un monstre, une nature exceptionnelle et bizarre. Qui dit trop ne dit rien. Ce sont des affirmations sans preuves.

Ils auraient pu, au contraire, constater que je suis entravée dans toutes mes volontés par mon père et par mon mari, qui seuls compromettent ma santé, ma fortune et ma vie. Ces insinuations, encore une fois, ne prouvent pas ma folie.

Quant à ma sensibilité morale et affective,

15° Il serait impossible de justifier son interdiction en se basant aux termes de l'article 489 du code civil, mais il est évident aussi qu'elle a besoin qu'on lui continue l'assistance, la protection que lui assure le conseil judiciaire dont elle s'est pourvue.

Sa situation est d'autant plus intéressante qu'elle est engagée dans des affaires où sa fortune est gravement compromise.

A notre avis, il importe qu'elle n'y soit point mêlée. D'abord, elle entraverait toute solution ; ensuite elle se trouverait au milieu de difficultés qui sont loin d'être aplanies, les causes qui ont provoqué l'accès aigu du mois d'août 1891.

16° Après un examen *prolongé* qui ne nous permet pas de trouver rien de plus qu'une *amélioration relative,* nous sommes en droit de conclure que Mme Esquiron, qui n'accepterait au dehors ni contrôle, ni direction, qui n'a près d'elle personne en qui elle ait confiance, est incapable de jouir sagement de la liberté qu'elle réclame ;

Qu'il y a lieu de la maintenir dans une maison de santé spéciale.

C'est là seulement qu'il sera possible de lui assurer la surveillance et les soins que son état réclame.

Et surtout de l'éloigner des embarras d'affaires qui, le jour où elle y sera directement engagée, provoqueraient certainement une rechute grave.

Ont signé :

MM. Mottet, Magnan, Voisin.

je la garde pour mes amis et non pour mes bourreaux.

15° J'ai recueilli ci-dessus l'aveu que je ne suis pas aliénée. Je constate, ici, que l'article 489 du code civil empêche mes adversaires de faire prononcer mon interdiction demandée par mon père et mon mari.

En lisant l'avis de MM. les docteurs, on voit qu'ils s'efforcent de trouver des raisons pour justifier ma séquestration et la prolonger le plus longtemps possible, ce qui équivaut à une interdiction perpétuelle, ce qui est contraire à l'article 489.

De quel droit ?

Les raisons produites n'ont pas de sens. La loi doit me protéger comme toute autre personne en France.

Le certificat d'aliénation mentale ne peut être en contradiction avec la loi, car ce serait l'abroger par voie indirecte.

16° Ce paragraphe a été longuement calculé et prémédité ; il démontre la résolution de faire prévaloir le *certificat d'aliénation mentale* sur le texte de l'article 489 du code civil, qui serait ainsi mis en oubli, par exception pour moi. C'est la théorie de mon père et son application.

Le certificat d'aliénation mentale obtenu à la suite d'une manœuvre déloyale de ma famille, que les médecins n'ont pu motiver que par des allégations insuffisantes de prétendues manies héréditaires, des affirmations contradictoires et surtout par l'oubli ou le mépris du devoir qu'ils avaient de m'appliquer le bénéfice de l'article 489 du code civil, ce certificat d'aliénation mentale n'est qu'une forfaiture bien caractérisée.

Ces Messieurs ont l'air de me porter de l'intérêt et ils disent que je ne puis jouir sagement de la liberté que je réclame.

Qu'en savent-ils ? Ont-ils le droit de juger l'avenir de mon existence ?

MA CONCLUSION

Je proteste donc, une fois de plus, contre le plaidoyer de MM. les aliénistes. J'ai réfuté leurs arguments complaisants avec assez de netteté pour prouver que je ne suis pas *aliénée*. Mon internement à perpétuité, qui comblerait de joie ma triste famille, ne leur sera pas accordé, sans un appel de ma part à la justice de mon pays qui me protégera.

Que vient-on parler encore des soins que mon état réclame, quand on a dû savoir que, chez M. le docteur Goujon, je n'ai été soumise à aucun traitement médical mental et que j'y suis privée de tous les soins que je puis me procurer chez moi, sans peine, ma fortune étant suffisante !

Que disent MM. les aliénistes experts ?

Ils affirment ceci :

1º Que je ne suis pas aliénée ;

2º Que je suis très intelligente ;

3º Que mon intelligence n'est pas amoindrie ;

4º Que j'ai une acuité d'esprit très grande ;

5º Que je discerne parfaitement ce que je dois dire de ce que je dois taire ;

6º Qu'il serait impossible de justifier mon interdiction en se basant aux termes de l'article 489 du code civil, n'étant ni démente, ni imbécile, ni en état de fureur.

Que disent-ils encore ?

Que malgré cet état mental satisfaisant, largement suffisant pour vivre en société, certes, il faut selon eux, selon leur avis, que je reste séquestrée à perpétuité dans une maison de fous, afin d'y recevoir les soins et la surveillance dont j'ai besoin, n'étant pas capable d'user sagement de la liberté que je réclame.

Après avoir pesé les raisons pour et contre, il n'est pas douteux que ma cause est gagnée devant la justice et devant le plus vulgaire jugement.

C'est pourquoi, Monsieur le Ministre, je viens insister auprès de vous pour ordonner la fin de mon supplice en me mettant en liberté immédiate.

MARIE ESQUIRON, née DE GASTÉ,

Séquestrée, depuis le 27 août 1891, chez le docteur Goujon,

90, rue Picpus, à Paris.

4

Pauline Lair Lamotte

'Je sens que la vérité est là'

The eminent psychologist, psychiatrist, philosopher, and Professor of the Collège de France, Pierre Janet, published a medical treatise in 1926 entitled *De l'angoisse à l'extase: études sur les croyances et les sentiments*.[1] The first volume of this work took as its principal case study a patient who came to Janet's attention at the Salpêtrière in 1896, and who had chosen for herself the alias 'Madeleine Lebouc'. She would stay in the asylum for eight years before being released in 1904, when she returned to her family home to live out her days. This doctor followed his patient's progress for twenty-two years, corresponding regularly with her until the end of her life. 'Madeleine' sent her last letter the day before she died in 1918 (1–43).

Janet sums up his patient's presenting symptoms as: 'délire religieux, avec crises extatiques' (6), and he found her strange behaviour intriguing:

Sa vie étrange, ses fugues, son délire religieux, son attitude, sa marche sur la pointe des pieds, les stigmates du Christ qu'elle a présentés aux pieds et aux mains à plusieurs [r]eprises et surtout les sentiments violents qu'elle éprouvait dans des crises d'angoisse et dans des crises d'extase, sa guérison relative à la fin de sa vie soulèvent à chaque instant des problèmes médicaux et psychologiques du plus grand intérêt. (1)

This story has been privileged in the history of female incarceration, and only comes to us because of Janet's avowed fascination with his patient. Catherine Clément points out that her case is unusual because, in contrast to the thousands of women whose madness could only be

---

[1] Janet (1926).

managed rather than treated at the Salpêtrière, 'un savant l'observa minutieusement'.[2]

All the biographical details given about 'Madeleine' are contained in the first chapter of the treatise. The third child of four sisters, and strongly influenced by her devout elder sister (named simply 'Madame X' in the text), the young girl is reputed to have asked: 'Si tu réussissais à m'enlever ma religion, qu'est-ce que tu me donnerais à la place?' (10). This suggests that the exaggerated centrality of her belief system appears to have been in place from a very early stage; indeed, she claims that her visions began around the age of nine (12).

Janet's case history states that 'Madeleine' left home in her late teens to pursue a 'carrière de pauvre fille': a life of anonymity among the poorest of the poor. He records that she spent some time working as a maid, and a few weeks in a convent, both places where according to Janet she felt 'trop surveillée', and in 1874 'Madeleine' moved to Paris. In the years that followed she was arrested on a number of occasions, each time giving her name as 'Madeleine Lebouc', claiming to be the lover of Christ and scapegoat for the sins of the world (21). She was sentenced to a year in prison for 'vagabondage'. Proving to be a model prisoner, she was released after six months but quickly rearrested and found guilty of 'escroquerie, vagabondage, prostitution, mendicité, rupture de ban'. She served five months of a prison sentence before being re-released, and then proceeded to write letters to the police that had her put under surveillance, being considered 'une folle probablement atteinte du délire de la persécution' (22).

Jacques Maître has investigated in detail the state of historical information regarding this case history, and points to a number of inaccuracies in Janet's account. This is partly because of Janet's concern to keep his patient's identity concealed, and partly because of his propensity to muddle dates and historical facts: 'Madeleine' would become his clinical secret and personal obsession. Maître discovered this woman's real name to be Pauline Lair Lamotte. Born in 1853 in Mayenne, she lived with her parents until 1873 when she left home to work for a

---

[2] Clément (1993: 17). Edelman (1995: 185) also notes the importance of Janet's discussion of 'Madeleine' in the context of acknowledging the importance of belief in mental functioning. The case of Pauline Lair Lamotte is now well documented and is frequently cited in discussions of hysteria, mysticism, and anorexia in the nineteenth century. See Maître (1993, 1997, 2001); Hamona (2008); Burton (2004).

family in London.[3] Lamotte's religious education was provided in the context of the Franciscan third order, which gave her a distaste for the cloistered life of the convent and a yearning for a life of absolute poverty. Her choice of lifestyle made her a subversive figure both in the religious community and in society at large, where she came into conflict with some of its core institutions: the law, the police, and the hospital. Her life would be marked by the social and political upheaval in which she existed: her youth under the Second Empire; the awakening of a vocation through seeing the poverty of the area around the Tower of London; two decades in Montmartre in the ruins of the Paris Commune of 1871; the Belle Époque; and, during her final years, the First World War.[4]

Lamotte's writing has some prophetic qualities to it, and as such can be aligned with contemporary women writers whose texts possess a mystical and indeed optimistic quality, such as Céline Renooz and Louise Michel.[5] The latter was a key figure in the Paris Commune and her memoir writing embodies a dynamic hope for change and multiple references to the future, in which Michel envisages a truly socialist revolution.[6] Lamotte's text to some extent reflects the concerns and feminist optimism of the era because she places her hope in a God that may redeem France. However, it is also true to say that much of her text, as well as being introspective in nature, is retrospective and pessimistic in tone, being concerned with the memory of the turbulent era of the early 1870s that preceded her incarceration. This was followed by the establishment of the comparatively stable Third Republic with its renewed rejection of Catholicism. Lamotte views revolution simply in terms of rebellion against God, and her concerns cannot be described as being specifically feminist in nature. However, her text may be read as a form of fiction of empowerment as an example of a woman writer representing an experience that enables her to evade the strictures of the society in which she lived.

---

[3] A chronological list of major events in Lamotte's life is provided in Maître (1993: 355–6). Several important biographical details are changed or simplified in Janet's treatise, such as Lamotte's family background. Lamotte's biographer has found repeated errors in Janet's recording of important facts, such as his patient's age in a given year. While these inaccuracies must be noted, they do not have a significant bearing on the analysis of her text in this chapter.

[4] Maître (1993: xxx).

[5] Renooz is discussed later in this chapter on page pp. 176–7.

[6] See Chapter 4 of Hart (2004: 131–70) for a full discussion of Louise Michel's memoirs.

Janet's study was published by the Librairie Félix Alcan, which produced most major medical treatises at this time, as well as works in the areas of philosophy, sociology, the history of medicine, the psychology and anthropology of religion, and psychoanalysis, from the late 1880s until the end of the 1930s. *De l'angoisse à l'extase* represents a synthesis of Janet's work on neurasthenia—a form of nervous exhaustion dubbed the 'maladie du siècle'—with a particular case of psychopathology. The study of Lamotte's behaviour serves to corroborate general observations made about patients troubled by doubts and obsessions: problems for which Janet coins the term 'délire psychasthénique' (7). His overall contribution to knowledge through this work is to demonstrate that 'mystical' religious experiences can be shown to be manifestations of a wider psychopathology.[7] Janet made progress in the treatment of mental illness by re-engaging with the possibility of curing psychiatric conditions, during the post-1870s era of increased anxiety about degeneration and social decline.

Lamotte wrote prolifically, her memoirs taking the form of a daily journal written for the attention of her doctor. Janet's commentary incorporates these writings in fairly long, uninterrupted excerpts of text within the main body of his case study, and they are the focal point of his analysis: 'J'attache une certaine importance aux lettres et au journal que Madeleine commença à rédiger à mon intention dès son entrée à l'hôpital [. . .] Madeleine prit l'habitude de rédiger tous les jours un long mémoire qu'elle me remettait le lendemain' (5). She at no point claimed ownership of these writings; rather, she 'bequeathed' them to Janet at the end of her stay at the Salpêtrière in acknowledgement of the fact that he had been the most significant human figure in her life for all this time:

Donc, mon père, tout en vous répétant que je n'aime pas que l'on parle de moi, je dois me résigner au sacrifice de mon désir le plus cher, celui de rester cachée, dans l'intérêt de la religion et de l'étude. La pauvreté d'esprit que Dieu me demande exige que je ne garde rien de ma propriété. Mes écrits ne m'appartiennent plus et vous avez le droit, mon père, d'en faire ce que vous voulez. (5–6)

These writings, together with the letters she sent after leaving hospital, comprise an 'œuvre' of well over two thousand pages (5). Lamotte's professed desire to remain hidden is directly contradicted by the action of giving her writing to her doctor for consideration, and indeed by the exhibitionism of her ecstasies. These reveal the opposite motivation of,

---

[7] On neurasthenia as the 'maladie du siècle' see Proust (1897).

in fact, wishing to be the object of psychiatric observation; this links the writer to Esquiron and Rouy in her desire for her ideas and beliefs to be taken seriously by her doctor, and indeed in her great verbal output that drew clinical attention to her case.[8]

We can only speculate on the reasons why Janet was so attracted to Lamotte as an object of study, but among these are likely to be the fact that she wrote so much and, despite a limited education, so well. Janet compliments Lamotte's 'remarquable facilité de style' (13), and notes: 'elle avait conservé malgré ses vingt années de misère à peu près sans lecture une grande facilité de rédaction et quelques mérites de style' (37). It is unlikely that the version we have of Lamotte's writing is exactly as she left it, for Janet felt it judicious to edit her writing, which is often 'trop longue et diffuse'; and just as Esquiron's complaint is judged 'interminable', so Lamotte's writing is criticized for being 'interminable dans la description de ses sentiments religieux' (37). He is, however, anxious to portray 'l'intelligence et la délicatesse morale de cette personne, ainsi que ses véritables qualités littéraires' (6), even though she had read relatively little (some seventeenth-century French literature; the Bible; the life of St Francis of Assisi, and part of Teresa of Avila's *Traité de la perfection*) (13).

Some argue that in a different era, or even in a different context, Lamotte's entourage might well have taken her adult 'mystical' experiences as authentic, which indeed closely resemble those of some of the most famous mystics.[9] Janet does not overtly deny this possibility, admitting that such experiences are not rare in religious contexts, although he doubts that her writing would ever be used seriously for the purposes of religious instruction (2–5). He views Lamotte's case as exceptional because her experiences occur in a secular context:

Ce que Madeleine présente à mes yeux d'un peu exceptionnel, c'est que pendant plusieurs années elle a vécu dans un hôpital laïque où les extases mystiques et les stigmates du Christ n'habitent pas d'ordinaire et qu'elle a été étudiée en dehors des influences qui agissent d'ordinaire sur les mystiques. (3)

---

[8] Maître's extensive research into the archive sources of Janet's treatise reveals that a series of unfortunate events has led to a dearth of primary information relating to Lamotte's life. Three boxes of notes containing the original writings were burnt at Janet's request by his daughter. Documents and photographs regarding the case of Lamotte have been lost or destroyed by the Archives de l'Assistance publique, the only remaining information being her admission records. The dossier on Lamotte created by the Carmelite Père Bruno de Jésus-Marie has disappeared, and the family papers from Pauline's sisters Sophie and Léontine were destroyed by one of their nieces. See Maître (1993: 358).

[9] Clément (1993: 25).

Maître argues, though, that Janet is too quick to dismiss the importance of the religious influences in Lamotte's life. Strong parallels can be drawn between what could be termed her 'trois pères symboliques': Janet himself and Lamotte's two spiritual directors, Père Conrad and Père Poulain.[10] Since Janet observed and may have inadvertently encouraged her activities, it is perhaps unsurprising that Lamotte continued to experience these phenomena so intensely for as long as she did.

Janet's claim that Lamotte's experiences occurred spontaneously and without external suggestion points to a parallel between Lamotte's writing and the quasi-mystical experience of scientific 'révélation' regarding the origin of species recounted by Céline Renooz, discussed in Chapter 1 and later in this chapter. Renooz purports to record her revelation 'telle que je l'avais vue dans mon esprit, sans aucun livre autour de moi, sans aucun document, sans avoir, même, un seul instant, l'idée de consulter les livres que les hommes avaient pu écrire sur ce sujet'.[11] Just as Lamotte lives these experiences away from religious influences, so Renooz claims to gain scientific insight without studying prior theories.

Lamotte describes oscillating between an 'état de consolation', a cataleptic state of ecstasy and union with God, and an 'état de torture', an extreme depressive state characterized by persecutory delusions. She names intermediary states 'tentation', a state of obsession and doubt; 'sécheresse', a feeling of emptiness and abandonment by God; and 'équilibre', a state that resembles sanity and is characterized by greater stability. She exhibits stigmata, has an intimate and sexual relationship with God, and walks around on tiptoes.[12] This is a physical manifestation of her belief that she will be taken up to heaven in the imminent future in a repetition of the Assumption of the Virgin Mary.[13] Although this woman's beliefs were delusional from a medical point of view, it is also the case that many of her religious ideas were shared by certain groups at that time.[14]

---

[10] Maître (1993: xxxi).

[11] Renooz (1888: 267).

[12] For a detailed discussion of the patient's stigmata see Apte (1903).

[13] From the fifth century the Church has honoured the death of the Virgin Mary, and first accounts of belief in the bodily assumption of the Virgin are found from the sixth century. Although not admitted as official dogma by the Catholic Church until 1950, as an event it was widely believed and celebrated. See the following articles on 'Assomption': GD: 810; GL: 660.

[14] G. Lantéri-Laura in preface to Maître (1993: xiv): 'Elle s'attache bien, à certains moments, à des convictions bien étranges; mais, pour les unes, J. Maître établit clairement qu'elles faisaient alors partie d'une piété assez répandue dans le tiers ordre, et, pour les autres, rien ne montre que leur bizarrerie appartînt indubitablement à la

In 1896, twenty-three years after leaving her family, Lamotte was admitted to the Salpêtrière, suffering from stiffening of the whole body, particularly the legs, thighs, and stomach. Prior to her admission Lamotte had been treated in various Parisian hospitals, where diverse speculations were made regarding her illness. At the Hôtel-Dieu doctors thought the problem had been caused by 'une névrite, suite d'une fausse couche'; at Bichat and Necker Lamotte was diagnosed as suffering from 'contractures hystériques', and was thought to be a dancer who did not want to divulge information about her dubious former profession (26–7).[15]

Janet gives a rather endearing first impression of this patient, 'cette petite femme trottinant indéfiniment sur la pointe des pieds', and appears to have been captivated by her strange story (1):

Elle ne donnait que des explications fort confuses sur l'origine et l'évolution de cette raideur des pieds qui avait débuté, racontait-elle, pendant une nuit de Noël; elle ajoutait des allusions bizarres à une force qui la soulevait au-dessus du sol et qui l'empêchait de toucher la terre davantage. (27)

Lamotte spent the whole of her first night at the Salpêtrière in the 'attitude de la crucifixion': stretched out on her back with her legs fully extended, both arms crossed over her chest (27). Janet, unable to rouse her from her stupor the following morning, was quickly taken with this new patient and within a few weeks had won her trust. Over the twenty-two years that followed the two main actors in this story were to form what would become a quite extraordinary clinical relationship.

Possible approaches to the text of a patient claiming to have mystical experiences vary according to the context in which it is read. The experiences related by 'Madeleine' can be read in a number of ways: as an authentic mystical religious experience; as some form of misguided or overzealous spiritual accident; as a psychotic episode *tout court*; or as a psychotic episode characterized by a specific 'mystical' element. The dividing line between these discursive positions is arguably porous, since they take as their starting point comparable human experiences; there is continuity, in terms of the root experience, in what different theoreticians

pathologie. Quand elle parle, par exemple, de sa lévitation, il s'agit d'une croyance en accord avec le milieu religieux qui l'inspirait.'

[15] The exact dates of Lamotte's hospitalization(s) are 3 November 1894–15 December 1894: Hôpital de l'Hôtel-Dieu; 15 December 1894–14 June 1895: Hôpital Bichat; 15 June 1895–11 February 1896: Hôpital Necker; 11 February 1896–1 December 1901: Hôpital de la Salpêtrière; 3 January 1903–7 March 1904: Hôpital de la Salpêtrière.

describe. Religious commentators, such as Evelyn Underhill, are sympathetic to mystical activity and critical of the dismissive attitude of psychiatry towards the subject, and most French clinicians in this era essentially viewed the 'mystical' experience as psychopathological. The approaches offered by existential psychiatry influenced by phenomenology, and psychoanalysis, will reveal that just as the psychotic experience can be understood as an authentic, if somehow problematic, manifestation of one aspect of the broad range of legitimate human experience, so the experience of mystics and 'false' mystics alike can be read as truthful in terms of the internal world out of which they are born. This analysis privileges the thinking of theorists such as Eugène Minkowski, Laing, and the Jungian analyst Morton Kelsey, as well as psychoanalysis, which all represent ideas that have in varying ways sought to get to the heart of the lived experience of the patient and the mystic.

Evelyn Underhill, in her landmark text *Mysticism*, defines this as 'the science or art of the spiritual life [...] The expression of the innate tendency of the human spirit towards complete harmony with the transcendental order'.[16] In line with this model, Lamotte's narrative is constructed around the movement of a central character who approaches and moves away from God, in a dynamic that reaches its zenith during absolute union and its nadir in a feeling of total abandonment by this same God. Underhill does not make explicit reference to Lamotte's case, but she is critical of the French psychological school's view of mystical experience: 'French psychology [...] would, if it had its way, fill the wards of the Salpêtrière with patients from the Roman Calendar.'[17] She denies that the 'problem' of mystical experience has been fathomed by psychiatry, and critiques in particular the work of Janet, Murisier, and Ribot, instead suggesting that 'the mystical temperament belong[s] as yet to the unsolved problem of humanity'.[18]

Indeed, French psychological thought equates mysticism with superstition and naivety, and parallels this experience with psychotic states. Moreau de Tours in 1859 wrote extensively on the subject of mysticism in his treatise on *La psychologie morbide*, in which he compares the mystical experience with madness: 'Les mystiques, les théosophes se croient réellement en relation avec Dieu, l'entendent dans leur

[16] Underhill (1911: xiv).
[17] Ibid. 267.
[18] Ibid. 60. See also Murisier 1901; and Ribot (1896: 297) on 'le sentiment religieux'.

conscience, conversent avec lui, en reçoivent les instructions. Elles expriment enfin un véritable état hallucinatoire.'[19]

Maxime de Montmorand, to whom Janet refers extensively, characterizes Christian mysticism as a 'sentiment et goût du mystère', exemplified by a 'tendance à subordonner le raisonnement à l'intuition [...] à rechercher, comme essentiellement révélateurs, des états purement affectifs'. The experience is further demeaned in Montmorand's second chapter, where he describes typical orthodox Catholic mystics as being women who are 'humbles et simples', 'nerveu[ses]', docile, uncultivated, and demonstrating a pathological need for direction.[20] Sérieux and Capgras also dismiss mysticism as a form of delusional ambition, and mystics as megalomaniacs whose ideas have been shaped by a religious upbringing.[21]

The predominance of this point of view is even reflected in texts that one would expect to take a more sympathetic approach to the mystical experience, such as the philosopher Henri Delacroix's *Les Grands mystiques chrétiens*, published in 1938. He differentiates between the psychological make-up of what he terms 'grands mystiques' and 'caractères inférieurs', who exhibit 'délires religieux'; 'accidents nerveux'; and 'l'hystérie ou la folie religieuses'. He warns: 'Les bas mystiques, dégénérés sans génie, névropathes sans puissance intellectuelle et volontaire, aliénés méconnus par un pieux entourage, pullulent et sont légion; les mystiques d'imitation et de second ordre sont nombreux aussi.'[22] Lamotte's case would, according to these criteria, presumably be placed in the second category.

Janet compares his patient's experiences to those of Thérèse Martin, Sainte Thérèse de l'Enfant-Jésus, who was canonized in record time and officially proclaimed by the Church in 1925 'la plus grande sainte des temps modernes'.[23] This woman was a member of a Carmelite religious community at Lisieux, and she received an order from her prioress,

---

[19] Moreau de Tours (1859: 228).
[20] Montmorand (1920: 2, 11, 16).
[21] Sérieux (1909: 121). It would be fair to say that patients exhibiting some form of 'délire mystique' were well represented in French asylums during this period, and that there is little evidence of any such experiences being seen as anything other than pathological by contemporary commentators. Réja (2000: 185, 180) discusses the case of a 'délirant mystique' and the phenomenon of 'stigmates délirants', and Rogues de Fursal (1905: 259) dedicates part of his treatise to 'le mysticisme pathologique'.
[22] Delacroix (1938: ii–iii).
[23] Maître (1986: 23).

Mère Agnès, to write a spiritual autobiography. In 1895 the twenty-two-year-old Thérèse obediently composed the text that would become *Histoire d'une âme*.[24] We shall later see that parallels can indeed be drawn between this text and the writings of Lamotte, but it is important at this stage also to note that the Church, and particularly the Carmelite order, distanced themselves from the figure of 'Madeleine'. They sought to prevent their saints from being tainted by the inevitable association with psychopathology.[25]

To the end of discrediting 'Madeleine Lebouc', in 1931 the Carmelite scholar Père Bruno de Jésus-Marie directed a series of articles on this subject in the journal *Études carmélitaines*. In these he objects to the way in which Janet conflates the experience described by Lamotte, a 'délire religieux', with 'legitimate' mystical occurrences, and like his predecessor Delacroix seeks to differentiate between the misguided 'Madeleine' and authentic mystics. He criticizes her excessively penitent lifestyle, in particular her self-deprivation and mortification, which he views paradoxically as intemperate and indulgent because of the masochistic pleasure gained from such activity. Jésus-Marie writes: 'La "petite voie" manquait d'attrait pour Madeleine. Son école de spiritualité, c'est l'école buissonnière où elle se roule dans les épines, où elle se détruit sans rien apprendre.'[26] For the religious community, Lamotte was a good, but seriously misguided, Christian woman.

Underhill argues: 'There is no trustworthy standard by which we can separate the "real" from the "unreal" aspects of phenomena [...] For practical purposes we have agreed that sanity consists in sharing the hallucinations of our neighbours.'[27] Laing reiterates this point of view in his account of psychotic breakdown in *The Divided Self*: 'Sanity or psychosis is tested by the degree of conjunction or disjunction between

---

[24] Ibid. 25.
[25] An interesting counter-example to this is an edition of the 'autobiography' of Jeanne des Anges, mother superior of a community of Ursulines at Loudun, written in 1644. An edition of this account was published in 1886 by historian Gabriel Legué and psychiatrist Gilles de la Tourette. The given title in the manuscript is 'La possession de la Sœur Jeanne des Anges', and the view of her editors is that the occurrence of possession here recounted was an example of hysteria. Jeanne des Anges is utterly demonized in their commentary. For a detailed discussion of this case, see Finn (2003). Ribot also examines the writings of Teresa of Avila as an example of the psychopathology of the mystical experience in a chapter on 'l'anéantissement de la volonté' (1888).
[26] Jésus-Marie (1931: 103).
[27] Underhill (1911: 7).

two persons where the one is sane by common consent.'[28] Both these approaches, which, although radically different in their philosophical underpinnings, attempt to validate what is true about 'psychotic' and 'mystical' mental occurrences, rather than focusing on what is unsettling about them to the outside observer.

Psychoanalysis also achieves this by demonstrating that there is continuity between normal, neurotic, and psychotic states and that the workings of the psyche do not alter as radically between these as is initially perceived.[29] Since neurosis and psychosis respectively entail either minor or major confusion between the internal world of the patient, her 'psychical reality', and the shared reality of the external world, Freud's thinking is useful to consider when validating the experience of the patient. Laplanche and Pontalis define the Freudian notion of psychical reality as follows:

When Freud speaks of psychical reality [...] he means everything in the psyche that takes on the force of reality for the subject. [...] Phantasies, even if they are not based on real events, now come to have the same pathogenic effect for the subject as that which Freud had at first attributed to 'reminiscences': ' ... phantasies possess *psychical* as contrasted with material reality [for] *in the world of the neuroses it is psychical reality which is the decisive kind*'. [...] Generally speaking, neurosis, and *a fortiori* psychosis, are characterized by the predominance of psychical reality in the life of the subject.[30]

We could similarly posit the idea that it is 'psychical reality', or perhaps internal, spiritual reality, that predominates in mystical experience.

The assertion that the 'real world' is one ordered by space and time is crucial when discussing the nature of psychopathology. Eugène

---

[28] Laing (1990: 36). Laing is a very problematic figure in the history of psychiatry because of the political dimension to his work. He emphasizes the necessity of placing mental health problems in a social context, and argues that conventional psychiatric diagnostic procedure is 'adapted to the elimination of the conditions of the possibility of understanding', because the psychiatrist's gaze is depersonalized and depersonalizing. See R. D. Laing, 'Laing's Understanding of Interpersonal Experience', in Gregory (1998: 417). Any reference to Laing's hugely influential work is conspicuously absent from many standard textbooks of psychiatry, such as the *Shorter Oxford Textbook of Psychiatry* (Gelder 2001). His ideas are useful in this analysis for the same reason that they are problematic for the psychiatric profession: his approach undermines the pathologizing gaze of the clinician and attempts to gauge something of the truth of the underlying mental disturbance.

[29] Kristeva (2001: 8): 'Psychoanalysis explores the logical processes underlying "normal" human experiences as well, and it thus learns to describe the conditions under which such processes degenerate into symptoms.'

[30] Laplanche (1988: 363).

Minkowski, influenced by French phenomenology, was a hugely innovative thinker in psychiatry who set out to describe the psychotic experience as lived by the patient, rather than in terms of how its symptoms appeared from the outside.[31] The French philosopher Henri Bergson, in whose thinking intuition is opposed to intelligence and time to space, heavily influences Minkowski's landmark text, *Le Temps vécu*. Bergson's notion of the 'élan vital', the mysterious force that drives life forward, is borrowed by the later thinker who describes delusions as the result of the breakdown of the 'élan vital', or of vital contact with reality. This text is a phenomenology of lived time combined with an analysis of the spatio-temporal structure of mental disorders, which ventures to understand what his translator terms 'the lived experience of the other, both normal and psychopathological'.[32]

According to Minkowski, psychiatry had thus far wrongly considered isolated affective symptoms and judgmental factors as central rather than secondary manifestations of mental illness.[33] In fact, the psychoses are distortions of lived time, and externally perceptible symptoms emanate from a disturbance in the way in which time, space, and causality are experienced. Nancy Metzel's introduction to the English translation of *Le Temps vécu* summarizes this point:

In the normal person the unity and continuity of life are fundamental [. . .] The true nature of the delusion has to be grasped phenomenologically. This idea led Minkowski to speak of 'phenomenological compensation'. The person experiencing such delusions, according to Minkowski, is experiencing a breakdown of the *élan vital* and, further, of the 'personal *élan*'; as a result, he attempts to compensate for this loss. This breakdown can be understood by examining the person's experience of space and time as well as the subcategories of space and time, such as materiality, causality, and spirituality.[34]

Metzel observes: 'The psychopathological personality has lost, or has never achieved, the normal equilibrium which is constituted between interior and exterior forces.'[35] What psychoanalysis contributes to this

---

[31] See also Ellenberger (1958: 16): 'the phenomenologist uses a categorial frame of reference; [he] attempts to reconstruct the inner world of his patients through an analysis of their manner of experiencing time, space, causality, materiality and other categories.'

[32] Translator Nancy Metzel in introduction to Minkowski (1970: xvii). Originally published in French as *Le Temps vécu: études phénoménologiques et psychopathologiques* (1934).

[33] Ibid. xviii.

[34] Ibid. xx–xxi.

[35] Ibid. xxii.

discussion is the conceptualization of a whole different order of truth that does not correspond with, and indeed departs from, historical reality. However, although psychoanalysis admits of the existence of psychical reality, mysticism is treated by Freud as a powerful illusion: 'Freud famously characterized religion as an illusion, and the mystical or oceanic feeling of "oneness with the universe" as a regressive return to the primary narcissism of the "infant at the breast" unable to distinguish between himself and the world around him.'[36] In his dismissal of the authenticity of religious experience, Freud arguably neglects 'its value in giving us means to express our inner world'.[37]

This value is embraced more fully by Jungian analysis, which views the inner or spiritual world and the mental realm of the unconscious as interchangeable ideas.[38] The Jungian point of view does not repudiate the generally accepted fact that Lamotte is mentally ill: 'One sign of mental illness is [the] inability to make distinctions between the two worlds. In certain forms of psychosis the person is so absorbed in what is going on inside that it becomes impossible to deal with outer reality.'[39] Indeed Janet describes Lamotte's saner moments as being the times when she is able to differentiate between the inner and outer worlds and to perceive time normally: 'En effet dans l'état d'équilibre elle est capable de distinguer l'externe, l'interne, l'avenir, le passé, le présent, l'imaginaire, le réel, la pensée, etc.' (451). What seems to be happening in the psychotic experience is that the individual concerned can only react to internal and external phenomena in an undifferentiated way, without being able to recognize that which is inner and that which belongs to the external world.

Janet's own training was initially as a philosopher, and he completed a 'thèse de médecine' on the subject of 'L'État mental des hystériques' in order to practise as a clinician.[40] Janet proposed the rather vague notion of 'psychasthenia' to describe a nervous exhaustion characterized by 'perte de la fonction du réel' and 'troubles de l'émotivité', in contrast to hysteria.[41] Lamotte's physical difficulties were not 'hysterical' as such, but caused by the injuries she inflicted on her own body as a result of acting on her delusional beliefs: her state of mind can more accurately

[36] Sayers (2002: 105). Sayers is here referring to Freud's statements made in 'Civilization and Its Discontents' (1930: 66, 72).

[37] Sayers (2002: 110).

[38] Kelsey (1976: 140).

[39] Ibid. 143.

[40] Janet (1894).

[41] Roudinesco (1986: 249).

be described as psychotic than hysteric. Like Freud, Janet cannot be viewed, as can some other psychiatrists, as a great 'silencer' of patients. His approach was based on three fundamental rules: the examination of the patient in a one-to-one situation, with no others present; the rigorous recording of the patient's words; and the exploration of antecedent causes in her life and medical history. Janet rejected psychoanalysis, however, and his analyses were not based on listening to the unconscious communications of the patient, nor on the examination of transference and counter-transference, which leaves an important level of interaction missing from clinical encounter he presents.[42] This level of insight is lacking in what is at times a sympathetic appraisal of the voice of the patient. We cannot argue in this case that medical treatment did not help Lamotte, for Janet's intervention did facilitate her re-integration into family life and created a healing environment. Importantly, also, unlike the other women studied here, being free to come and go as she pleased, Lamotte did not have to struggle to gain freedom. It would seem that Lamotte is the exception that proves the rule: because she was given favoured access to a sensitive clinician the treatment she received was, to some extent, therapeutic. However, most patients did not enjoy this singular privilege.

But the achievement of mental stability was at the expense of Lamotte's most heightened human experiences, which occur during her retreat into the internal world and in her rejection of 'normality' and 'reality'. Lamotte's apparent motivations differ from those of Rouy and Esquiron, in that she does not seem to have sought emancipation or escape from the asylum. However, her textual voice can be paralleled with theirs because, in a similar way, she enters into dialogue with the clinician and challenges and resists his diagnostic procedure: she testifies to a realm of human experience that he is unable to fully validate.

The theories privileged in this analysis have in common the acknowledgement of the fact that the self is complex, and comprised of at least two possible realms of experience, whether these are called the internal world and the external, the unconscious and the conscious, or the temporal and the spiritual. They also all demonstrate that the psychotic experience is to some extent the confusion of the individual's internal world with external or shared reality, but vitally attempt to understand how this is lived by the subject, and hence recognize the validity of such

---

[42] Janet's approach is summarized ibid. 247.

altered states of subjectivity in the wide range of possible human experience. These approaches have made the lived experience of the patient the focus of much useful analysis, and in the sense that they attempt to see what is true in the content of so-called 'delusions' instead of emphasizing their untruth in terms of the shared reality of the outside world, a connection can be posited between such viewpoints and those that validate the mystical experience.

'LE DÉLIRE D'UNION AVEC DIEU'

Since Lamotte was viewed as inauthentic by the Church, and mentally disturbed by secular society, she was as a subject doubly alienated and isolated by spiritual and medical authorities. She says of the Bible: 'Je sens que la vérité est là [. . .] Je sens à [la] lire une lumière intérieure qui m'éclaire sur bien des choses', insisting that what she feels can be equated with what is true (13). In her text, and in the accompanying commentary by Janet, the concept of truth is fraught with complexity. The figure of 'Madeleine', as first-person narrator and protagonist, demonstrates a shifting, unstable, and unreliable understanding of truth that alters according to her emotional state.[43] In the dialogue portrayed between clinician and patient in this text, the notions of 'truth' and 'sanity', 'falsity' and 'madness' cannot be viewed as simplistically concurrent terms. Instead, there is evidence of narrative authenticity in 'delusional' accounts that exhibit a sense of existential truth about experiences related by a speaking subject.[44]

---

[43] In this section I refer to the protagonist as she appears as the narrator of her text, exclusively as 'Madeleine'.

[44] Ideas and beliefs considered to be 'sane' or, by contrast, 'mad' correlate directly with the philosophical notions of 'truth' and 'falsity' taken for granted as axiomatic by the majority of sane, speaking subjects. That which common consensus deems to be sane can be married with what is termed the 'correspondence theory' of truth: for a proposition to be true it must correspond with externally verifiable facts. Janet is concerned to demonstrate that his patient's ideas do not correspond with material facts, and it is evidence of this 'material reality' that he presents to Madeleine when he tries and fails to persuade her that her beliefs are erroneous. The correspondence theory, however, runs aground when the notion of 'fact' is itself problematized: if we can argue that the whole concept of truth is a problematic one, surely the same can be said of the 'facts' of this case. As Blackburn and Simmons (1999: 8) assert:

Facts have logical complexity: not surprisingly, they have exactly as much complexity as the propositions we choose to assert. And the real world—the world of dated, particular, events and things in specific spatial and temporal orderings—just does not seem able to

Though inherently paradoxical because the text offers historically false claims, its assertions are made in complete 'bonne foi', being true at least in the internal world of the individual who makes them.[45] This chapter examines the shifting mental states described by 'Madeleine' in three sections: first, an examination of her 'état de consolation' will read the 'délire d'union avec Dieu' (170) as a manifestation of narrative energy being inwardly directed, constructing a textual refusal of reality and retreat into blissful isolation; second, the 'état de torture' or 'délire de séparation avec Dieu' (170) will be considered as a painful form of refusal, in which energy is outwardly directed: these states are viewed as two sides of the same coin, and are held to be subversive of the discourse of her observer because they are characterized by the rejection of his truth; and finally, the intermediary states are examined as manifesting both an angry, subversive voice in dialogue and a passive voice of resignation. The common ground that the textual voice of 'Madeleine' shares with that of Hersilie Rouy and Marie Esquiron is in her rejection of clinical 'truth', and in the vitality of her resistance on a linguistic level.

The experiences of 'Madeleine' represent a creative retreat from a world in which she could find no place, and a metaphorical compensation for the poverty of her real human relationships; the regrettable fact seems to be that when she conforms to the norms of the world her creative freedom is stifled. Her introspective retreat into her internal world represents an emancipatory strategy that proves limited in its outcomes. Even though her personal campaign of resistance against psychiatric 'normality' did little to really subvert the course that the emergent science would take, the madwoman did nevertheless speak, and her testimony, together with that of Janet, gives us a view of 'reality' richer than that to which we would otherwise have access, had the patient remained silent.

Madeleine's state of 'consolation' is subdivided into the substates of 'recueillement' (recollection), a preliminary phase before entering the state of ecstasy proper; 'extase', characterized by complete immobility; and 'ravissement' (rapture), a state that resembles deep sleep during which even internal activity seems to cease (45). A feeling of inner joy

---

contain anything of this kind of complexity; negative, or disjunctive, or counterfactual situations, for example.

[45] Since existential philosophy rejects the validity of the psychoanalytical notion of the internal world, commentators such as Simone de Beauvoir (1976: 582–593) would actually argue the opposite, that mystical experiences are in fact a strategy of 'mauvaise foi' that leads to limitation of experience rather than true freedom.

and ecstasy is common to all these states, and the boundary between them is fluid since they are all aspects of the same phenomenon: oneness with God. As the basis of mystical belief is that reality is oneness and the dissolution of illusory boundaries between self and world or self and God, Madeleine's sense of reality reaches its paroxysm during her 'consolations'. This state is reached only periodically, and in phenomenological terms closely resembles the classical 'mystical' experience of union with the Absolute.

The state of 'recueillement' is imperceptible to the outside observer, but is characterized by a sense of the splitting of body and mind, which Laing describes as a symptom of the 'ontological insecurity' that precedes psychotic breakdown. The subject 'may feel more insubstantial than substantial, and unable to assume that the stuff he is made of is genuine, good, valuable. And he may feel his self as partially divorced from his body.'[46] It is a controlled and hidden state, in which the spirit is affected with the impression of the body being left behind. While the body still functions, unlike during the immobile phase of 'extase', Madeleine senses that it is operating independently of the mind.

This state of recollection is common to all mystical experiences. Underhill describes it as 'a condition which is peculiarly characteristic of the mystical consciousness, and is the necessary prelude to pure contemplation, that state in which the mystic enters into communion with Reality'.[47] Madeleine compares 'recueillement' to the discreet sense of joy she imagines Mary and Joseph experienced when contemplating the Christ-child:

L'extase peut devenir moins visible aux regards humains et elle est pourtant profonde avec beaucoup de belles pensées et une joie intense. [...] Bien que leurs cœurs fussent intimement et très parfaitement unis dans un commun amour, leurs corps cependant agissent, travaillent. (46)

The outward appearance of normal activity is accompanied by the inner sensation that the mind is separating from the body, which becomes depersonalized and automated. Laing identifies the key notions of depersonalization and engulfment in his description of this process, evoking 'petrification' and 'depersonalization' as 'the act[s] whereby one negates the other person's autonomy, ignores his feelings, regards him as a thing, kills the life in him. [...] One treats him not as a person,

---

[46] Laing (1990: 42).
[47] Underhill (1911: 48).

as a free agent, but as an it.'[48] Engulfment, on the other hand, describes the occurrence where 'the individual dreads relatedness as such, with anyone or anything or, indeed, even with himself, because his uncertainty about the stability of his autonomy lays him open to the dread lest in any relationship he will lose his autonomy and identity.'[49] Madeleine reduces her role during this state to that of an 'it', a machine: 'Mon esprit n'est pas aux mouvements que je fais, c'est mon corps seul qui agit comme une machine'. The adjective 'paralysée' is used to evoke this sense of loss of control over bodily movement, and Madeleine uses the equally concrete term 'absorbée' in a metaphorical sense to describe the effect of God's all-consuming presence upon her. The image of engulfment prior to the inertia of 'extase' is accompanied by Madeleine's insistence that she experiences herself as fundamentally split, and alienated from herself: 'je ne m'appartiens pas davantage, mes sens sont aliénés'; 'C'est un être qui marche en moi' (66). 'Recueillement' is a dynamic state, during which the subject moves from a sense of cohesion to an awareness of the mind being radically split from the body.[50]

During 'recueillement' Madeleine depicts the feeling of automatism as being caused by a transcendental force that guides her, as if she were a puppet:

Ma vie extraordinaire a été dirigée par une **volonté supérieure** contre laquelle je ne pouvais pas essayer de lutter. J'ai obéi sans comprendre aux voix que j'entendais et j'ai accepté tout ce qui résultait de mon obéissance. L'assurance donnée par la voix que j'étais le bouc émissaire me faisait donner franchement mon nouveau nom, je ne regardais pas cela comme un mensonge, car un mensonge, c'est ce que l'on dit soi-même et ce n'était pas moi qui le disais. (94)

This voice speaks instructions to her, and demands obedience, resulting in the complete evacuation of a sense of personal choice and agency in

---

[48] Laing (1990: 46).

[49] Ibid. 44.

[50] The postures taken up by Madeleine during 'consolation' are consonant with the phenomenon of the 'waxy flexibility' characteristic of catatonic schizophrenia: 'The patient allows himself to be placed in an awkward posture, which he then maintains apparently without distress for much longer than most people could achieve without severe discomfort. This phenomenon is also called *catalepsy* [...] At times these postures have obvious symbolic significance (for example crucifixion).' Janet's description of Madeleine's movements and behaviour conforms to the textbook picture: 'A patient in stupor is immobile, mute, and unresponsive, although fully conscious. Stupor may change (sometimes quickly) to a state of uncontrolled motor activity and excitement' (Gelder 2001: 333).

relation to the outside world. Here we can note considerable slippage
between the experience of hearing the voice of God, as many claim to
do, and the auditory hallucinations of the psychotic.

The states of 'extase' and 'ravissement' are difficult to distinguish,
because Madeleine appears to slip from one to the other with relative
ease and frequency. 'Ravissement' entails the complete detachment of
soul and body in a deep, sleep-like state. Like a regression to the pre-
Oedipal, the period of Freud's 'primary narcissism', the feeling of
oneness between infant and mother prevails: 'Je suis comme un enfant
dans les bras de sa mère' (47). Madeleine switches between wakefulness
and sleep, for she is like the child 'qui de temps en temps ouvre les yeux
et goûte le bonheur d'être dorloté, puis se rendort' (47). An impression
of the total loss of self is established through liquid images such as
drunkenness and the flowing grace of God: 'Elle retombe dans l'assou-
pissement de l'**ivresse**, elle se perd dans les **flots** de la grâce' (48). The
use of the third-person pronoun 'elle' refers to the aforementioned child
(47), and significantly marks a gradual effacing of the coherent sense of
self that exists in Madeleine's intermediary or balanced states. Accompanied by the image of an enveloping liquid, this reinforces the elimination of ego boundaries that seems to occur in 'extase': 'Je sors de ces
états n'ayant qu'un souvenir vague, c'est celui qui j'étais avec Dieu' (48).
The powerful image of drunkenness and oblivion seems to represent a
pleasurable means of forgetting a world that could not accept her, and of
mitigating the difficulty Madeleine experiences in forging meaningful
human relationships.

The phrase 'j'étais avec Dieu' is a literary echo in human terms of the
description of the relation of Christ to the godhead described at the
beginning of St John's gospel. The mystical notions of being with God
and being God are paralleled, or juxtaposed, in this gospel, generally
considered by theological commentators to be the most 'mystical' of all
New Testament texts. As William Inge asserted at the close of the
nineteenth century: 'The Gospel of St John [...] is the charter of
Christian Mysticism. Indeed, Christian Mysticism, as I understand it,
might almost be called Johannine Christianity.'[51] The French translation
of these opening lines read: 'Au commencement était la Parole | et la
Parole était avec Dieu | et la Parole était Dieu. | Elle était au commence-
ment avec Dieu.'[52] Here, Madeleine's statement that she was 'with' God,

---

[51] Inge (1899: 44).
[52] Évangile selon Saint Jean 1. 1–2. SB: 85.

'j'étais avec Dieu', clearly postulates a mystical union of the form outlined in these verses, during which the boundary between self and other is held to be illusory and is ultimately dismantled.

'Ravissement', or rapture, is an extreme catatonic state characterized by complete inertia and the total inability to tend to the needs of everyday life: 'je ne sais pas comment je vis'. Madeleine says that 'ravissement' is a state against which she struggles: 'Je lutte de toutes mes forces contre les états de sommeil dans la journée.' It is, however, a state that she can at times control and conceal by effectively maintaining and extending 'recueillement': 'J'arrive ainsi à dominer ce sommeil et à cacher mes impressions', even though the delicious feeling of 'consolation' is just as intense: 'Les délices intérieures n'en sont pas moins de plus en plus grandes.' Madeleine allows herself to be taken over by the effects of 'ravissement' only when she feels secure enough to allow the process of engulfment to take place: 'Si je me sens à l'abri je cesse de me mouvoir et je tombe tout de suite dans un ravissement dont rien ne peut plus me tirer' (48). To give herself over to this immobility is to divest herself of the power to return to the relatively neutral state of 'recueillement'.

Where 'recueillement' can be either concealed or controlled, Janet demonstrates that: '*L'extase*, au contraire, ne peut pas se dissimuler et Madeleine essayait [...] de ne pas s'y abandonner ou de n'y céder que la nuit, ou dans l'isolement' (46). The state of ecstasy to which Madeleine succumbs is the ultimate stage of 'union avec Dieu'. Janet describes what occurs during 'extase' as being 'un long drame aux actes divers' revolving around the couple of Madeleine and God, calling this relationship 'la vie d'un ménage'. This state of union is described by Madeleine as her reified soul being the receptacle of God: 'Il habite en mon âme devenue son palais et son autel.' The latent image of penetration is accompanied by further evidence of Madeleine's sense of self becoming increasingly incoherent, where the splitting off of parts of the body, such as the heart, is followed by the personification of those same parts: 'Dieu parle sans cesse à mon cœur et mon cœur lui répond.' The image of dialogue with God is reinforced by statements declaring the eternal nature of this union, which have echoes in biblical and liturgical notions of the eternal and unshakeable relationship between the Christian God and his subjects: 'rien ne peut plus nous séparer'. The anaphoric appearance of the phrase 'qui donc pourrait...?' in the same passage echoes St Paul's repetition of a similar interrogative structure in his epistle to the Romans: 'Si Dieu est pour nous, qui sera contre nous? [...] Qui accusera les élus de Dieu? [...] Qui les condamnera? [...]

Qui nous séparera de l'amour du Christ?'[53] Madeleine appears to emulate this assertion, asking: 'Qui donc pourrait m'empêcher de lui être unie? Qui donc pourrait m'empêcher de jouir de sa présence et de son amour?' (69). This question brings to the fore her reading of the Bible, or at least a knowledge of its better known texts.

God overwhelms Madeleine entirely, and she calls him 'mon centre', 'ma fin', and 'mon tout', every part of her being consumed. A series of physical and physiological metaphors act as counterpoint to these more abstract notions of God and his relationship with Madeleine. Combining the concrete image of breathing and the abstract notion of the 'soul' this union is 'la respiration de mon âme'; 'le battement de mon cœur'; 'ma nourriture'; and finally, 'ma vie' (69). Like a lover, Madeleine is unable to stop thinking about God, and her voice appears to exist on a continuum between herself and God on which occurs the dissolution of identity and fragmentation of the self.

The joining of the two selves, Madeleine and God, is represented in explicitly sexual and uterine metaphors that describe two processes: containment within or envelopment by the other, and penetration by the other: 'Le souffle divin m'enveloppe et me pénètre tout entière' (108). Janet relates Madeleine's account of containment, within the setting of the Bethlehem stable, as follows:

Dieu m'a mise [...] dans un singulier endroit, dans une sorte d'armoire comme on enferme un objet précieux, une statue; mon état tout passif me permet de rester dans la position où il m'a mise, je me sens bien au chaud et je ne souffre pas du manque d'air. Mon esprit est bien vivant dans ce tabernacle et je songe au sacrifice à accomplir. (75)

Janet, ordinarily a sceptic when it comes to Freudian ideas, advocates a psychoanalytical reading of her description of containment. In 'The Interpretation of Dreams', Freud discusses cases of individuals who dream of being enclosed in soft, warm cases, chests, cupboards, and ovens, and claims that this represents a reversion to an intrauterine space.[54] Here, Janet argues, Madeleine is the infant Jesus, 'en train de se mettre dans le sein de Marie' (75). Madeleine's fluid sense of identity also permeates her text when the 'je' of the story shifts from being the Christ child to the mother of God, and finally to being his lover: 'Madeleine [...] nous montre brutalement qu'elle est non seulement la fille de Dieu, la mère

---

[53] Épître de Paul aux Romains 8. 31–5. SB: 148.
[54] These objects are referred to in Freud (1900–1: 154, 354, 684).

de Dieu, mais qu'elle est encore la maîtresse ou, si l'on veut, l'épouse de Dieu et qu'elle sait l'être complètement' (76). During these contemplative moments Madeleine exhibits a serious disturbance in her perception of time:

> Madeleine ne comprenait guère la distinction usuelle des temps et réunissait le passé et le présent sans craindre la contradiction. [...] Ainsi elle est donc encore Madeleine âgée de 40 ans en 1898 et elle est en même temps Jésus qui vient de naître il y a vingt siècles et en plus Marie enceinte. (452–3)

Madeleine is able to project herself backwards and forwards in time, and to a different spatial realm, without experiencing this as contradictory. This disrupted experience of time recalls Minkowski's description of the psychotic experience as a disturbance of the 'élan vital' that normally regulates the subject's ability to conceive of a past, present, and future for herself in a harmonious relation with external reality.

Madeleine's sexual union with God is expressed primarily in terms of intoxication, and through the image of the 'baiser perpétuel' (76). Describing the oral thrill of heart-to-heart interaction with the beloved, Madeleine writes: 'Mes lèvres se collent l'une contre l'autre [...] Ma bouche se remplit de délices [...] Mon être est enivré par les baisers divins' (76–7). Incorporated into this sexually charged image is the idea of 'folie', itself a term invested with positive affect: 'Je viens de passer une nuit d'amour et de **folie** [...] Dieu me rend **folle** d'amour' (77). It is marked by an attitude of indifference to the implications of being called 'folle' by the rest of the world, whose standards of health and sickness she rejects: 'c'est bien vrai que je suis **folle**, que j'ai la **folie** de l'amour et je ne veux pas en guérir' (80). The orgasmic delight of 'extase' is equated with the idea of madness as delicious abandon: 'c'est une **folie** bien douce et ceux qui cherchent des jouissances en ce monde devraient faire leur possible pour en être atteints car il n'y a aucun plaisir, aucune joie qui puisse lui être comparée!' (104). This oxymoronic, almost Petrarchan comparison of the idea of madness with love and 'douceur' is reflected in the writings of Sainte Thérèse de l'Enfant-Jésus, and in those of Teresa of Avila, who speaks of 'sweetness caused me by this intense pain'.[55] Sainte Thérèse calls herself a happy victim, and juxtaposes love with the idea of violence:

---

[55] Peers (2002: 193).

O mon Jésus! que ce soit *moi* cette **heureuse victime**, consumez votre holocauste par le feu de votre Divin Amour!

Je commençais mon Chemin de Croix, et voilà que tout-à-coup, j'ai été prise d'un si **violent amour** pour le bon Dieu que je ne puis expliquer cela qu'en disant que c'était comme si on m'avait plongée tout entière dans le feu. Oh! **quel feu et quelle douceur** en même temps.[56]

Similarly, Madeleine seeks to legitimize her experience of the ecstasy of madness by invoking the folly of the cross: 'Oui je suis **folle**, l'amour me brûle jusqu'à la moelle des os, mais Dieu n'est-il pas lui-même le premier et le plus grand **fou**? Les trois personnes de la sainte Trinité, mystère de notre foi, n'ont-elles pas au suprême degré cette **folie** de l'amour?' (109). Laing describes the feeling of annihilation and engulfment experienced during psychotic breakdown as the sensation of being burned: 'Some psychotics say in the acute phase that they are on fire, that their bodies are being burned up. A patient describes himself as cold and dry. Yet he dreads warmth or wet. He will be engulfed by the fire or the water, and either way be destroyed.'[57] Similarly, here Madeleine claims to feel burnt to the very core of her being by God's love.

Madeleine's union with God is unequivocally sexual, during which she exhibits the physical sensations of orgasm:

J'ai des douceurs énormes sur les lèvres et au ventre qui se resserre des secousses vraiment divines... J'ai des frémissements de tout le corps quand Dieu applique partout ses mains brûlantes qu'il promène doucement, c'est indéfinissable, il me semble que je m'évanouis dans la jouissance que je ressens. Je me sens de plus en plus soulevée en l'air, on dirait que tout mon corps porte sur une grosse corde passée entre les jambes et que cette corde comprime les parties qu'elle fait rentrer à l'intérieur. [...] J'éprouve trop souvent à l'intérieur comme à l'extérieur des frémissements suaves qui sont si particuliers que je ne peux les expliquer. J'aimerais mieux ne plus rien dire de ces sensations qui sont trop étranges pour que vous puissiez comprendre, il y a là un grand mystère. (109–10)

Many of the nouns used here are almost interchangeable within the general paradigm of physical pleasure: 'douceurs'; 'secousses'; 'frémissements'; 'jouissance'. These together create a heady image of intense bodily gratification, and are accompanied by the—literally—uplifting description of Madeleine who feels so ecstatic as to be 'soulevée'. This is probably Madeleine's most explicitly sexual piece of writing, and the image of the

---

[56] Quoted in Maître (1986: 26).
[57] Laing (1990: 45).

'grosse corde passée entre les jambes' that penetrates her and elicits sensations rendered by the adjectives 'suaves'; 'particuliers'; 'indéfinissable'; 'étranges', is barely euphemistic, although her claimed inability to describe her experience gives the impression that she is genuinely unaware of the sexually explicit nature of her descriptions.[58] Beauvoir, in her discussion of mysticism in *Le deuxième sexe*, usefully parallels the strategy of the female lover with that of the mystic:

On prétend parfois avec piété que la pauvreté du langage oblige la mystique à emprunter ce vocabulaire érotique; mais elle ne dispose aussi que d'un seul corps, elle a pour s'offrir à Dieu les mêmes conduites que lorsqu'elle s'offre à un homme. Cela ne diminue d'ailleurs en rien la valeur de ses sentiments.[59]

So as the female mystic has the same body as the lover, she experiences the same range of corporeal pleasures. Madeleine here enters a realm of physical enrichment that would be impossible for her to experience outside of her 'mystical' experiences.

The image of penetration can, of course, be compared to Teresa of Avila's most famous vision, illustrated in *The Life of the Holy Mother Teresa of Jesus*, in which she describes a beautiful angel:

In his hands I saw a long golden spear and at the end of the iron tip I seemed to see a point of fire. With this he seemed to pierce my heart several times so that it penetrated my entrails. When he drew it out, I thought he was drawing them out with it and he left me completely afire with a great love for God. The pain was so sharp that it made me utter several moans; and so excessive was the sweetness caused me by this intense pain that one can never wish to lose it, nor will one's soul be content with anything less than God.[60]

The parallel that can be drawn between the image of penetration related by St Teresa and Madeleine's orgasmic rapture is only too clear. A bizarre side effect of these heady unions is that Madeleine feels 'sealed' by God: 'Dieu en mettant des baisers partout a mis un sceau et je ne

---

[58] Madeleine's repeated insistence that the sensations she experiences are 'indéfinissables' and 'ineffables' call to mind William James's celebrated 'four marks' of the mystic state: ineffability, noetic quality, transience, and passivity (Underhill 1911: 81).

[59] Beauvoir (1949: 587).

[60] Peers (2002: 192–3). *The Life* was principally written during 1565. Lacan's comments (1975b: 70–1) on Bernini's famous depiction of St Teresa's vision further parallels Madeleine's orgasmic vision with the experiences of other mystics, viewed as authentic by the Church. Lacan writes: '[C]'est comme pour Sainte Thérèse—vous n'avez qu'à aller regarder à Rome la statue du Bernin pour comprendre tout de suite qu'elle jouit, ça ne fait pas de doute. Et de quoi jouit-elle? Il est clair que le témoignage essentiel des mystiques, c'est justement de dire qu'ils l'éprouvent, mais qu'ils en savent rien.'

pourrai plus jamais uriner' (77). In addition, the remnants of her habitual chastity, although relinquished during these encounters, nevertheless remain in her mind as an ideal to be aimed at: 'Non, ce ne sont pas des caresses, ni des délices que je recherche dans la prière, le bon Dieu le sait bien, s'il me les donne ce n'est pas sans résistance de ma part' (78). This process of rationalization represents a return for Madeleine to the state of 'recueillement' where, although irrevocably marked by God, she is all the same re-establishing a separate, semi-unified self.

This image of oneness with God has a detrimental effect on dialogue with Janet, which occurs rarely during 'extase' and not at all during 'ravissement'. During 'extase' Madeleine sometimes murmurs statements for her doctor's ears only, but communication only actually occurs during the preparatory and cooling-off stages of 'recueillement'. Madeleine's attitude when she engages in dialogue with Janet is characterized by indifference and a refusal of the external world. She rises above rational reality, and as a result narrative energy is in her text concentrated on the internal world. Conversation between clinician and patient during 'consolation' is superficial and relatively poor, and can be read in contrast to the intense sense of communication, and thus union, with God. According to Beauvoir, what motivates this process in female mystics is narcissism. The mystic uses retreat into ecstasy as a strategy to bolster and indeed inflate her sense of self: 'La femme cherche d'abord dans l'amour divin ce que l'amoureuse demande à celui de l'homme: l'apothéose de son narcissisme; c'est pour elle une miraculeuse aubaine que ce souveraine regard attentivement, amoureusement fixé sur elle.'[61] With Madeleine, this strategy, as with Rouy's delusions of grandeur, represents an attempt to ensure the survival and perpetuation of the self for all eternity. This offers a temporary remedy to the limitations offered by the sane world: 'On comprend l'ivresse qui envahit le cœur de la narcissiste quand le ciel tout entier devient son miroir; son image divinisée est infinie comme Dieu même, elle ne s'éteindra jamais.'[62] However, the joy experienced in these states is fleeting and illusory, because it is sought at the expense of vital relatedness to other human beings.

During the state of 'recueillement', Madeleine expresses a lack of concern with external events, including her communications with Janet. She does not actively engage in dialogue, but instead produces a spontaneous and unstructured 'focalisation interne' that is heard and

---

[61] Beauvoir (1976: 587).
[62] Ibid. 588.

analysed by Janet.[63] Entering the state of 'consolation' in fact involves a gradual reduction of contact with the outside world, characterized by total indifference: 'Je ne m'intéresse en réalité à rien de ce que je fais, tout continue à m'être indifférent' (67). During 'recueillement' and 'extase', Madeleine is still able to describe what she feels internally, the essential difference being that the first can be concealed whilst the second, as Janet affirms, 'ne peut pas se dissimuler' (46).

Despite the relative poverty of dialogue in this state, the clinical relationship is nevertheless represented as a close and intimate one. Although the immobility of 'extase' is taken to cataleptic extremes during 'ravissement', her sense of being cut off from the outside world is never in fact complete: the retention of this link is always mediated through the figure of Janet. He observes that even when Madeleine no longer reacts to external stimuli, there is one important exception: 'quand il s'agit de mes propres commandements', supporting the suggestion that Janet functions as a pseudo spiritual director figure in Madeleine's story (47).

This privileged position is reflected, also, in Madeleine's response to Janet's request to use her writing as clinical case material. Despite a profound anxiety of exposure she gives her permission: 'Je dois me résigner au sacrifice de mon désir le plus cher, celui de rester cachée, dans l'intérêt de la religion et de l'étude' (5). This desire to remain hidden conflicts with the showy nature of her 'extases', over which she effectively has no control. She emphatically feels the need to 'cacher [ses] impressions' and to dissimulate as much as possible in order simply to function (48).[64] She writes:

Alors je ne sais pas comment je vis... Il me faut un grand secours de la grâce pour continuer d'agir un peu quand même... Je lutte de toutes mes forces contre les états de sommeil dans la journée. [...] J'évite d'être tranquille quand je ne suis pas dans ma chambre et qu'il peut y avoir des témoins. J'arrive ainsi à

---

[63] Genette (1972: 206–7). The form of 'focalisation interne' exhibited here is what Genette terms 'fixe', in other words characterized by 'limitation du champ'. Later we shall see that in different states Madeleine's narrative shifts to become a 'focalisation zéro', adopting a detached viewpoint and narrating her story in the third person, referring to 'Madeleine' rather than the pronoun 'je'.

[64] This reaction is widely observed elsewhere in the tradition of spiritual autobiography. Writing about Madame Guyon in the seventeenth century, Hart (2004: 22) writes: 'Frequently the female spiritual autobiographer protests in her text that she lacks the authority to write about herself or her faith.'

dominer ce sommeil et à cacher mes impressions, mais les délices intérieures n'en sont pas moins de plus en plus grandes. (48)

Madeleine expends a huge amount of effort simply to function in daily life, and is able to 'dissimulate' only to a limited extent, for she is unable to resist the force of 'ravissement' when no external constraint requires it to be suppressed: 'Si je me sens un peu à l'abri je cesse de me mouvoir et je tombe tout de suite dans un ravissement dont rien ne peut plus me tirer' (48). On several different levels, Janet's privileged access to the workings of Madeleine's inner world is parallel to the admittance accorded to God. The sense that he must mediate between Madeleine and the world reveals a profound 'anxiety of authorship': the unconscious fear that women have of writing and therefore becoming precursors.[65] Madeleine's stance is intensely ambivalent, for she does express a wish for her writing to be published, for her voice to be heard, but this desire is couched in an attitude of feigned humility, expressed through the rationalizing formula that she agrees to this only for the greater good, claiming: 'je n'aime pas que l'on parle de moi' (5).

During the state of 'consolation' verbal dialogue is rather poor, despite the relative lack of conflict in the clinical relationship. Reality is refused by declining to engage in dialogue, and by turning energy inwards away from the world of objects. Madeleine succeeds in exploring a creative realm of experience that would, as a metaphorical reversal of the limitations of the 'real' world, appear to compensate for her absolute lack of agency and role in that realm with its religious, moral, police, and medical constraints. She does to some extent find creative freedom and she certainly experiences intense joy, but as Beauvoir affirms, as a truly emancipatory strategy this fails to offer her a feminine role that will be taken seriously by her entourage, in the widest sense:

[E]n soi ces efforts de salut individuel ne sauraient aboutir qu'à des echecs; ou la femme se met en rapport avec un irréel: son double, ou Dieu; ou elle crée un irréel rapport avec un être réel; elle n'a en tout cas pas de prise sur le monde; elle ne s'evade pas de sa subjectivité; sa liberté demeure mystifiée.[66]

The ecstasy of union with God contrasts sharply with the modes of thought present in the state of 'torture', during which the 'délire

[65] Gilbert (1979: 49).
[66] Beauvoir (1976: 593).

d'union' translates into a 'délire de rupture'. This rupture is evinced dramatically in a dialogical exchange marked by conflict and strife, and it is to the examination of this state that we shall now turn.

'LE DÉLIRE DE SÉPARATION AVEC DIEU'

Janet translates Madeleine's 'état de torture' into clinical terms as a 'délire de séparation avec Dieu' (170). 'Torture' is Madeleine's 'dark night of the soul', and is a state as extreme as her most ecstatic moments of 'consolation'. Indeed, many common points can be identified between these apparently disparate states. The most immediately obvious transformation that takes place is the shift in tone from the description of closeness with God, an experience presented in terms of abundance and joy, to the description of punishment by God, described in terms of deficit and pain. Madeleine's visions are now replete with images of '*choses terribles*' (168).

Toute la nuit j'ai vu des *choses terribles. Dieu nous châtiait.* Des monstres déchaînés jetaient l'effroi partout. Je voyais les hommes se réunir pour essayer de les combattre, mais ils luttaient en vain. Ils étaient enlevés, piétinés: c'était *horrible.* [...] Enfin des maisons s'écroulaient et j'étais témoin de grands malheurs.

The image created is achieved in part through the use of negative adjectives: Madeleine's vision is 'horrible' (168); this might reflect of the era of great political instability through which this woman had lived, most notably the Paris Commune of 1871 and its aftermath. France is described as 'coupable' (169; 424), 'divisée' and 'décrépite', and her punishment will be 'douloureux' (424). A sense of terror and paranoia inflects Madeleine's discourse at these points in the text, and the punishment to be meted out will be applied to her as an individual as much as to unbelieving France: 'J'aurai à subir les persécutions les plus pénibles pour un cœur chrétien [...] Je serai frappé d'excommunication majeure' (169).

During 'torture', instead of communicating with God or Janet, Madeleine represents herself as being besieged by Satan: 'J'ai passé une nuit d'enfer' (169). She apostrophizes Satan as Christ does in the gospel account: 'Arrière, Satan!', and in the following lines counteracts his perceived presence with the image of the cross and the love of God as evoked during periods of ecstasy: 'Place à la Croix! Place à l'amour! Arrière!' (424). As 'torture' and 'consolation' are opposite but common states, the role of God in the latter is played by his traditional enemy, the devil, in the former.[67]

In the third part of Janet's text, entitled 'Les troubles intellectuels dans le délire religieux', he devotes a chapter to 'Les troubles de la croyance' in which he draws an interesting parallel between the characteristics of the states of 'consolation' and 'torture': 'C'est la malade elle-même qui nous enseigne à réunir les tortures et les consolations qui forment dans son esprit une unité' (424). As Madeleine's pleasure during 'extase' is intensely physical, so her pain during 'torture' is described in corporal terms. The sensation of burning is once more evoked to describe this pain, and the feeling of being tortured extends to all parts of the body. During 'extase' Madeleine paradoxically writes: 'l'amour me brûle, mais s'il fait mon tourment il est en même temps ma félicité' (491), but during 'torture' any sense of joy is effaced by the suffering inflicted during these hellish periods.

As during 'consolation' the phallic image of the 'grosse corde' penetrating between her legs is transformed during torture into a graphic anal image of abusive penetration:

> Les tortures s'étendent à toutes les parties du corps, ce que je souffre à l'anus, au coccyx, aux parties est inimaginable, on me brûle, on m'enfonce de gros objets rougis au feu et on envoie des rayons électriques sur les plaies... Quel supplice du fouet sur les fesses qui se pétrifient... On me taillade la chair dans tous les sens, des chiens me dévorent et broient mes os... Quel supplice n'invente-t-on pas, je suis suspendue au plafond par le bout des seins, c'est atroce. (169)

Orgasmic pleasure is displaced by unbearable pain, and despicable torture is inflicted on the body's other erogenous areas. The euphemistic and elliptical reference to the penetrating phallus in Madeleine's previous account of her sexual encounter with God, 'une grosse corde passée entre les jambes' (109), in this context is more graphic, although it retains the elliptical statement 'ce que je souffre [...] aux parties' (169). The adjectives used to express the indescribability of these experiences are uncannily similar in the states of 'consolation' and 'torture'. Here, the pain is 'inimaginable', where previously her pleasure had been 'ineffable' (78; 491) and 'indéfinissable' (109). 'Torture' is a more simplistically horrific experience than 'extase': in it the heady mixture of delight and agony has

---

[67] Évangile selon Matthieu 16.23. 'Arrière de moi, Satan! tu m'es scandale; car tes pensées ne sont pas les pensées de Dieu, mais celles des hommes.' SB (Nouveau Testament): 17.

been lost. However, the author retains a stable image of God as an omnipotent, good and just figure even though he is in this context punishing rather than blessing: Madeleine speaks of 'la bonté divine qui aura transformé la France et l'aura ramenée à son amour' and predicts that 'après les châtiments douloureux vient l'heure de la miséricorde, du pardon et de la joie' (424). The ubiquitous notion of God's love and mercy provide a further sense of continuity between the states of 'consolation' and 'torture'.

As clinical dialogue during the state of 'consolation' is supplanted by Madeleine's all-consuming preoccupation with oneness with God, during 'torture' she remains impervious to her doctor's claims and throws scorn upon his attempts at rational explanation. Where previously she was indifferent she is now dismissive, but there is continuity in her belief in God's nature and his centrality to her existence. Both 'consolation' and 'torture' represent states during which her awareness of God and of all things spiritual is heightened. As she oscillates between feelings of 'jouissance' and 'souffrance', God's role remains fairly consistent, and her reliance on Janet as a guiding figure is diminished. In one sense, we can affirm that during these more extreme states, Madeleine leans less on Janet and his supporting system of reason and achieves a level of creative independence that relies on the unreason that she fails to reach in other states. The Jungian view is that the unconscious is 'the source of humanity's creative power and energy', and indeed the workings of Madeleine's inner world are indeed a great source of creative energy.[68]

Janet's discussion with Madeleine centres upon her belief in the Assumption of the Virgin Mary. The sensation that accompanies this is a feeling of being lifted upwards, for Madeleine believes that God wants to subject her to the same experience:

Le soulèvement de ces saints personnages est historique, il a été constaté dans des procès-verbaux religieux. La seule chose qui puisse m'étonner c'est que cela m'arrive à moi-même . . . Mais puisque je sais que cela doit m'arriver, puisque je le constate, je dois me rendre à l'évidence . . . Il me faut tendre les pieds pour toucher la terre, je ne fais plus qu'effleurer le sol, à de certains moments, je ne le touche plus du tout, mes sandales ne sont plus mouillés même quand le sol est détrempé . . . je ne marche plus, je vole . . . Je comprends, je sais que Dieu veut donner en moi un signe sensible de sa volonté en faisant *un peu* pour moi ce qu'il a fait pour Marie, en m'élevant au-dessus des nuages. (98)

---

[68] Kelsey (1976: 141).

Madeleine insists on walking around on tiptoes, which is an elevation in proportion to the humble claim that God wants her to know '*un peu*' the experience of the Virgin Mary. Since Janet discourages her strange habit, the question of Madeleine's elevation is a good example through which to examine the functioning of dialogue during 'torture'.

As we saw in Chapter 2 on Hersilie Rouy, the model of dialogue offered by Diderot's *Le Neveu de Rameau* is one of discursive slippage between the speakers 'lui' and 'moi' beneath the appearance of light-hearted banter. Similarly, the question of the nature of reality being discussed in this text is couched in everyday exchanges and seemingly banal statements. These exchanges follow the same pattern: Madeleine's central delusion is that she is being lifted up by God; Janet attempts to demonstrate that this is not the case by weighing her regularly and systematically, and Madeleine then dismisses his claims as inappropriate in the appreciation of divine phenomena. She writes: 'M. Janet veut des signes absolument indiscutables [...] Quelle singulière idée de mettre des mesures dans les choses divines!' (146). At these points in Madeleine's text dialogue is strained, and a fundamental tension between Janet's rational, empirical reality and Madeleine's frustration at the dismissal of her truth becomes clear. It is at these points that the speaker's resistance to the totalizing discourse of the clinician is most animated, and the strategies employed resemble the compelling rejection of medical diagnosis offered by Rouy and Esquiron.

The importance of the notion of 'folie' and related terms is rendered in a radically different way during 'torture'. Instead of being a term loaded with positive affect, as it is during her 'consolations', Madeleine takes terminology from the discourse of psychiatry and distances herself from it. As Esquiron makes ironic use of such terminology, Madeleine applies epithets such as 'folle' and nouns such as 'manie', clearly terms drawn from the jargon of her guardians, to individuals and objects other than herself. Where Madeleine found 'folie' to be a delicious form of abandon, she now uses the idea to pour scorn on the ideas that threaten her sense of reality. 'Le diable' is responsible for Janet reading her weight as constant, and this result is attributed to the fact that 'la balance est devenue **folle**'. The doctor previously viewed as a spiritual director is now rebuked for his attempts to challenge Madeleine's delusional belief: 'Vous devriez bien renoncer à cette **manie** de me peser, pourquoi faire? Dieu me soulève, il m'emporte, ce n'est pas respectueux de lui opposer une balance' (431). Madeleine's borrowing of such terminology reveals the complexity of the double bind in which she, along with Rouy and

Esquiron, found themselves. Although the psychiatrist is able to label inconvenient beliefs using terms such as 'manie' or 'folie' in their creation of an acceptable reality, when the reverse process is used by the patient to vigorously expose the rigid and limiting belief systems of her incarcerators it is taken as symptomatic of illness.

Madeleine's refusal of scientific proof here resonates with Moreau de Tours's comparison of mystical experience and insanity. He identifies as part of their psychic intransigence 'leur mépris pour la science officielle, pour toute science qui n'émane pas d'eux (c'est-à-dire de Dieu même!), la violence de leur prosélytisme, la férocité de leur intolérance, [...] tous ces mystères de l'intelligence, en un mot, que la psychologie morbide a seule le pouvoir de pénétrer'.[69]

Where Madeleine is apostrophizing Janet, she turns the notion of 'manie' back on her interlocutor. Using the psychiatrist's terminology in order to highlight the inadequacies of his process of reasoning effectively reverses the process of pathologization, and distances the patient's claims from the denigrating notion of mania. This process is extremely important, for it provides evidence of the lack of the possibility to symbolize positively the experience of 'madness' in language. As Lyndall Gordon, speaking about Virginia Woolf's psychosis, puts it: 'Our language has, as yet, no term for madness which is not demeaning.'[70] Laing also bemoans this deficit when he speaks in *The Divided Self* of 'a language of denigration'.[71] The effect of this in the text of the psychiatric memoir is the creation of a certain space in language where the discourse of the incarcerator and the discourse of the patient merge.

During these moments of conflict the doctor is unable to 'reason' with his patient and to impact the progress of her ideas in any way. Although when ensconced in the sleepy depths of 'ravissement' Madeleine will still respond to her doctor–priest's commands, during 'torture' she remains completely unmoved. Janet writes:

Il me paraît clair que d'abord elle ne comprend rien au raisonnement, quoi-qu'elle l'ait compris les jours précédents et surtout que mon argument et mon expérience n'ont aucune influence sur sa croyance qui est fixée définitivement avant la discussion et qui ne change pas du tout par la discussion. (431)

---

[69] Moreau de Tours (1859: 229–30).
[70] Claridge (1990: 27).
[71] Laing (1990: 27), quoting Hendrik van den Berg (1955).

This statement affirms that dialogue has broken down during 'torture', but not in the same way as it breaks down during 'consolation'. Ecstasy causes indifference, silence, inertia, and refusal to engage in dialogue; 'torture', on the other hand, produces a more defiant, angry and frustrated—a more 'true'—form of refusal. Janet's statement that his patient's belief system is 'fixée définitivement' during 'torture' is somewhat paradoxical, because whilst it is true within this state it is not the case throughout the range of feelings Madeleine experiences. Rather, it is Janet's beliefs about the untruth of his subject's claims that are definitively fixed in a rigid system of medical knowledge. We have seen that her understanding of terms such as 'folie', and therefore her sense of reality, are shifting and dependent upon the 'here and now' within which she constructs a context of utterance: what Minkowski terms the 'me-here-now' factor in the life of an individual, the personal 'élan', which when disturbed entails 'the *loss of vital contact with reality*'.[72]

Madeleine's statements when engaging in conversation with her doctor are marked with a sense of urgency. The eternal and mysterious power of God is set in direct opposition to the insignificant proofs of those who deny the existence of the presence so overwhelmingly known by the narrator of this story. She emphatically insists: 'Quelle importance cela a-t-il pour nous que la balance marque tel ou tel chiffre? Qu'est-ce que peut bien signifier une balance des hommes devant le souffle de Dieu?' (431). As the events of a dream are pointedly real to the dreamer when she is dreaming, the events of Madeleine's internal world are 'vrai' even though not 'vraisemblable', because the details of her intrapsychic experience are so immediate and undifferentiated from outer reality.

One point of comparison that can be drawn between the functioning of dialogue in the two states is in the use of 'shifters' (deixis). Deixis is defined primarily in terms of the use of demonstrative determiners and pronouns: 'Selon sa valeur fondamentale, le démonstratif indique que l'être ou l'objet désignés par le nom sont localisés par rapport au locuteur.'[73] 'Shifters' in language place the speaker, or the object referred to by the speaker, firmly in the context of utterance. During 'consolation' and therefore 'extase', the use of the first-person pronoun 'je' predominates, and the text is littered with the personal pronoun 'me' and the possessive determiners mon/ma/mes, and the stressed pronoun

---

[72] Minkowski (1970: 273).
[73] Grévisse (1993: 919, 1021).

'moi': 'c'est **mon** corps seul qui agit'; '**Mon** âme n'est pas à **moi**'; 'c'est un être qui marche **en moi**' (66). Psychic energy is, at these points, inwardly directed, constructing an impression of narcissistic pleasure, which therefore underlines the ecstatic effect achieved.

This passage is also a fine example of the textual rendering of the sense of oneness with God experienced during mystical union. The frequent occurrence of the personal pronouns 'je', 'me', 'il', 'lui', 'moi', and possessive determiners 'son/sa', 'mon/ma' creates a sense of proximity between the speaker, 'je', and the object of her attention, 'lui', through the use of demonstrative determiners: '**je** suis unie à Dieu et **il** est uni à **moi**, **nous** jouissons de cette union et **mon** âme se perd dans cette jouissance' (69).

By contrast, the use of deixis during 'torture' differs radically. Where during 'consolation' there is a concentration on the internal world at the expense of the external world, in 'torture' there is a confusion between these two realms. Both these states inflate the importance of the internal world, but 'torture' does this by giving meaning to external phenomena in terms of the internal space, giving the impression that energy is aggressive and outwardly directed. The use of the first-person pronoun 'je' is markedly reduced at these points in the text, and appears at times to be supplanted by the increased frequency of the impersonal pronoun 'on' and the more inclusive first-person plural 'nous': '**Nous** allons bien patauger dans la boue et le sang'; '**On** me brûle [...] **On** me taillade la chair dans tous les sens'. Madeleine's state of 'torture' here reflects 'le terrible *on*' so feared by Hersilie Rouy in her most delusional state. The nonspecific 'on' is the agent of suffering and absolute constraint.

Further evidence that narrative energy becomes outwardly directed during 'torture' is exhibited through the use of the vocative. A sense of 'rapprochement' between Madeleine and the other agents in her story, most notably antagonists such as Satan, contrasts sharply with the blissful ecstasy of union with God. It is only during 'torture' that the second person possessive determiners 'ton' and 'ta' are used: '**Ton** triomphe, Satan, sera de peu de durée' (424). In addition, where the present tense is constant during 'consolation', in 'torture' the narrative shifts between the imperfect describing the dreadful visions of the night: 'Des monstres déchaînés **jetaient** l'effroi partout [...] C'était *horrible*' (168) and the use of the progressively more complex prophetic future tense: 'Dieu **fera** naître une nation nouvelle [...] Plus le scandale et le martyre auront été grands, plus éclatera la bonté divine qui aura transformé la France et l'aura ramené à son amour' (424).

Madeleine calls these prophecies 'ces noires révélations', and exhibits a sense of fear: 'J'en ai trop horreur' (432). The narrator of these dreadful divinations plays on the assonance and alliteration in French between 'rêve' and 'révélation', stating 'J'ai des rêves révélateurs', repeating the noun within the epithet used to describe its nature suggesting a semantic slippage between the notion of dream and reality, truth, and fiction.

Somewhat paradoxically, the metaphor of light is evoked to illustrate further the notion of 'révélation': 'une lumière particulière qui m'éclaire', even though the image portrayed is a shattering one: 'j'ai eu la révélation de la guerre civile et de la division du pays contre lui-même' (432). This prophecy warns of a year that will be 'sombre' and not 'calme', and links the notions of truth, revelation, inspiration, and feelings in a coherent but devastating whole. Madeleine asserts that 'il n'y a pas d'erreurs dans les vraies révélations' and that this feeling is 'un pressentiment qui ne trompe jamais'. 'Révélation' in her terms is a form of communication that takes the form of an extrasensory experience of clairvoyance. She claims: 'Je ne le vois pas par les sens [...] C'est une intuition de l'âme, c'est une inspiration qui vient du ciel et qui n'a aucune analogie avec les communications humaines' (432). The notion of 'folie' is once again centred upon as a negatively connoted term, this time through the ironic dismissal of the fact that her 'révélations' are themselves rejected by her interlocutor and psychiatrist: 'On verra bien si ce que je dis est de la **folie**, les événements parleront' (432).

This description of interior revelation can be compared to the way in which another author, Céline Renooz, uses the metaphor of light. She writes: 'Il se fit, tout d'un coup, dans mon esprit, une grande lumière.' This insistence on the experience of revelation being an internal realization, occurring as the result of some external revelatory force, is repeated and emphasized throughout this short text, also. Renooz thus describes the phenomenon: 'Cette révélation subite fut très rapide et, en quelques minutes, éveilla dans mon esprit une telle multitude d'idées qu'il me fallut, depuis, plusieurs années pour les développer.' This author also describes the experience of inner revelation as being the passive object of a penetrating external power, much like Madeleine during 'consolation'. This further reinforces the parallel drawn between the states of 'torture' and 'consolation' through the experience of revelation. Renooz writes:

C'était dans le silence de la nuit, surtout, que j'étais **envahie** par une étrange impression, en considérant que j'étais l'objet d'une pareille découverte. Et je dis improprement l'objet et non le sujet, parce qu'il me semblait que j'étais

étrangère à ce qui s'était passé dans mon cerveau, puisque ma volonté n'y avait été pour rien.[74]

The projection of an internal-world process on to an external force is evidence of the confusion between phenomena occurring from within and without that occurs in these states of mind.

'Torture' is not a state of doubt, but rather one of profound and pointedly felt belief. Divine punishment and devastation are central to this belief system, and are a projection on to the outside world of the experience of melancholic persecution felt by Madeleine. The centrality of belief, as opposed to doubt, is underlined by the outright denial of the possibility of error. As Renooz dismisses the power of doubt, 'Tout cela me fut instantanément révélé, et avec un tel caractère d'évidence qu'aucun doute n'était possible', so Madeleine asks: 'Comment pouvez-vous dire que l'erreur est possible? Il n'y a pas d'erreur possible pour une pensée qui est la vérité' (428). Here the notions of thinking and truth are conceptually linked, making an overall connection in Madeleine's thought processes during 'consolation' and 'torture' between what she thinks, what she feels, and that which she holds to be true.

Janet affirms that it is during these states that his arguments are greeted with a reaction of either flat denial ('torture') or complete indifference ('consolation'), and it is at these moments in the text that the tension between these these two opposing notions of truth is most pronounced. He writes: 'Elle vient de dire qu'elle admet l'existence de gens qui doutent, mais dès qu'on insiste elle retire cette concession [. . .] A ce moment en effet je ne puis pas arriver à lui faire entrevoir la possibilité d'une erreur' (428). Janet here refers to Madeleine's attempt to understand what it is to truly doubt, in other words to be sceptical about the actual existence of God, where this knowledge completely fails to impinge on her reality: 'Je dois comprendre, quoique ce soit difficile, que les autres puissent douter; mais en réalité cela me paraît absurde, mon cœur a maintenant une certitude que rien au monde ne peut troubler' (426). The irony of Madeleine's insistence that nothing in the world can disturb the certainty of her beliefs in 'consolation' and 'torture' is that in the intermediary states her sense of truth is deeply challenged. 'Consolation' and 'torture' represent metaphorical expressions of Madeleine's reaction to the real world: either a blissful reversal of her experience of the world or an agonized metaphorical

---

[74] Renooz (1888: 267).

representation of how painful she finds relatedness and engagement with that world. The strategy of using retreat into her internal world is shown, in the intermediary states, to be limited and ultimately unsatisfactory.

THE INTERMEDIARY STATES: 'TENTATION', 'SÉCHERESSE', AND 'ÉQUILIBRE'

As we have seen, true scepticism does not enter Madeleine's range of possible feelings. However, Janet describes the state of 'tentation' as being characterized by doubt, where Madeleine's uncertainty is centred not upon a questioning of the existence of an all-powerful God, but rather upon a crisis of confidence in her ability to carry out her mission of the pilgrimage to Rome on tiptoes: a necessary voyage in order to have the miracle of her divine elevation recognized by the Pope. Madeleine first doubts Janet, and the legitimacy of his 'absolution', and then extends this anxiety to authority figures through the hierarchy of the Catholic Church: priests, bishops, and even the Pope himself. Madeleine questions her doctor, whose reality she refuses, and her spiritual superiors in the same terms, further reinforcing the parallel that can be drawn between the roles of these figures in her life. She perhaps also inscribes here some the anxiety of her time, characterized by the dismantling of hierarchies and the challenging of traditional authority through successive periods of revolution.

In 'tentation' dialogue between the two protagonists is very animated, and the reader gains a real sense of drama between the clashing belief systems being upheld. Madeleine's troublesome doubts about her mission initially permeate the text through the proliferation of interrogative sentences: 'Est-ce que je suis digne de la communion que je pratique tous les jours depuis vingt ans? Est-ce que je dois me confesser?' (142). This doubting of the rudimentary practices of faith for the devout Catholic is pursued later in the text in the form of a rhetorical question that functions as a challenge to Janet's sceptical attitude, but that in fact thinly veils Madeleine's uncertainty: 'Pour la toute puissance divine faut-il plus de trois ans pour soulever de dix centimètres une petite femme de quarante kilos?' (146).

During 'tentation' the author uses conjunctions textually as qualifying connections between statements. The effect this has on these sections of text is to cast doubt upon the validity of the values and beliefs that this woman holds dear, which is a reflection consistent with her general attitude at these times. Janet's role and function as priest-figure is once again foregrounded, and the conjunction 'puisque' and the indefinite pronoun 'quoi que' are used with the doubt-casting subjunctive construction, to undermine this aspect of the part he plays in her story: 'vous me dites d'aller me confesser **puisque** je ne me contente pas de votre absolution. Vous donnez l'absolution à toutes les malades, **quoi qu**'elles aient fait, ce n'est pas sérieux.' This dismissal of Janet's attitude that is not 'sérieux' is immediately contrasted with her evocation of the Pope, who is 'infaillible' (142). However, even this description is coloured with doubt, for Madeleine fears the Pope will be incorrectly informed and therefore unable to make an infallible judgement: '**mais** il est infaillible **quand** il décide d'après des informations et jamais il ne sera bien informé sur moi' (142). This portrayal of lack of faith in the papal entourage allows Madeleine to project her own doubts and fears that her beliefs may be erroneous on to negligent external agents, which leaves her relationship with God and faith in the Pope intact, and reveals an ability to situate herself in the context of a wider set of power structures that go beyond those of the medical profession.

As well as the fact that Madeleine's periods of 'tentation' are marked by her loss of faith in the primary figures in whom she had formerly placed her trust—her doctor and various authority figures in the Catholic Church—this phase in her mental life is characterized by excessive reasoning. A technique used by Madeleine that serves to present these beliefs in what could be termed a more objective and rational manner is to shift from the use of the pronouns 'je' and 'vous' when referring to herself and Janet in conversation or debate to the use of 'il' and 'elle'. This has the effect of displacing rather an intimate dialogic relationship into the realm of the hypothetical and the objective:

M. Janet veut des signes absolument indiscutables, **il** ne veut pas entendre parler de cette ascension [. . .] Il est vrai que c'est lent, fixons une date: mercredi matin **Madeleine** ne portera plus du tout sur la terre [. . .] Quelle insolence de fixer ainsi des dates à Dieu [. . .] Comment en sortir? (146–7)

Although in a previous paragraph Madeleine avows obedience to God, it is clear that her behaviour towards God's alter ego—Janet—is more disobedient and rebellious than docile. Madeleine has become argumentative and defensive because the very foundation of her belief system, of her psychical reality, has come dangerously under threat.

One example of the feeling of doubt that seeps through Madeleine's text through seemingly inconsequential words is the extensive use of the conjunction 'si': '**si** je n'obéis pas aveuglément'; '**si** je continue à me taire je vais encourir la colère de Dieu'; 'c'est une lâcheté de ma part de ne pas partir, **si** c'est vraiment Dieu qui m'inspire' (144). These statements betray Madeleine's profound sense of doubt in relation to her God and her knowledge of him. Nagging dilemmas, in which she can only speculate on what the terrifying consequences of disobedience or ignorance might be, have displaced the proximity and intimacy of 'consolation'.

During 'tentation' Madeleine requires more than just her own feelings, and seeks also the external endorsement of the Pope. At this point in the text we become increasingly aware of a sense of vulnerability and fear, where our protagonist no longer knows whom she can trust. She writes: 'Je dois chercher les moyens de parler au Pape. C'est *absolument nécessaire*... [...] Je crains d'être très coupable si je n'obéis pas aveuglément' (144). The suggestion that she desires or needs to obey blindly implies that this would remove the need for her to think for herself about the reality of her experience—a process simply too difficult for her to face, since her internal world would fall apart if she found the potential for non-belief within her worldview. The use of the adverb 'absolument' accentuates the sense of urgency precipitated by the onset of 'tentation', and the need to obey 'aveuglément' underlines Madeleine's fear of insight and need to feel led by a superior spiritual force.

The state of 'tentation' is superseded by 'sécheresse', and Madeleine's feelings of doubt are transformed into an overall sense of emptiness and despair. 'Torture' and 'sécheresse' are both depressive states, the former being characterized by anguish and pain, and the latter by absence and the annihilation of feeling. Madeleine's paranoid ranting during 'torture' is replaced by a period of what Janet terms 'obsession interrogatoire', revolving again around the argument over her claimed 'assumption' and her questioning of Janet's scepticism.

Throughout 'sécheresse' Madeleine is utterly disconsolate, and her usual sources of comfort offer no reprieve:

Rien, absolument rien n'est capable de me consoler, je me sens toute abandonnée dans une *solitude* effrayante. Dieu s'est retiré, le ciel, la terre, tout me manque. Je n'ai plus de foi, plus d'espérance, plus d'amour, plus rien qu'un affreux désespoir intérieur. (161–2)

The use of the negative constructions 'ne... rien' and 'ne... plus' repeatedly in this extract reinforce the claim that this state is fundamentally one of loss and lack. In the second of these sentences, the emphatic reiteration of the negation 'plus': '**plus** de foi, **plus** d'espérance, **plus** d'amour, **plus** rien' elicits the removal of each of Madeleine's sources of happiness. These things fall away one by one, leaving only 'un affreux désespoir intérieur'.

'Sécheresse' is a state of disillusionment, despair, and bewilderment which leaves the subject confounded by the apparent abandonment by a God in whom she had placed her trust. Madeleine addresses some of her verse to this God, and her lines are dominated by interrogative forms:

> Pourquoi, divin époux, te cacher à mes yeux?
> Pourquoi fuir ainsi, tandis que ta présence
> Enlèverait les maux de mon âme en souffrance?
> Oh! pourquoi rester sourd à mes cris douloureux?
>
> Si tu ne réponds pas à mes cris suppliants,
> Si tu me fuis encore, je ne saurai plus vivre;
> J'ai tout abandonné, bon Jésus, pour te suivre,
> Ne veux-tu plus guider mes pauvres pas errants? ... (162)

The anaphoric repetition of the adverb/conjunction 'pourquoi' and the conjunction 'si' in the first lines of each stanza of this excerpt reveals an overwhelming sense that the questions and doubts raised during 'tentation' remain unanswered, and the questioner ultimately unsatisfied. And yet, Madeleine continues valiantly to defend her claims, even though her feelings do not at this stage correspond to her beliefs.

This would suggest that we could indeed credit Madeleine with a more sophisticated grasp of what 'truth' is. Rather than being the straightforward translation of feelings into dogma, Madeleine still propounds the idea of her 'assumption' even when she feels abandoned. However, it could be argued that, when she reaches this stage, the ceaseless interrogation that the narrator addresses to her doctor–priest interlocutor is as much a form of rhetorical questioning aimed at, in fact, convincing herself. Madeleine is chasing away the feelings of emptiness and abandonment, trying to re-establish a sense of oneness with her beloved God.

Janet tells us that Madeleine, when not preoccupied with her dynamic inner world, slips periodically into the state of 'équilibre'. There is very little textual commentary to be made on this comparatively 'sane' state because it does not conduce Madeleine to write. This fact evinces a very straightforward connection between the Jungian notion that the inner or spiritual world is a creative force to be tapped into, and

Madeleine's ceasing productivity during 'équilibre'. This is a source of great frustration for Janet, who requests material from Madeleine and feels justified in writing her a 'mot de reproche' about the lack of potentially analysable matter in her letters:

J'arrivai même un jour à être mécontent de ces lettres qui ne contenaient plus rien sur ses croyances, sur ses doutes, sur ses joies ineffables et qui devenaient banales et je lui ai écrit un mot de reproche en demandant une lettre plus détaillée. (177)

What is poignant about this observation is that the moment Madeleine reaches 'équilibre', or sanity, or the ability to differentiate effectively between her inner world and the shared reality of the outside world, she ceases to be an object of clinical interest. What has actually happened during 'équilibre' is not so much that Madeleine has developed a sophisticated grasp of what is internal, unconscious, or spiritual and what is external, rational, and material, but that there is a numbing of her inner world. This drive to stasis, and Madeleine's mediocrity in this state, is the whole tragedy of her case.

Janet's treatise acts as an arena within which two competing notions of truth are played out. Madeleine's text is paradoxical because it is simultaneously truthful and delusional: in good faith, it describes inner experiences mistaken for the shared reality of the sane world. Her writing offers textual evidence of the outer immobility accompanied by intense psychical, or creative, activity characteristic of the withdrawal and introspection of the state described in clinical language as 'catatonic schizophrenia'. The narrative dynamism of the complementary states of 'consolation' and 'torture' is counteracted by the stilted frustration of the intermediary states of 'sécheresse' and 'tentation', and by the stasis of sanity that determines Madeleine's activity during 'équilibre'. As a result of her inability to differentiate between inner and outer reality, Madeleine's text even at the most creative stage of thinking is severely limited. The protagonist 'je' is dominant and the figure of the 'other' is conflated into an indistinct character represented either by the indistinct but ominous 'on' or by the predictable binary opposition of God and Satan, translated into the simultaneously good and bad object: Janet. Madeleine achieves a certain level of creativity and expressiveness, and at times she experiences joy in life. However, she does not achieve true relatedness or connectedness with the world of people and objects, because there would appear to be no place for a woman like her in that world.

What is most 'psychotic' about Madeleine's text is her failure to see any inconsistency between the apparent contradictions in her claims. However, it is this ability to shift in time and space, and the fluid and subversive application of medical terminology, that sets the protagonist's sense of truth radically apart from her doctor's rigid understanding, which is constrained by the demands of 'reality'. It is this flexibility that enables her to evade the double bind of the patient's utterance, and to construct a compelling challenge to psychiatric 'truth'. This argument was and is valid, because since the time of the composition of these texts this notion of truth has gone on to be challenged and undermined by revisionist theorists of the twentieth century. In this sense, as a female-authored text of the Belle Époque we can assert retrospectively that, although she was a marginal and not a serious member of the women's movement, Lamotte's writing did embody some of the feminist concerns of the era: hope for change and a challenge to the hegemony of patriarchy. Her delusions serve the purpose of metaphorically reversing her limited status as a woman who could or would not conform to the norms of the society in which she lived, as they offer her a realm of rich and dramatic experience that was denied her in 'reality'.

Janet and Madeleine both fail to differentiate between the inner and the outer worlds, because Janet, despite his sensitive approach, does not acknowledge the widely recognized validity of the internal world—as do thinkers such as Freud, Jung, Minkowski, Laing, and Underhill. The views of both parties are restrictive and limiting, but arguably function as complementary perspectives that in juxtaposition offer perhaps a more complete and complex view of the world inhabited by these two radically different characters. If the experiences of the so-called insane are to be understood more extensively by social historiography, then what is needed, in addition to a historical understanding of the medical world and the raw data of the case material, is an appreciation of the multifaceted nature of the texts involved. The story of Pauline Lair Lamotte, or 'Madeleine', is a case in point. This narrative addresses the reader in her humanity through an explosion of the inner world of a human being on to the pages of a medical treatise: a unique account that would otherwise have fallen irretrievably into oblivion.

5

Camille Claudel

'Du rêve que fut ma vie, ceci est le cauchemar'

The name Camille Claudel finds a modest place in twentieth-century French biographical dictionaries and encyclopaedias next to that of her brother, the celebrated French poet Paul Claudel (1868–1955), who at the end of his life was hailed as 'le plus grand des poètes français vivants'.[1] Although she was a well-known sculptor whose artistic genius was recognized by many during her productive lifetime, the entry one finds on Camille, if there is one at all, is invariably the shorter one: within a few lines or even words it places her in relation to the other important man in her life: her teacher, lover, artistic collaborator, and eventually, in her mind, absolute antagonist, Auguste Rodin. Her greatly reduced status in the collective memory of France, prior to her resurrection as an important figure in the history of French sculpture in the 1980s, is reflected in the glaring mistakes contained in such reference works as the *Grand Larousse encylopédique* and the *Dictionnaire de biographie française*, which as late as 1960 erroneously inform us that Claudel was born in 1856 and died 'around' 1920. There is no mention of the fact that she spent the last thirty years of her life in an asylum.[2] Today, however, if you visit the ground-floor apartment where Claudel lived and worked at 19, quai Bourbon, on the Île Saint-Louis in Paris, you will find a plaque giving her correct birth and death dates, and which laments the fact that she was taken from that very place in 1913 to begin 'la longue nuit de l'internement'.

---

[1] GL: 182. The title citation is taken from a letter written by Claudel in 1935, and is quoted in Rivière (2003: 307).

[2] GL: 181; DBF: 1382–1383. I refer to the author as 'Camille' only in the context of discussing her as part of the Claudel family, so as to avoid confusion as to which member I refer.

In fact, Claudel was born on 8 December 1864, in Fère-en-Tardenois, Aisne, the second child of Louise-Athanaïse Cerveau and Louis-Prosper Claudel, in the shadow of a mother's grief, their firstborn beloved son, Charles-Henri, having perished in infancy in 1863. A sister, Louise, was born in 1866, and a cherished brother, Paul, in 1868. Camille was a highly gifted but capricious youngster who showed signs of artistic genius from a very early age. Paul Claudel does not hesitate to assert that it was she who was at this stage 'le génie de la famille'.[3] Claudel produced her first clay sculptures in 1876, depicting the somewhat belligerent figures of *David et Goliath*, *Bismarck*, and *Napoléon*. In 1879, she met the sculptor Alfred Boucher, who was her first teacher, and in the spring of 1881 Louise Claudel and her children moved to Paris to enable Camille to begin work at the Académie Colarossi. In 1882 she rented a studio with some other young women artists, among them the English sculptor Jessie Lipscomb, who would become a lifelong friend.[4] Boucher continued to teach these young women regularly, and in the same year introduced Claudel to Paul Dubois, director of the École Nationale des Beaux-Arts. Dubois, upon seeing her work, is reputed to have exclaimed: 'Vous avez pris des cours avec Monsieur Rodin?'[5] But she had at this stage never met Rodin, suggesting that her artistic style pre-existed their relationship, and that there may have been something inexpressible in the aesthetic quality of their art that would later draw them to each other.

Claudel began working in Rodin's studio in 1883, and eventually became his lover. Theirs was an initially passionate relationship that soon grew troubled and emotionally strenuous, eventually breaking down in about 1899. Claudel's artistic activity in the public eye lasted from about 1882 until 1905, and during this time her work was regularly exhibited at the Salon des Artistes français. However, these two artists, neither of whose 'genius' has ever really been contested, would have very different destinies: Rodin's reward would be international renown, Claudel's would be oblivion. This apparently gendered injustice is also repeated in the unfolding of her brother's life. As Pierre Claudel very aptly said at the unveiling of a commemorative plaque to Paul and Camille in the cemetery of Villeneuve-sur-Fère: 'Une double

---

[3] Paul Claudel is quoted in Cassar (1987: 27).
[4] Grunfeld (1989: 231).
[5] Cassar (1987: 50–9, 459).

vocation s'est éveillée dans ce village même, pour la plus grande gloire de l'un et le plus grand malheur de l'autre.'[6]

Commentary on Claudel's life and work, even that which seeks to bring her work to light, is inflected with a prevailing attitude of anxiety about the fact that she might have been or become, although a woman, a very great artist. Despite being a champion of her work, the critic Octave Mirbeau still qualified his enthusiastic declaration of her genius ('C'est la femme la plus géniale de son temps') with the opinion, still regrettably prevalent in the twenty-first century, that for a woman to be great she must be like a man: 'Elle a du génie, comme un homme qui en aurait beaucoup.' Camille Mauclair, in an article on 'L'Art des femmes peintres et sculpteurs', declared: 'Mademoiselle Claudel est la femme artiste la plus considérable de l'heure présente.' Mirbeau even suggested that there was something unnatural and disconcerting about her work, which represented: 'Une révolte de la nature: la femme de génie'.[7] To assert that Rodin was simply the greater genius is an easy answer to the problem, but the value of comparing the two artists is highly questionable: it seems grossly unfair to compare one artist who has left a huge body of work, because he managed to reach artistic maturity, with another whose working life was tragically cut short by debilitating mental illness.

The psychiatrists François Lhermitte and Jean-François Allilaire provide 'expert' opinions on Claudel's mental illness in Reine-Marie Paris's biography of the artist. Although arguably less than qualified to comment on artistic matters, they take it as read that Rodin was the greater artist. Her already subordinate position to the master, in their opinion, is reflected in the use of the forename 'Camille' to refer to Claudel, where the appearance of the name 'Auguste' used to refer to the great Rodin never occurs. Despite there being no reliable means of assessing how the two artists influenced each other, they confidently assert: 'Rodin apporta plus à Camille que celle-ci à Rodin.' They do, however, concede that Rodin signed some sculptures that Claudel had worked on, and therefore that the accusation that he stole her work is grounded in something resembling reality. They also speculate: 'L'œuvre de Camille, délicate par nature ou puissante par l'influence de Rodin, ne pût l'atteindre et donc la dépasser plus tard, dans la plus optimiste des hypothèses.'[8] We will never know how Claudel might have developed as

[6] Cassar 4.
[7] Ibid. 17 and 35.
[8] Lhermitte (1984: 181–2).

an artist, but the fact that these opinions can still be aired in important biographical works justifies a renewed attempt to validate the only creative work, powerful in expression and deeply troubled in nature, that Claudel was able to produce after her committal to the asylum: her writing.

Even supposing Claudel's 'genius' matched that of her master, her position in society as an unmarried, independent female artist was simply unsustainable.[9] As Paul Claudel laments: 'Le métier de sculpteur est pour un homme une espèce de défi perpétuel au bon sens, il est pour une femme isolée et pour une femme du tempérament de ma sœur une pure impossibilité.'[10] Rodin, on the other hand, throughout the vicissitudes of an animated love life and a precarious career, had a mistress at his side: the ever-loyal Rose Beuret. Claudel stood to lose so much more from the breakdown of relations with Rodin. Although he is said to have been tortured by the memory of her, and to have tried to continue supporting her, it would seem ultimately that where Claudel needed Rodin, he needed Rose Beuret.[11] Claudel's social status as an unmarried woman carrying on a scandalous affair was significantly inferior to Rodin's; the stress of this situation, coupled with the wish to break away from his artistic influence, eventually pushed her to issue an ultimatum: marry me, or lose me.

Rodin chose not to leave Beuret, and he and Claudel went their separate ways. It is very likely that Claudel fell pregnant at least once by Rodin, and that she had an abortion or a miscarriage.[12] The pressure of a series of unhappy events meant that by 1905 she had ceased to produce work that would be seen in public, and in the years that followed Claudel began systematically to destroy the work she did

[9] The British artist Richard Nevinson (1937: 45–6) observed a great disparity in status between female artists in London compared to their Parisian counterparts. He records in his autobiography an incident in 1912, when he met a young woman who was studying at the Sorbonne and trying 'to live a life à l'anglaise' in the manner of his student friend Dora Carrington. But 'the treatment she experienced and the insults that were heaped on her would simply be disbelieved in England. She had ventured down Boulevard Saint Michel alone and on foot, and as a result of what was said and done she cried the whole way.'

[10] Cited in Cassar (1987: 229).

[11] Champigneule (1967: 242).

[12] Lhermitte and Allilaire (1984: 165) say it is likely Claudel lost a child in 1893, but agree this is not a verifiable fact. Paul Claudel (quoted in Antoine 1988: 166) also alludes to this event in a letter to Marie Romain-Rolland, writing: 'Sachez qu'une personne dont je suis très proche a commis le même crime que vous et qu'elle l'expie depuis 26 ans dans une maison de fous.'

produce. Her lifestyle became progressively more misanthropic, and she grew increasingly suspicious of the outside world, accusing Rodin and other artists of stealing her work and ideas, and people around her of colluding with the 'bande à Rodin': those she held responsible for her demise and inability to make a success of her career. One cannot help feeling now that Claudel's ruin, as an artist and indeed as a human being, need not have been a human tragedy of such immense propor-tions, but it is difficult to speculate on how events could have turned out differently.

Claudel was committed to the asylum at Ville-Évrard following her father's death in 1913. In August 1914, because of the war, Claudel was transferred to an asylum at Montdevergues in Montfavet, near Avignon, where she would remain until her death, thirty years after her commit-tal, in 1943. She never saw her mother or sister again, and received only intermittent visits from her brother, Paul, who worked abroad in the French diplomatic service. Neither did she work again, and the only remnants we have of her life from 1913 onwards are her letters.[13] She corresponded regularly with her mother, brother, and several friends until the end of her life.

At the time that Claudel was writing her correspondence, significant progress had been made in France by the educational reforms of the Third Republic. Jules Ferry's 1882 law instituting obligatory, secular, and free education for all meant that women's illiteracy had fallen by the early twentieth century. Feminist activism pre- and post-1900 had improved women's status in terms of education, divorce, and their financial affairs. It was an era when much was hoped for, but that was ultimately characterized by disappointment when women failed to gain the vote in post-1918 France.[14] Although Claudel took no formal part in the women's movement, this premature and ultimately frustrated hope for change reflects her desire for change in her own status and personal emancipation, a move forward that would never come about. The mood of her correspondence and her ultimate disap-pointment exemplify the dynamic of frustrated hope experienced by the women of her time.

---

[13] Although Claudel was allowed and even encouraged to work, she refused. A letter to her mother in 1913 (Rivière 2003: 257) gives an explanation for this: 'Veuillez s.v.p. souhaiter le bonjour de ma part à Mlle de Vertus. Vous lui direz pourquoi je n'ai pu continuer à lui faire de beaux marbres. Depuis que je suis folle, mes facultés intellec-tuelles ayant perdu leur équilibre.'

[14] See Alex Hughes, '1900–1969: Writing the Void', in Stephens (2000: 148).

As Claudel slipped into the asylum and was abandoned by those she loved, so her work fell quickly into oblivion. Rodin had died in 1917, and only in 1951 would Claudel's work be seen again in public, when Paul Claudel organized an exhibition of his sister's work at the Musée Rodin in Paris. However, only much later, after the publication of the novel *Une femme* by Anne Delbée in 1982, based on Claudel's life, would the level of interest in her work rise dramatically.[15] This book captured the attention of the French public, which soon grew concerned with reclaiming and making an emblematic feminist figure of her memory. Exhibitions of Claudel's work in Paris and Poitiers followed in 1984, and in the same year Reine-Marie Paris published a biography entitled *Camille Claudel.*[16] Jacques Cassar's *Dossier Camille Claudel* was published posthumously in 1987, and provided the first comprehensive account and catalogue of her life and career. In addition to Anne Delbée's novel, it was Bruno Nuytten's hugely successful film, *Camille Claudel,* released in 1989, featuring French superstars Gérard Depardieu and Isabelle Adjani in the roles of Rodin and Claudel, which made Camille Claudel a household name in France.[17] A major exhibition of Claudel's work was also organized at the Musée Rodin in Paris from April to July 2008, and this was accompanied by an 'hors-série' special dossier produced by *Le Figaro* in March 2008. Ironically, given her fate, Camille Claudel is now a highly celebrated figure in France.

Excerpts of her letters have been reproduced in many biographical and critical works on Claudel and Rodin. However, the appearance in 2003 of a definitive and complete edition of Camille Claudel's correspondence, edited by Anne Rivière and Bruno Gaudichon, for the purposes of this study and further analysis of her writing was a fortuitous event. The editors have reproduced the letters in chronological order, the dating of each piece being backed up with the use of as much secondary material as possible. Each letter is reproduced exactly as it appears, with spelling and grammatical mistakes left uncorrected and general formatting unchanged. Claudel's written word has been reproduced in this edition exactly as she left it.

At the time of her committal to the asylum at Ville-Évrard, just eight days after the death of her beloved father in 1913, Claudel had in the preceding years become increasingly antisocial and neglectful of her

---

[15] Delbée (1982).
[16] Gaudichon (1984); Paris (1984).
[17] Nuytten (1989).

own health and well-being, eventually living in utter squalor and isolation in her home.[18] A doctor who knew her, Docteur Michaux, diagnosed Claudel as suffering from 'psychose paranoïde'.[19] The 'certificat d'internement' reads as follows:

Je soussigné [...] certifie que Mademoiselle Camille Claudel est atteinte de troubles intellectuels très sérieux; qu'elle porte des habits misérables; qu'elle est absolument sale, ne se lavant certainement jamais; qu'elle a vendu tous ses meubles, sauf un fauteuil et un lit; [...] qu'elle passe sa vie complètement renfermée dans son logement et privée d'air, les volets étant hermétiquement fermés; que depuis plusieurs mois elle ne sort plus dans la journée, mais qu'elle fait de rares sorties au milieu de la nuit; que d'après ses lettres écrites tout récemment à son frère, d'après ses propos tenus à la concierge, elle a toujours la terreur de la bande à "Rodin", que j'ai déjà constaté chez elle à plusieurs reprises depuis 7 à 8 ans qu'elle se figure être persécutée, que son état déjà dangereux pour elle à cause du manque de soins et même parfois de nourriture est également dangereux pour ses voisins et qu'il serait nécessaire de l'interner dans une Maison de Santé.

Paris, le 7 mars 1913.

Signé docteur Michaux.

Claudel was committed under the law of 1838 as a 'placement volontaire'. The diagnosis of paranoid psychosis remained unchanged until the end of her life.[20]

The term 'paranoia' was given its modern meaning by the German psychiatrist Kahlbaum in 1863, and was later introduced into French psychiatry by Jules Séglas.[21] He gave a definition of paranoia that is still applied in French clinical practice today:

On désigne sous le nom de *paranoïa*—folie systématique—un état psycho-pathique fonctionnel, caractérisé par une déviation particulière des fonctions

---

[18] The British painter Gwen John would become Rodin's lover in around 1906, and her fate would be similar: 'After converting to Roman Catholicism in 1913 she lived at Meudon, where she became increasingly religious and reclusive' (McGovern 2002: 808).

[19] It is unclear whether this diagnosis, which was made by a general practitioner, takes into account the distinction in French psychiatry between 'psychose paranoïde' and 'psychose paranoïaque'. The former indicates a serious form of the illness, linked to diagnoses of schizophrenia and eventual dementia; the latter is evidence of a 'constitution paranoïaque' and was not thought to be degenerative (Claude 1925: 146–7).

[20] Claudel's medical records are reproduced in Paris (1984: 193–208). From 1913 to 1942 they record no change in her mental state. In 1943, a decline is noted prior to her death.

[21] From Charles Rycroft's entry on 'paranoia', in Gregory (1987: 576).

intellectuelles les plus élevées, n'impliquant ni une décadence profonde ni un désordre général, s'accompagnant presque toujours d'idées délirantes systématisées et permanentes. Ce délire [...] se présente comme une sorte de perception inexacte de l'humanité, échappant à la loi du consensus universel, comme une interprétation particulière du monde extérieur dans ses relations avec la personnalité du malade qui rapporte tout à lui, soit en mal, soit en bien [...] et il s'accompagne toujours d'un manque de critique, de contrôle, d'une foi absolue, bien que la lucidité reste complète en dehors du délire.[22]

French psychiatrists had, over the years, found different labels for similar groups of symptoms: Pinel proposed the term 'délire partiel' in 1800; Lasègue was the first to use the term 'délire de persécution' in 1852; Trélat proffered the concept of 'folie lucide' in 1861; the same symptoms were placed within Esquirol's monomania thesis in 1838 as 'monomanie de persécution' or 'monomanie ambitieuse'; and Sérieux and Capgras described paranoid symptoms as 'le délire d'interprétation' or 'la folie raisonnante' in 1909. In France, as early as 1834 Leuret had made a distinction between incoherent delusional states and so-called 'arrangeurs', distinguishing between what now might be recognized as schizophrenic mental disintegration and simple paranoia, where delusional ideas are systematically organized.[23] Kraepelin was careful to limit the label 'paranoia' to those mental states that developed in a systematic style without any sign of dementia. Bleuler then appropriated Kraepelin's theory of dementia praecox in 1911 into his theory of schizophrenia, which led to the category of schizophrenia encompassing almost all chronic psychotic states in Anglo-American and German psychiatry. However, in France, and at the time of Claudel's diagnosis, theories about chronic delusional states remained clearly distinct from the category of dementia praecox, or schizophrenia.[24]

The principal themes that can be drawn from these descriptions are that paranoia is a state where the subject moves successively from feelings of depression or disappointment, to feelings of persecution, and finally to ideas of grandeur, or megalomania. That megalomania results from delusions of persecution is usually thought to be via a process of erroneous reasoning: the subject feels she is being persecuted, and therefore deduces that this must be because she is a person of great

---

[22] Séglas, 'Leçons cliniques', 1895, quoted in EU: 504.

[23] See Pinel (1800); Leuret (1834); Esquirol (1838); Lasègue (1852); Ott (1854); Trélat (1861); Séglas (1893); Sérieux (1909).

[24] Rancher (1993: 16).

importance. The clinical history of Hersilie Rouy is a good example of the process resulting in delusions of grandeur, although the term 'paranoia' had not been coined at the time of her diagnosis. This textbook description represents an attempt to theorize how frequently observed symptoms can be seen as having common causes, but is not an explanation accepted by all. Others, particularly those from the psychoanalytical tradition, as we shall now see, argue that such radical affective corollaries cannot be attributed to the conscious process of rationalization.

We saw in our discussion of the Rouy case that in his famous analysis of Judge Schreber's autobiographical writings, Freud argues that megalomania is the result of libido being withdrawn from external objects and reinvested in the ego: 'In paranoia the liberated libido becomes attached to the ego, and is used for the aggrandizement of the ego. A return is thus made to the stage of narcissism [. . .], in which a person's only sexual object is his own ego.'[25] Freud argues that paranoia is a neurosis of defence, and that its main mechanism is projection, his thesis being that Schreber's delusions of persecution were a defence against unconscious (and would-be consciously intolerable) homosexual feelings.[26] There is a reversal of affect, and feelings are not recognized consciously as originating internally, but perceived as persecutory attitudes emanating from an external source. In this case, the feeling 'I love him' is unconsciously transformed into 'I hate him'. However, through the unconscious process of projective identification, this manifests itself at a conscious level as 'He persecutes me', which forms the basis of delusions of persecution.[27]

Jacques Lacan's doctoral thesis, *De la psychose paranoïaque dans ses rapports avec la personnalité*, published in 1932, examines the writings of a woman he calls 'Aimée', detained because she had acted on paranoid delusions and attacked a famous actress. Lacan argues that the approaches of his predecessors are limited for this reason: 'L'analyse de la psychose s'est fondée jusqu'à ce jour sur les symptômes du délire.'[28] He suggests the following as an alternative way of proceeding:

---

[25] Freud (1911–13: 72).

[26] Freud's interpretation of Schreber's delusions is far from being universally accepted. For a criticism of the reading of paranoia as a defence against unconscious homosexual urges, see Macalpine (1956).

[27] The concept of projective identification was introduced by Klein in 1932 (Laplanche 1973: 356–7).

[28] Lacan (1975a: 345).

La clef du problème nosologique, pronostique et thérapeutique de la psychose paranoïaque doit être cherchée dans une analyse psychologique *concrète*, qui s'applique à tout le *développement de la personnalité* du sujet, c'est-à-dire aux évènements de son *histoire*, aux progrès de sa *conscience*, à ses réactions dans le milieu *social*.[29]

The answer lies, it would appear, in a new approach to the subject not based entirely on pathological symptoms externalized in psychotic episodes, but with equal emphasis on the latency period preceding these acute moments. However, in his close analysis of Aimée's writing, Lacan fails to adopt the very approach he favours in his concluding remarks. Although Freud and Lacan begin the important process of giving a voice to the psychiatric patient, and both suggest that there is much to be gained from looking behind the mask of an individual's presenting symptoms to the experience itself, and to the formation of the personality, neither successfully manages to do what they claim needs to be done.[30] This is perhaps because, as Freud himself suggests, there is a rather embarrassing resemblance between feelings or sensations described by paranoiacs and the psychoanalytical process itself, and the work of the psychoanalyst through the analysis of the transference:

Schreber's 'rays of God' [. . .], are in reality nothing else than a concrete representation and projection outwards of libidinal cathexes; and they thus lend his delusions a striking conformity with our theory. [. . .] It remains for the future to decide whether there is more delusion in my theory than I should like to admit, or whether there is more truth in Schreber's delusion than other people are as yet prepared to believe.[31]

Others from the psychoanalytical tradition identify a problematic like-ness between the claims of paranoiacs and those of great artists, proph-ets, and political and religious leaders.[32] This observation, coupled with the fact that Freud disappointingly only concedes on the final page of his discussion that there could be more truth in delusion than we can comfortably admit, reveals an alternative point of entry into Claudel's

---

[29] Ibid. 346.

[30] Lacan attempts to approach his patient with 'un regard aussi direct, aussi nu, aussi objectif que possible' (Allouch 1994: 20), but concedes that his approach only gives insights from one point of view, which is 'un point de vue *doctrinal*' (Lacan 1975a: 307).

[31] Freud (1911–13: 78–9).

[32] Rycroft in Gregory (1987: 577). Rycroft also notes that many contemporary analysts hold that narcissistic self-overestimation is a compensatory reaction to humili-ation in infancy and childhood.

writing for the literary critic. It suggests that her work is potentially more complex on a textual level than at first it might appear. Her profound sense of the importance of her own existence and of the significance of her work has, with the irony afforded by hindsight, been shown to be more full of truth than megalomania in the heroine she has become in the collective mind of the French people, and indeed internationally, since the 1980s.

It is beyond the reach of this study to undertake detailed critical analysis of Claudel's artwork, but neither is it possible to discuss her writing without putting it in the context of her artistic production. Claudel's most acclaimed pieces date from around 1888 to 1905, and many critics view her work as being initially closely embroiled with the relationship with Rodin, and eventually moving away from this influence to the beginnings of artistic maturity and independence: a blossoming sadly interrupted by the onset of her mental illness. In the context of discussing her writing, I refer to two of her sculptures, *L'Âge mûr* and *Les Causeuses* (1894–5), the first relative to her liaison with Rodin, and the second, which is mentioned in her text, in relation to her attitude to other artists.

The remainder of this chapter will be based on the analysis of two items in Claudel's correspondence from 1909 and 1917–18, respectively.[33] The first letter from Camille to Paul, written before her committal to the asylum, is strongly themed along the lines of her feelings of persecution by Rodin. The second letter from Claudel to Docteur Michaux, the doctor who wrote her 'certificat d'internement', gives a detailed and compelling account of the reality of her artistically unproductive and pitiful life in the asylum, and appears—superficially, at least—as an attempt at a more plausibly 'sane' request for clemency on the part of the medical establishment.

CAMILLE CLAUDEL TO PAUL CLAUDEL, BEFORE 7 DECEMBER 1909

The letter to be discussed in this first section was written four years prior to Claudel's committal to the asylum at Ville-Évrard, during a time when her family was becoming increasingly concerned about her mental

----

[33] These dates are estimated since both letters are undated.

health. Camille's way of life was placing considerable strain on the Claudel family, upon whom she was still completely financially dependent, and the tone of Louis-Prosper Claudel's letters to his son Paul is concerned, if somewhat exasperated. He writes:

Jusqu'ici personne n'a voulu s'occuper d'elle. [...] Nous payons son loyer, ses contributions, et jusqu'à ses traites de boucher, et de menues sommes que nous lui envoyons de temps en temps, demandées ou non par lettres non affranchies. [...] Je voudrais que Camille vienne nous voir de temps en temps. Ta mère ne veut pas entendre parler de ça, mais je me demande si ce ne serait pas le moyen de calmer sinon de guérir cette folle enragée.[34]

Her father's letter brings to light the sacrifices incurred by the Claudel family as a result of Camille's insistence on pursuing her career at considerable cost to those upon whom she remained dependent, and reveals that her mental state had been deteriorating for some time before her committal. Later in the same year, Camille wrote the following letter to her brother:[35]

N'emmènes pas mes sculptures à Prague, je ne veux pas du tout exposer dans ce pays-là: les admirateurs de calibre-là m'intéressent nullement. Je désirerais bientôt avoir la reconnaissance de l'Aurore, comme ce n'est que 15^f, je la retirerai le mois prochain et je vais essayer de la vendre. Renvoie-la moi le plus tôt possible.

Tu as raison, la justice ne pourrait rien contre le sieur Hebrardt et les brigands de son acabit, ce qu'il faut avec ces gens-là, c'est le révolver, seul et unique argument.

C'est ce qu'il faudrait car note bien qu'en laissant celui-là sans punition, cela encourage les autres qui exposent effrontément mes œuvres et se font de l'argent avec sous la direction du sieur Rodin.

Mais ce qu'il y a de plus drôle, c'est qu'il s'est permis l'autre année d'exposer en Italie une œuvre qui n'était pas de moi, signée de moi et à qui il a fait donner une médaille d'or pour pousser l'ironie jusqu'au bout. Je tiens maintenant le bout de l'oreille.

Le gredin s'empare de toutes mes sculptures par différentes voies, il les donne à ces copains les artistes chics qui en échange lui distribuent des décorations, des ovations, etc.

---

[34] This excerpt is taken from a letter to Paul Claudel from his father written during the summer of 1909 (Rivière 2003: 241).

[35] Ibid. 239–43. The letter is undated, but estimated to be before 7 December 1909. The pages of the letter are not numbered, so again the editor has attempted to place the parts in the correct order. Errors of spelling, punctuation, and grammar have deliberately been left uncorrected.

En entrant chez nous il a ruiné Chacrise et s'est fait 300 000^F avec les tapisseries, il n'a pas perdu son temps de s'entendre avec Collin pour me faire venir à Paris.

Ma prétendue vocation lui en a rapporté!

A bientôt

Camille

Je tremble du sort de l'Age Mûr, ce qui va lui arriver, c'est incroyable! Si j'en juge par ce qui est arrivé aux Causeuses. Exposées en 1890. Depuis ce moment divers individus s'en servent pour se faire des rentes. Entre autres une Suédoise (Stalhelberg de Frumerie) qui depuis cette époque expose tous les ans un groupe de Causeuses plus ou moins modifié; et bien d'autres, peintres et sculpteurs qui exposent des 'Potins' 'conversations'

Après quoi la Petite cheminée, cette année-là dans tout Paris on ne voyait que des Cheminées avec femme assise, debout, couchée, etc.

L'Age Mûr, ce sera de même, ils vont tous le faire les uns après les autres. Chaque fois que je mets un modèle nouveau dans la circulation, ce sont des millions qui roulent, pour les fondeurs, les mouleurs, les artistes et les marchands et pour moi... $0 + 0 = 0$.

Après cela ils s'étonnent que je leur ferme la porte de mon atelier et que je refuse de leur donner ces modèles qui rapportent à tout le monde excepté à moi... ça fait les étonnés. L'année dernière, mon voisin le sieur Picard (copain de Rodin) frère d'un inspecteur de la sûreté, pénétrait chez moi avec une fausse clef, il y avait contre le mur une femme en jaune; Depuis il a fait plusieurs femmes en jaunes grandeur nature exactement pareilles à la mienne qu'il a exposées, rapport au bas mot = 100 000^f. Depuis ils font tous des femmes en jaune et quand je voudrai exposer la mienne ils feront la contrepartie et me la feront interdire. Le même jour le sieur Picard vit chez moi un monument que j'étais en train de faire et le passa à ses bons copains les sculpteurs, on partage en frères entre francs-maçons.

[En marge] c'est moi la voleuse

Un autre année je me servais d'un gamin qui m'apportait du bois, il vit une esquisse que j'étais en train de faire ("une femme avec un biche") tous les Dimanches il allait à Meudon rendre compte au sieur R. de ce qu'il avait vu. Résultat = rien que cette année il y avait au salon 3 femmes à la biche textuellement modelées sur la mienne, en grandeur nature, rapport au bas mot = 100 000^f.

Une autre fois une femme de ménage me donnait un narcotique dans mon café qui me fit dormir 12 heures sans arrêter. Pendant ce temps, la femme pénétrait dans mon cabinet de toilette et prenait la femme à la croix, résultat, 3 figures de femme à la croix rapport = 100 000^f.

Le triste sire puise chez moi par différents moyens et partage avec ses copains les artistes chics qui en l'échange le font décorer, lui font des ovations, des banquets, etc.

Les ovations de cet homme célèbre m'ont coûté les yeux de la tête, et pour moi rien de rien!...

Depuis il a attiré les Cartereau à Paris et leur a volé tous leurs meubles rapport au bas mot 500 000^f.

Le gaillard vit à nos crochets et se taille un belle pâtée. Et quand je rue dans les brancards il se sert de vous pour me donner des coups de fouet. Le mécanisme est facile à comprendre.

Garde tout cela pour toi, inutile de crier, il vaut mieux agir en dessous. Quand ils te parleront de moi, tu leur diras "ça vous étonne qu'elle se refuse à ce système-là, c'est pourtant assez logique tout le monde en ferait autant, il y a l'amour propre d'artiste, cela se comprend et jamais rien pour elle?"

Et avoir le toupet après s'être servi de mes groupes depuis plus de 20 ans, de me faire terminer ma carrière à la charité de mes parents; du toupet! Tu leur diras "vous lui devez quelque chose pour tout ce que vous lui avez pris depuis des années, sans cela son atelier restera dorénavant hermétiquement fermé, je n'y peux rien"

Les huguenots sont aussi malins que féroces. Ils m'ont élevé exprès pour leur fournir des idées, connaissant la nullité de leur imagination. Je suis dans la position d'un chou qui est rongé par les chenilles; à mesure que je pousse une feuille elles la mangent.

La férocité des hugenots était légendaire au moment de la Renaissance. Depuis ça n'a pas changé.

Ne montre ma lettre à personne, méfie-toi des suppôts que l'on te soudoie.

Mes amitiés pour toi et Reine et Chouchette.

Ne parle de rien et surtout ne dis pas de nom, sans cela ils arriveraient me menacer.

The prevailing theme that comes through Camille Claudel's first letter is the author's feeling of persecution. This provides the basic structuring principle behind the writing of this excerpt, and produces fascinating textual effects because of its complex, intertwined relationship with the truth of her life situation. The text can simultaneously be held to be characterized by a delusional sense of order, being 'systematized' in nature, and chaos, by being the unbridled expression of a powerful and true affective experience. Claudel's writing is fraught with paradoxes, but its apparently contradictory nature must be supported. We must tolerate the insanity of the narrative in order to reach its sanity, and we must identify how the system works in order to observe those points in the text where it breaks down, representing, in fact, moments of breakthrough. Here, the writing subject oscillates between two positions which will be examined in turn: first, that of the overdetermination of the internal world, as a result of which reality is abandoned; and second, the 'real' injustice of life experiences, which lend their themes to the delusions.

In the first case, the textual signs and symptoms that betray the writer's pathological state of mind render it restricted and closed, stifled and stifling, repetitive, and frustrating to read. The system imposed on the world depicted in these pieces of writing is excessively reductive, where all is brought down to the persecutory figure of Rodin, and the meaning of 'real' events repeatedly shackled to a reality-sidelining system. In the second, we shall see that the sense of order imposed on the world is in fact never complete, because this ordering, described by psychoanalysis as an attempt at reparation, fails. Always bubbling beneath the surface is the devastating immediacy of the psychic experience, of the breakdown of manageable relations with other human beings. The frustrating reality of existence as a woman artist, barely able to make her way in a society antagonistic to her talent, provides sufficient motivation to pass over the shared reality of other people, and to create a new order of truth as a means of holding on to a sense of one's value as a human being. Despite the imposition of a reductive system, there is also strong evidence here of what Freud poetically terms 'the irruption of the repressed', and it is here that we can bear witness to the real writerly drama of the text.[36] Claudel's letter is a text that breaks out of its own system, because the affective event it relates is rooted in an authentic experience. It is this rootedness that can lead us to a sympathetic reading of the delusion as metaphor in this text: the beliefs put forward, as part of a restrictive and limiting system, in fact function as symbols or metaphors representative of real injustices. This text is discomforting, bewildering, and even tedious and repetitive to read at times, and the 'irruption of the repressed' challenges the reader's comforting assurance of her own subjectivity—from a position of sanity—in relation to the text. It invites her to participate actively in the construction

---

[36] Freud (1911–13: 68); Barthes (1973: 22–3). Barthes describes the 'writerly' text as 'celui qui met en état de perte, celui qui déconforte [...], fait vaciller les assises historiques, culturelles, psychologiques, du lecteur, la consistance de ses goûts, de ses valeurs et de ses souvenirs, met en crise son rapport au langage'.

of meaning, which in contrast to the pathologizing reading of the psychiatrist, who would reduce meaning to a constellation of symptoms, will be left open, and will lead us to a new level of understanding and indeed tolerance of the psychotic experience.

The textual paralysis of systematized delusions

According to the psychoanalytical description of paranoia, what has occurred here is that the erstwhile love object has been set up as the persecutor. The passionate love once felt for the figure of 'Rodin' has been repressed, and, having been unconsciously contradicted and transformed into hate feelings, is then projected onto an external figure and experienced as persecution. In this piece of writing the system imposed on events is simple and seemingly uncreative: Rodin is an enemy, and almost every other character invoked is in league with him. These malevolent figures are set in opposition to the 'je' of the text, the only benign 'other' figure being the addressee of the letter, Paul. At the beginning, Paul is addressed explicitly via the pronoun 'tu'; in the middle section, as the 'moi' of the text grows progressively more enmeshed in the terrifying story of her own victimization, the enemy figures are foregrounded; and in the concluding section the addressee 'tu' reappears as if to signal a return to a sense of equilibrium.

Several different figures appear as persecutory agents, and these range from very vague references to groups, such as 'les admirateurs' in the second line of the text, to specific, real individuals such as '[le] sieur Rodin', 'Collin', and 'le sieur Hébrardt [*sic*]'. These figures are not developed as 'characters' as such, but are portrayed as one-dimensional persecutory figures that function as ciphers to indicate that nuisance actions are being carried out. For example, the complexity of the real relationship with Rodin is left aside, for the historical person has come to represent the external force responsible for Claudel's terrible suffering. The repeated use of the title 'sieur' in these lines is also surely ironic, and strikes the reader as archaic, almost courtly language used to sardonic effect, the result being to further undermine and pour scorn on these hateful figures.[37]

---

[37] French dictionaries identify one of the uses of the term 'sieur' as being ironic: 'S'emploie par mépris ou par plaisanterie, dans le langage ordinaire'. GD: 697.

These malicious characters are frequently evoked in the plural, and are also portrayed as being friends among themselves, implying a conspiratorial factor in their relationship. They are referred to as 'ces gens-là'; 'les autres'; 'ses copains les artistes chics'; 'divers individus'; 'd'autres peintres et sculpteurs'. The use of the adverb 'là' in the expressions 'ces gens-là' and 'celui-là' is a reinforced use of the demonstratives 'ces' and 'celui', and imposes a sense of distance between the speaking 'je' and her perceived persecutors, very definitely in her mind forces coming from the outside, beyond the reach of her control or will.

Where the state of affairs presented here is narrated in rather simple, one-dimensional terms, Claudel's artwork finds means other than words to represent complexity between relationships. The same system that limits her capacity to write fuels her artistic creativity. Claudel's sculpture *L'Âge mûr*, produced between 1894 and 1895, depicts a group of three figures that represent different stages of life. The central mature male figure is held in the grasp of a heavily draped, deathly old woman, and is simultaneously entreated through an imploring gesture by a young female nude. Such characters are not developed, in the literary sense, for they represent the universal experience of ageing and the appeal and seduction of youth. The relationship between the figures is, however, worked out in an intensely complex way. The male is held firmly in the grip of a powerful, rough and manly pair of female hands, and the group is drawn towards the abyss of death. The man's hand has slipped from the tender clutches of a nubile and appealing young woman, whose posture is weak and open where her elder counterpart's is enclosing and oppressive. The man's face turns agonizingly away from her gaze, and abandons the youth.

One reading of this image could be that it presents the original affective incident that lies behind both the composition of this sculpture and the paranoid structure of the text. The young Claudel, despite the appeal of youth and beauty, unable to entice Rodin away from the clutches of another woman, whose status has been made significant through time and the ageing process through which the young woman has not yet lived. This ordering of the world is reconstructed in the text where love is transformed into hatred through rejection, and is experienced as persecution. Claudel's three-dimensional work is traditionally viewed as a repetition in art of her own drama at the moment of composition, a view confirmed by her brother Paul: 'une œuvre de Camille Claudel est [...] une espèce de monument de la pensée intérieure, la touffe d'un thème proposé à tous les rêves.'[38] However, this reading of the image could be expanded to view the protagonist as all three characters. The young figure is Claudel, denied the person she desires by the older woman. But this image also has a prophetic quality that prefigures Claudel the older woman clinging to the memory of Rodin, whom she will never release from the grasp of her internal world. And the figure of Rodin, held in another's grip, mirrors the 'je' of the text, trapped by a restricting and delusional system of belief.[39]

Some of the other ill-intentioned characters in the text are the typical stuff of paranoid delusion and indeed conspiracy theory: 'francs-maçons' and 'huguenots'. These figures, too, are all portrayed in terms of affiliation, and a single poorly constructed sentence contains suggestions that there are links of fraternity or friendship between two indistinct groups: 'Le même jour **le sieur Picard** vit chez moi un monument que j'étais en train de faire et le passa à ses bons **copains** les **sculpteurs**, on partage en **frères** entre **francs-maçons**.' Simon's comments on the writing of paranoiacs resonates with these aspects of Claudel's writing:

> Ces aliénés ont un langage qui leur est essentiellement propre et qu'on rencontre identiquement chez la plupart d'entre eux: les Jésuites, les francs-maçons les persécutent; ils sont en butte à la malveillance des *médecins*; une bande les poursuit dont le *chef* joue dans leur esprit un rôle considérable et qu'ils désignent fréquemment par cette appellation générique.[40]

---

[38] Claudel (1905: 276).

[39] Anne Pingeot (2002: 939) discusses the idea that Claudel's *Âge mûr* represents the sculptor's own predicament. This reading of the piece as an autobiographical expression is, of course, only one approach. Counter-readings—or expanded readings—of the same work do exist. In a different discussion of the piece Pingeot (1988: 73) argues that the image is at once personal and indicative of a more universal truth, and was influenced by contemporary artistic trends:

La seconde moitié du XIXe siècle voit se développer en plein air, un art funéraire réservé, aux siècles précédents, à l'intérieur des lieux de culte. De véritables statues, figures allégoriques ou portraits des défunts, marquent le lieu de la sépulture, assurent le souvenir du disparu et parfois même donnent au spectateur la possibilité de s'identifier à celui-ci.

Ainsi peut-on lire le groupe de Camille Claudel de la façon suivante. Le défunt c'est Rodin entraîné par la Mort (la figure de vieille femme est à rapprocher, par exemple, de 'La Patrie' du Départ des volontaires de Rude, du Génie de la guerre de Rodin ou de 'La Mort' sur le Tombeau du Maréchal de Saxe par Pigalle). Perdu pour l'Amour, il l'est aussi pour l'Art. Désespérée, la figure de jeune femme—autoportrait de Camille mais aussi allégorie de l'Inspiration—le laisse à son destin. Cette 'Implorante' est voisine des figures de Douleur présentes dans les compositions allégoriques qui se multiplient sur les tombeaux des grands cimetières parisiens à la fin du XIXe siècle.

[40] Simon (1888: 322).

In addition to powerful organized groups such as the Freemasons and the Huguenots, the writer feels pursued by 'une bande', an indistinct group headed up by Rodin, and indeed Claudel very frequently invokes the same words, or uses synonyms, to designate these figures. Frequent reference is made to Rodin's 'copains' or 'frères', and to her persecution by 'sculpteurs' and 'artistes'. These disparate figures are arranged into groups, producing a picture of complete alienation, of one individual alone against the whole world. 'Le sieur Hébrardt [*sic*]' is accompanied by 'les brigands de son acabit'; 'divers individus' are thought to be profiting from Claudel's ideas; 'tout le monde' is making money out of her work, with the important qualifying statement: 'excepté à moi'. On a paradigmatic level we note a certain metaphorical disability: just as the system that restricts and observes her—the asylum and the clinician—reduces all of her utterances to their system called 'délire de persécution', so a limited view of the world is produced by the inability to select and substitute signs and to apply a multiplicity of meanings. This is because, in terms of their function in the text, every external figure equals Rodin. However, at the same time we can observe metonymic hyperactivity on a syntagmatic level: all these figures, in reality disparate, are presented in terms of connection, affiliation, and influence.[41]

Claudel does give very precise examples of occasions where she claims that specific objects have been stolen from her, or times when those around her have been used in Rodin's schemes, such as the time she claims 'une femme de ménage me donnait un narcotique dans mon café', and subsequently stole various sculptures. However, in many ways this piece does not conform to the clinical picture, and is potentially less systematized than we have initially seen. Indeed, what undermines the internal consistency of Claudel's complaint here is the juxtaposition of apparently specific references with vague statements. For example, we have the occasion where a child stole an idea from the sculptor, followed by an estimation of how much money this cost expressed through a definite sum of money: 100,000 francs. However, the sentence is begun

---

[41] Jakobson (1971: 67–96) observes that aphasia is characterized by either a similarity disorder, problems with selection and substitution (paradigmatic axis), or a contiguity disorder, problems with combination and contexture (syntagmatic axis). Where a disorder such as schizophrenia might be overactive in terms of paradigmatic connection and deficient on a syntagmatic level, producing 'nonsense' utterances, paranoia represents syntagmatic overactivity, where combination is imposed to the point of juxtaposition, which is the reason the combination of the figures in this story reveal it to be written by an individual with a disturbed view of the world.

with the confusingly imprecise reference: 'Un [*sic*] autre année', instead of a definite date.

The repetition of terminology identified by Simon as being typical of such writing is a feature of Claudel's text that applies to the use of nouns to designate groups, such as Rodin's 'copains'. It can also be seen in the manner in which key verbs are used to create an image of violation. One striking example is the repeated use of the verb 'pénétrer' to describe the literal event of individuals breaking into her home: 'L'année dernière, mon voisin [...] **pénétrait** chez moi avec une fausse clef'; '[...] la femme **pénétrait** dans mon cabinet de toilette'. The use of this verb is deceptively concrete, and is revelatory of the devastatingly profound psychic event taking place. The writer of these lines creates a sense of terror, that she is literally cornered, persecuted, and harassed. Her life is threatened, and the feeling that others are stealing her livelihood is terrifyingly real, so as to be unbearable. The use of the verb 'pénétrer' exposes the feeling that the speaker's very sense of self is under threat, that her inability to live and work effectively is caused by the malicious actions of others. It is ironic that her brother Paul should choose the very same term to describe the event that Camille feared: her incarceration.

Un beau jour, les employés de l'hôpital **pénétrèrent** par le fond de la pièce et mirent la main sur l'habitante terrifiée qui depuis longtemps les attendait au milieu de plâtres et de glaises desséchées. [...] Dehors, l'ambulance attendait.[42]

The picture we have of the world through this first piece of writing is of one divided sharply in two: there is the figure of 'je' or 'moi' set in direct opposition to the figure of the 'other(s)': 'il'; 'lui'; 'ils'; 'on'. The benign addressee of the letter, Paul, is not simply a neutral character. He is clearly portrayed as a defender of the speaker, but one who only appears in the opening and concluding sections of the letter—if we can really speak of there being a beginning and an end—and who is not rendered as a character on an equal footing with Camille. There is little to imply that this is really a text in dialogue, for the character 'Paul' is given orders and instructed on how to act, and there is no hint of an awareness of his complicity in the decision that will lead to her perpetual detention. It is as though this possibility is not one that can even be entertained, so necessary is his participation and support in the struggle to defend Camille from those who are causing her downfall: the real

[42] Claudel (1951: 277).

tragedy, however, is that her closest allies are her true enemies. The bossy commands given to Paul are indicative of an intense and controlling relationship, one that had become obsolete for this brother but that remains in Camille's mind. She uses imperatives such as: 'Garde tout cela pour toi'; 'méfie-toi'; and twice repeats the command: 'tu leur diras'. The use of the unambiguous future tense as opposed to the more 'vraisemblable'—given the subject under discussion—conditional tense is again indicative of the lack of insight the writer has into her own difference of mind, and how this is perceived by others. As the torturing shadow of death hangs over the characters depicted in her sculpture, her words in dialogue here are dead weight.

The metaphorical truth of delusions

We have seen therefore that the paranoid system structuring this piece of writing is on one level excessively reductive. Psychiatrists through history have observed that such texts, in contrast to the disintegration and nonsensical effect characteristic of the schizophrenic text, are constructed via a system that has reeled out of control.[43] However, the text also breaks out of its own system, which is shattered by the force of the affective experience being related. As Freud hints, at the end of his analysis of Judge Schreber's memoir, there is perhaps truth in delusion, and it remains to be seen where that truth lies. Arguably, a reductive system of meaning exists simultaneously in this text with that which has been repressed, which makes inroads into this order of meaning. It is the experience of rejection, failure, and injustice that is repressed, and it is this emergent truth that is unsettling and destabilizing for the reader who has initially been able to reassuringly distance her sane point of view from the paranoid one evident here. Reality is unbearable, just as the image of 'woman' brought out in this piece of correspondence is, as we shall now see, dislocated and dislocating. In this sense, the claims made in this excerpt must be read as metaphorical expressions of real repression and the annihilation of the self by the world.

We are presented with a chaotic series of images of women, in the form of Claudel's sculptures, which to varying degrees represent the

---

[43] For an exploration of the incoherent language forms characteristic of 'schizophrenia', see Lacan (1931).

experiences related by the writer. Several figures are referred to: 'Les Causeuses'; 'Petite Cheminée'; 'L'Âge mûr'; 'Femme en jaune'; 'une femme avec une biche'; and 'femme à la croix'. Some of these titles are underlined, some placed in inverted commas, and some inserted in the text without emphasis. These images of females are successively presented as being stolen, copied, abused, and potentially destroyed, and the artist's integrity is progressively undermined. The 'Causeuses' are appropriated for illegal profit: 'divers individus s'en servent'. The 'Petite Cheminée' is copied and cheapened by counterfeit images being exhibited 'dans tout Paris', and her 'Femme en jaune' is shamelessly copied and the source of profit for others.

The image of 'woman' as depicted in these images, which are passed between disrespectful hands and put to work to the profit of others, and that of the artist who finds herself repeatedly to be the loser in the story, is dislocated because it is wrenched from the position of merit and recognition that it deserves. However, these ideas are also dislocating for the modern reader, who knows the recognition the figure of Claudel has now been given, and the huge value of an estate that has been generated by a veritable Claudel industry since the 1980s. This unsettles and challenges the reader, and places her in a position of tension as a potential sympathetic re-evaluator of this person's written production: for every person who writes about her is working in the context of a well-established tradition, and could profit both financially and in personal recognition from making Claudel's work better known. Irrespective of the critical appreciation of Claudel's sculpture, if Claudel's current status in art history is a reliable indicator, she deserved both recognition and financial remuneration. In her lifetime both would prove elusive, and she was right to feel exploited.

Towards the end of this first letter we are told: 'Le **mécanisme** est facile à comprendre.' The 'system' previously discussed is directly alluded to here as a mechanism to which facts, or events experienced, can be easily reduced. Crucially, however, we are also informed, in a following sentence, 'elle se refuse à ce **système**-là'. This is the system that others impose: that which says a woman of genius is an aberration, which dictates when she should be deprived of her freedom, and which prescribes what a woman should want and reasonably expect. This system is defied by the psychotic process, and is the one to which female sanity defers.

Camille instructs Paul to tell those whom she accuses: 'Vous lui devez quelque chose pour tout ce que vous lui avez pris depuis des années'. We too owe something to the legacy of Claudel: to believe her when she says she has been robbed. However, a striking detail contained in this letter that could almost be passed over is the marginal annotation, placed between two paragraphs describing the theft of her work, which reads: 'c'est moi la voleuse'. The use of the stressed pronoun 'moi' and the noun, marked as feminine to produce the unsettling concept, by analogy with her unnatural status as a woman of genius, 'voleuse', turns the tables on the male figures presented in the preceding paragraph as violators. It betrays an underlying anxiety of authorship, a sense that the appreciation of her own self-worth has fallen drastically, and a sense of doubt about the importance of the artist's work.

The strange assertion 'C'est moi la voleuse' is an indication of what later psychoanalytical thinking identifies as being at the root of ideas of grandeur: feelings of low self-worth are the result of humiliation in childhood and constitute a motivation to construct a new reality based on a foundation of the over-evaluation of the self. Arguably, however, this only constitutes a valuing of a self undervalued by society, and indeed the other way this statement could be read is as her perception of 'their' accusation. Here is a point in the text where the reader appears to be obliged to construct meaning out of a perplexing statement: if we read this statement as meaning 'they say I stole it from them', it reinforces the narrator's status as thief or disrupter of that value system. The belief that Rodin and others have singled her out at least gives Claudel a sense of status: if somebody is at pains to make her suffer, it means that she is worth persecuting.

While the common view in paranoia is that delusions of persecution develop into delusions of grandeur, the suggestion that the ideas propounded in this text are those of a megalomaniac is a thornier issue. The paranoid structure of this letter can be shown to exist on both a superficial and a more profound level, but ideas of grandeur are, in the case of a potentially great artist, difficult to disentangle from the narrative of greatness and genius that surrounds the person of Camille Claudel, both the living person before her dramatic disappearance from the public eye and the enduring mythical figure she has become in recent years. If Claudel can be said to have held ideas of grandeur, it is because she claimed her work was copied, and more important than it was perceived to be. But there is more than a grain of truth in this claim. Lhermitte and Allilaire do say that Rodin probably signed some of Claudel's sculptures, and it seems to be little contested that she contributed to some of his major works for which Rodin alone received credit. There is also evidence that sculptures exist, in various parts of the world that Claudel produced but which have been attributed to Rodin.[44] However, these psychiatrists suggest that to believe anything Claudel says is to enter into some form of 'folie à deux': '*A fortiori*, devant un délirant, celui ou celle qui est convaincu peut aller jusqu'à adhérer au délire de l'autre et, même, le renforcer (délire à deux).'[45] If Claudel rages at those who 'exposent effrontément mes œuvres et se font de l'argent avec sous la direction du sieur Rodin', it is because this claim bears an uncanny resemblance to what was probably the truth: her artistic production, and that of other sculptors who worked for Rodin, had in some measure been stolen from them because it remained, and remains, unacknowledged.

In 1877, Lasègue and Falret contributed an article entitled 'La Folie à deux' to the *Archives générales de médecine*, in which they argue that the difference between an error of judgement and a delusion is that the former can be corrected by persuasion, through reasoned argument, and the latter cannot.[46] One way of proceeding is for the modern reader to enter into a pact of complicity with Claudel's text, and to consciously

---

[44] Lhermitte (1984: 181). These psychiatrists argue that, since it was common practice for established artists—particularly sculptors—to use assistants in their work, Claudel's complaints are largely unjustified. If these assistants were not acknowledged, since the overall artistic direction of the work was assumed by one artist, it follows that Claudel's suggestion that her work was stolen is both true and false. Her work, and that of others in Rodin's studio, was accredited by the art world as the work of Rodin. However, in this text the feeling of having been cheated is translated into the accusation of Rodin having literally, physically stolen work from her studio, which is unlikely to have happened. However, some of Claudel's sculptures have been attributed to Rodin, which in retrospect lends a certain credibility to her accusation:

Les nombreuses années de Camille passées au service de Rodin furent vécues généreusement dans l'indivision artistique [...] La *Tête d'esclave* en terre cuite, aux yeux clos et à la bouche criante, sera signée par Camille et fondue par Alexis Rudier après la rupture, sous la signature de Rodin. *L'Homme aux bras croisés*, terre cuite conservée à Villeneuve, réapparaît avec ses yeux caves sous la signature de Rodin; au musée de Philadelphie avec le titre *Figure assise*, au musée de San Francisco sous le nom de *Petite Tête d'homme* dite aussi *Giganti*. Quant au vrai Giganti de Camille, un exemplaire en bronze est encore exposé aujourd'hui au musée de Brême sous le nom usurpé de Rodin. (Paris 1990: 34)

Morhardt (cited in Bouté 1995: 24–5) also suggests that Claudel's contribution to Rodin's *Porte de l'Enfer* was significant: '[elle] pose, elle compose; elle prête son corps à plus d'une damnée et plusieurs figures sont probablement à sa main'.

[45] Lhermitte (1984: 169).

[46] Lasègue (1877: 1).

cross the threshold into a 'folie à deux': Claudel's writing therefore challenges the reader's sanity and destabilizes our values and truths, and invites us to ascribe meaning to the authentic human experience lying behind the disturbing expression of paranoid ideas. In this sense, the paranoid text can be argued to be a metaphorical representation of historical reality.

Claudel was not, as is evidenced by comments made by critics of her work, just another workshop assistant. Her talent was outstanding, and Rodin recognized this. And it is also true that by any standard her destiny as a human being was wretched: one cannot help but feel that she was talented enough to be financially independent, and yet she still lived in poverty. This, exacerbated by the stress of the rupture with Rodin, caused her to place herself in self-imposed solitary confinement in her home. From this point, it is difficult to see how Claudel could have been brought out of her living hell. It is therefore essential for us to validate what in this context can be read as believable assertions: Claudel feels robbed; she feels unsupported; and most of all she knows that she is a brilliant artist, has worked relentlessly for years, and yet has nothing to show for it. These are compelling claims, but the narrative within which they find expression is, according to the shared reality of the sane world, a delusional one. This weaving of the truth of her experience into a fictional narrative of immediate threat and danger compels the reader to disentangle the threads of Claudel's utterance in order to establish the truth of what she was trying to express to us.

The predominant feeling that pervades the lines of this letter is one of immediate threat, which is a facet of the paranoid text that Lacan points up in his thesis: 'Ces phénomènes [. . .] se présentent dans la conscience avec une portée *convictionnelle* immédiate, une signification *objective d'emblée* ou [. . .] un caractère de *hantise*.'[47] Claudel makes three claims that can be read as metaphorical representations of events in her life: Rodin has stolen from her; other artists have copied her work; and she has not received sufficient financial remuneration for her efforts. The overall effect of these accusations is a sense of depletion, produced because the world has drained her of money, time, work, and emotional resources, and she has received nothing in return. The verbs used to describe the actions of enemy figures in this text reveal precisely how

---

[47] Lacan (1975a: 346).

they are portrayed as agents that lessen the narrator's ability to succeed in life and work. Many of these verbs fall within the general paradigm of destruction, violation, and diminution: 'pour **pousser** l'ironie jusqu'au bout'; 'le gredin **s'empare de** toutes mes sculptures'; 'il les **donne** à ses copains'; 'il a **ruiné** Chacrise'. In addition, the verb 'exposer' is used repeatedly in this piece, in the concrete sense of works of art being exhibited, but interestingly betrays a sense of violation of the speaker's sense of self: 'les autres qui **exposent** [...] mes œuvres'; 'une Suédoise [...] qui depuis cette époque **expose** tous les ans [...] et bien d'autres peintres et sculpteurs qui **exposent** des "Potins" "conversations"'; 'il a fait plusieurs femmes en jaune [...] qu'il a **exposées**'. The common theme running through these claims is that of others exhibiting works that in some way resemble Claudel's own. This creates a powerful feeling of distorted and uncontrolled exposure, in a way that diminishes her position of hegemony in relation to her artistic production, and a sense of being negated as a person through not being acknowledged.

Claudel's *Causeuses*, created in 1895, portrays the scene of two pairs of women seated opposite each other on two benches, as if in a train carriage. These figures appear to be holding an intimate conversation, three of them being positioned facing a fourth speaker. The sense of intimacy and complicity between women depicted here is harshly and ironically reversed in the text, where it is transformed into spiteful and bitter accusations against female colleagues. Rather than a spirit of cooperation and support, what is disclosed here is a sense of fierce competition and sheer struggle for survival, of each woman for herself, which is a dimension of human relations that might be latently present in the image of the *Causeuses*, but which is only brought to the fore in this piece of text. This lack of a sense of sisterhood with other artists seems to place Claudel in an anti-feminist position, which reflects that avowedly taken by writers of the Decadent movement such as Rachilde. As we have seen, Claudel's *L'Âge mûr* depicts a typically Decadent vision of woman as dangerous and monstrous, who in her youth and old age overpowers and fatally threatens the central male protagonist of the narrative. Claudel's self-imposed isolation, her representation of woman as dangerous and destructive, and her wilful sabotage of any sense of sorority and support between herself and other women artists echoes the inefficacy and implosion of the women's movement towards the end of the Belle Époque in France. However, although Rachilde claimed not to be a feminist, as Porter argues her writing is an important indicator of the mood of the times for women, as 'several of her novels dramatise a

feminine protest against gender inequity in important ways'.[48] Similarly, even though Claudel fails to align herself sympathetically with
other women artists, her message about the injustice of the outcome of
her life compared to male artists—and in particular Rodin—is a valid
and important one.

A second verb used repeatedly in this piece is 'rapporter', and particularly noticeable is the emphatic repetition of the expression 'rapport au
bas mot' to imply once again Claudel's own lack of recognition through
financial remuneration for her work. Her sense of vocation is called into
question by employing the notion of bringing back or retrieval of a prize
collected by somebody else: 'Ma prétendue vocation lui en a **rapporté!**'.
And the reward that Claudel is denied is extended to others also: 'ces
modèles qui **rapportent** à tout le monde excepté à moi'. The attempt to
appear plausible and rooted in reality is made evident through the use of
concrete numerical figures such as the '300,000F' Rodin is accused of
having made from Claudel's stolen works, and is set in ironic contrast to
the simple calculation of her own earnings: '0 + 0 = 0'. The money is
instead portrayed as passing through the hands of everybody else, and
the writer's consistent use of hyperbole accentuates her position as the
loser in all this: 'ce sont des millions qui roulent, pour les fondeurs, les
mouleurs, les artistes et les marchands'. Indeed, everybody else profits
and Claudel only loses: 'je refuse de leur donner ces modèles qui
rapportent à tout le monde excepté à moi'. For her 'Femme en
jaune', big money for lesser artists: '**rapport** au bas mot = 100,000^f;
for the thief of her 'Femme à la croix': 'rapport = 100,000^f.

While the ideas expressed here are to some extent reduced to a
system, that of the conviction of persecution, its written format lacks
structure to the extent that the editors of Claudel's *Correspondance* are
not even sure in which order the pages should appear. The sentences are
badly formed, and lack punctuation and stylistically coherent connections between clauses. Ideas and threats spill onto the page uncensored,
and afterthoughts or reasoned arguments rarely appear in any cogent
way. The overall appearance of the letter stands in contrast to the
depiction of these individuals as an organized group, and a powerful
force to be reckoned with. This contributes to the overall feeling of
depletion and weakening of the central figure, the 'moi' of this text,
which is consonant with the common notion that the psychotic experience entails a disturbance of the mental integrity of the subject.

[48] Laurence M. Porter, 'Decadence and the *fin de siècle* novel', in Unwin (1997: 104).

The final chaotic impression with which we are left is that of the ambivalent feelings associated with, on the one hand, seeking an advocate in the figure of Paul, and, on the other, a profound anxiety of exposure. The emphatic imperative 'Tu leur **diras**', from a preceding paragraph, is flatly contradicted in the final line of the letter: 'Ne parle de rien et surtout ne **dis** pas de nom'. This expression of a need to feel protected and concealed also contrasts with the metaphorical presentation of herself as 'un chou qui est rongé par les chenilles'. As soon as she grows and produces leaves that are viable, her enemies eat these up. That she is kept hidden from view is presented paradoxically as an adverse position and one that is desired. This reveals the chaotic, constantly shifting, insecure sense of her own integrity: a far more complex picture than that appreciated by doctors, who for thirty years routinely recorded her mental state as unchanging and unchanged, stuck in the rut of a 'délire de persécution'.[49] This paradoxical position mirrors Lamotte's professed desire to remain concealed: the act of writing is evidence of a strong revelatory and indeed emancipatory agenda, and yet the writing subject fears exposure like the terror of annihilation.

This first piece of writing is ordered because it does evince structural patterns that conform to the description of the systematized delusions common to paranoid mindsets. However, there is arguably as much 'reality', in experiential terms, behind the 'crazy' ideas propounded by Claudel in her private letters, as madness. The affective experience related is therefore characterized by paradox, and this invites the reader to disentangle the existential reality that constitutes the motivating factor behind the text's construction. The author's use of metaphor can be heavy-handed and reductive, and even unconscious; 'Rodin' and other menacing figures are interchangeable figures. However, the text is also highly creative in its handling of metaphor, for tragic, real-life experience is rendered in a delusional construct that bolsters the writer's subjectivity. Perhaps it is more bearable to believe that you are persecuted because you and your work are important, than to accept that you have been abandoned and forgotten. The system imposed on the interpretation of external events produces a stifled, stunted, and tortured view of the world: a view that had once fired her creative zeal and had provided the experiential matter behind the production of such works as *L'Âge mûr*.

[49] See n. 21.

Here is the case of an objectively brilliant artist who passionately loved Rodin, in everybody's reality, and in this text the fullness of this encounter is experienced instead as persecution and loss. For the last thirty years of her life Claudel was not free, was prevented from working by the symbolic restriction that her incarceration represented, and who would never in her lifetime know the extent her fame and fortune would reach in our times. If she says that she feels robbed, it is because she was robbed; if she says she feels persecuted by Rodin, it is because he neglected her and left her behind, while she never managed to purge his memory from her mind; if she says she feels other artists profit from her failure, it might be because others managed to exist in a world that she could not bear. Perhaps, also, on a more global level Claudel speaks on behalf of a generation of women artists who struggled to be accepted and whose achievements were limited by the inequitable social conditions imposed upon them.

CAMILLE CLAUDEL TO DR MICHAUX, 25 JUNE 1917 OR 1918

Being written four or five years after Claudel's internment, the context of the next letter differs considerably from the first one discussed. It is a letter from Claudel to the doctor who diagnosed her illness and who fulfilled part of the requirement according to the law of 1838, with her family's agreement, for her 'placement volontaire'. Ironically, perhaps, the principal theme of this piece of writing is the less than 'voluntary' nature of Claudel's detention, for she is writing to ask Dr Michaux to act on her behalf in order to help secure her release. The central speaking 'je' here mirrors the position occupied by the 'implorante' of *L'Âge mûr*, engaged in dialogue with her oppressor. This piece of writing contrasts greatly with the first one examined, in that it is clearly structured and seems to have been written during a period of less acute mental disturbance than the first. It remains clear, however, that Claudel's ideas of persecution have not been relinquished.

Monsieur le Docteur,

Vous ne vous souvenez peut-être plus de votre ex-cliente et voisine, Melle Claudel, qui fut enlevée de chez elle le 3 mars 1913 et transportée dans les asiles d'aliénés d'où elle ne sortira peut-être jamais. Cela fait cinq ans, bientôt six, que je subis cet affreux martyre. Je fus d'abord transportée dans l'asile d'aliénés de Ville-Evrard puis, de là, dans celui de Montdevergues près Montfavet (Vaucluse). Inutile de vous dépeindre quelles furent mes souffrances. J'ai écrit dernièrement à monsieur Adam, avocat, à qui vous aviez bien voulu me recommander, et qui a plaidé autrefois pour moi avec tant de succès; je le prie de vouloir bien s'occuper de moi. Mais dans cette circonstance vos bons conseils me seraient nécessaires car vous êtes un homme de grande expérience et comme docteur en médecine très au courant de la question. Je vous prie donc de vouloir bien causer de moi avec monsieur Adam et réfléchir à ce que vous pourriez faire pour moi. Du côté de ma famille il n'y a rien à faire; sous l'influence de mauvaises personnes, ma mère, mon frère et ma sœur n'écoutent que les calomnies dont on m'a couverte.

On me reproche (ô crime épouvantable) d'avoir vécu toute seule, de passer ma vie avec des chats, d'avoir la manie de la persécution! C'est sur la foi de ces accusations que je suis incarcérée depuis 5 ans 1/2 comme une criminelle, privée de liberté, privée de nourriture, de feu et des plus élémentaires commodités. J'ai expliqué à monsieur Adam, dans une longue lettre les autres motifs qui ont contribué à mon incarcération, je vous prie de la lire attentivement pour vous rendre compte des tenants et aboutissants de cette affaire.

Peut-être pourriez-vous comme docteur en médecine user de votre influence en ma faveur. Dans tous les cas, si on ne veut pas me rendre ma liberté de suite, je préfèrerais être transférée à la Salpêtrière ou à Ste-Anne ou dans un hôpital ordinaire où vous puissiez venir me voir et vous rendre compte de ma santé. On donne ici pour moi 150 f par mois et il faut voir comme je suis traitée, mes parents ne s'occupent pas de moi et ne répondent à mes plaintes que par le mutisme le plus complet, ainsi on fait de moi ce qu'on veut. C'est affreux d'être abandonnée de cette façon, je ne puis résister au chagrin qui m'accable. Enfin j'espère que vous pourrez faire quelque chose pour moi et il est bien entendu que si vous avez quelques frais à faire, vous voudrez bien en faire la note et je vous rembourserai intégralement.

J'espère que vous n'avez pas eu de malheur à déplorer par suite de cette maudite guerre, que m^r votre fils n'a pas eu à souffrir dans les tranchées et que Madame Michaux et vos deux jeunes filles sont en bonne santé. Il y a une chose que je vous demande aussi, c'est quand vous irez dans la famille Merklen, de dire à tout le monde ce que je suis devenue.

Maman et ma sœur ont donné l'ordre de me séquestrer de la façon la plus complète, aucune de mes lettres ne part, aucune visite ne pénètre.

À la faveur de tout cela, ma sœur s'est emparée de mon héritage et tient beaucoup à ce que je ne sorte jamais de prison. Aussi je vous prie de ne pas m'écrire ici et de ne pas dire que je vous ai écrit, car je vous écris en secret contre les règlements de l'établissement et si on le savait, on me ferait bien des ennuis!

Si quelquefois, vous croyez possible de venir me voir, comme mon docteur, cela me ferait bien plaisir de causer avec vous; en vous adressant au docteur

Clément, il vous donnerait l'autorisation. Enfin je m'en remets à votre sagesse et à votre inspiration; mais je n'y compte pas beaucoup car ici c'est bien loin et vous êtes toujours si occupé que je doute que vous puissiez entreprendre un pareil voyage.

Je vous en prie faites tout ce que vous pourrez pour moi car vous m'avez montré plusieurs fois que vous aviez beaucoup de prudence et j'ai bien confiance en vous.

Recevez, monsieur le Docteur, mes meilleurs souvenirs

C. Claudel

Je dois vous mettre en garde contre les balivernes dont on se sert pour prolonger ma séquestration. On prétend que l'on va me laisser enfermée jusqu'à la fin de la guerre; c'est une blague et un moyen de m'abuser par de fausses promesses car cette guerre-là n'est pas pour finir et d'ici-là je serai finie moi-même: Ah! si vous saviez ce qu'il faut endurer? c'est à faire frémir!

Si quelquefois je ne pouvais plus vous écrire veuillez tout de même ne pas m'abandonner et agir si vous pouvez le plus tôt possible

Ce qui gêne dans cette circonstance c'est l'influence secrète des étrangers qui se sont emparés de mon atelier et qui tiennent maman dans leurs griffes pour l'empêcher de venir me voir[50]

In many ways the claims made in this letter are highly plausible, and there is very little in it that can, on a superficial level, be identified as 'delusional'. However, it is the very attempt to do this on the part of the writer, and the way in which the effect of plausibility is achieved textually, that in the alienist doctor's book betrays the madness of its author. Paranoid patients, we are warned, can be very convincing. The effort to appear plausible was termed 'dissimulation' by alienists, and is indicative of the patient's awareness that her ideas are not believed. Sérieux and Capgras tell us: 'La dissimulation est si fréquente qu'on pourrait presque la considérer comme un symptôme.'[51] The close analysis of the process of dissimulation will link Claudel to the three other authors studied in terms of the double bind in which the psychiatric patient is locked: the desperate attempt in writing—through dissimulation—to place oneself outside the category of 'la folie' in fact reinforces one's status as mad.

This piece represents an attempt to construct an illusion of sanity, which on a superficial level fails, but which on the unconscious level of

---

[50] Rivière (2003: 277–9).
[51] Sérieux (1909: 26).

its motivation, and when interpreted on a metaphorical level, succeeds in communicating a compelling story. Two aspects of the excerpt merit further analysis: first, the creation of an effect of plausibility and the attempt to downplay ideas of persecution through dissimulation, a strategy that therefore places the author in the double bind of psychiatric diagnosis; second, the way in which the effect of plausibility breaks down. When this effect breaks down, the text reveals itself as an utterance that invites the reader to construct meaning out of delusions, and to disentangle the persuasive story that lies beneath the disjointed and confusing expression of morbid ideas. This process may appear contradictory, but it reveals that Claudel unconsciously succeeds in what she is attempting to do. Although she fails to appear truly 'sane', there is a metaphorical level of truth in the delusional claims she makes.

The use of dissimulation

As noted in the analysis of the first letter, the psychotic individual is generally held to lack insight into her condition.[52] It is therefore ironic that the existence of dissimulation reveals a painfully clear form of insight on the part of the patient, who knows that her ideas are not endorsed by those with whom she communicates. The mental process revealed through this excerpt is confusing and paradoxical, because it reveals both the existence of insight and the lack of insight: not knowing that one's ideas are objectively incorrect, but knowing that these are disbelieved. It is as though delusional ideas are placed metaphorically under cloches, protected from negation by the sane observer, and the attempt to appear sane is merely a tactic to get out of the asylum.

The effect of plausibility is achieved in part through the placing of the 'je' of the piece in a position of subordination to the addressee. Indeed the opening pronoun of the letter is 'vous', as opposed to the 'je' one might expect, and the author appears keen to display an attitude of humility. In contrast to the process of elevation of the self that supposedly occurs in megalomania, the author reduces the importance of her own status by suggesting: 'Vous ne vous souvenez peut-être plus de votre ex-cliente et voisine'. She defines herself in terms of how she as a patient crossed the doctor's path, rather than in terms of the work she

---

[52] Parant (1888: 219) claims that only 3 out of every 100 patients could be said to have insight into their illness.

had done or the position she occupied in society. The status of this doctor is further strengthened through the repeated use of the pronoun 'vous' followed by the superfluous 'comme docteur en médecine'. The status of the medical profession, where we might expect it to be undermined by an individual held firmly in its grasp, is reinforced. The use of terms of address such as 'Monsieur le Docteur', 'monsieur Adam', and '[le] docteur Clément' reveal a deferential and humble attitude, showing that the tactics of the incarcerated person have changed: where before her detention accusations had flown about uncontrolled, here she realizes that deferring to authority may be a strategy more likely to produce the results she seeks.

The author stresses her own position of subordination, in contrast to the relative might of the medical establishment, through the use of passive constructions and by initially referring to herself in the third person: '**Melle Claudel**, qui fut enlevée de chez elle [. . .] et transportée dans les asiles d'aliénés d'où **elle** ne sortira peut-être jamais.' The writer sets herself up as a plausible victim, the passive object of malevolent actions: 'Je suis **incarcérée** depuis 5 ans 1/2 comme une criminelle, **privée** de liberté, **privée** de nourriture, de feu et des plus élémentaires commodités.' This is a confusing statement from someone whose medical records state that she had refused 'first class' treatment, opting for 'third class' status where patients could cook for themselves. Lhermitte and Allilaire write: 'Parmi les persécutions qu'elle redoutait, l'une s'imposa à elle malgré la protection de l'asile: l'empoisonnement par "la bande à Rodin". Elle se mit à accuser les infirmières d'en être les entremetteuses.'[53] The central contradiction at the heart of these ideas is that, on the one hand, the author portrays a compelling sense of loss and injustice, but on the other, those responsible for her persecution and suffering are always placed at a distance.

Claudel does not in this letter name Rodin, or those she accuses of being in league with him. Aware that these ideas have been repeatedly dismissed, she chooses to keep them concealed: but the dissimulation is unsuccessful. What feels like a lesser accusation, that her family is merely 'sous l'influence de mauvaises personnes', is evidence to the medical eye of delusional ideas: those who actually have some influence over her destiny are portrayed as weak agents, unwittingly taken over by nonspecific, powerful external forces. The opening sentence of the

---

[53] Lhermitte (1984: 171–3).

second paragraph is for this reason extremely important, for it is textual evidence of the double bind in which the asylum resident repeatedly finds herself in the medical textbooks: the claim to be sane is taken as further evidence of madness. We are offered the ironic statement: 'On me reproche (ô crime épouvantable) d'avoir vécu seule, de passer ma vie avec des chats, d'avoir la manie de la persécution!' To the reader, however, the irony of this declaration is in the use of the exclamation mark; this suggests that the addressee might share her sense of indignation and surprise that there is any justification behind her incarceration. Although the reader can easily appreciate the psychiatric assessment of these ideas as paranoid or delusional, there is also a clear and compelling truth being told here. Rouy, Esquiron, and Claudel all protest that their treatment is unwarranted and unpleasant, to say the least. Their vociferous resistance is interpreted straightforwardly as symptomatic of illness. However, in terms of Claudel's personal experience as a result of her family's decision—absolute lack of freedom, creative stasis—the accusation that they are 'sous l'influence de mauvaises personnes' is quite true in terms of the power they have over her life.

The sense that an effort has been made to appear 'normal' is one device that betrays this writing as motivated by a disturbed pattern of thinking. An example of this is the attempt by the author to establish an amicable link between herself and the doctor, through the allusion to his family, which stands out as a desperate attempt to forge a link with the outside world. Her personal approach to Michaux could be part of a strategy to demonstrate how normal and no-longer-inward-looking she is now. The first sentence of the fourth paragraph is marked by the effort to show solidarity with the war effort: 'J'espère que vous n'avez pas eu de malheur à déplorer par suite de cette maudite guerre, que m^r votre fils n'a pas eu à souffrir dans les tranchées'. Although a sense of personal suffering is at the forefront of this tormented mind, she is at pains to demonstrate that her isolation from society is not complete.

The private nature of correspondence leaves the reader with a distinct feeling of discomfort, that one is crossing the public–private boundary, despite the fact that these letters have been published. With this in mind, the author's own thematization of writing, and of its contraband quality, is all the more striking. The knowledge that this letter is now available for anybody to read renders this aspect of the text very poignant. Claudel writes: 'Aussi je vous prie de ne pas m'écrire ici et de ne pas dire que je vous ai écrit, car je vous écris en secret contre les règlements de l'établissement [...].' We as readers are party to something that the words of this letter explicitly repudiate. The putatively sympathetic reader and the addressee of the letter are uncomfortable bedfellows, because we know that this doctor did not act on the requests contained therein, in the way in which its author appears to have wished, and because we know this piece of writing is private.

It is nevertheless true that this piece amounts to a form of primitive cry from the heart that does not fail to move, even if on one level it does fail to convince. Infantilized by an incarcerating system that effectively left patients with the status of a minor, Claudel here plays the role of the child crying out for somebody to care for her. Recalling the way in which Esquiron was infantilized by her father's and then her doctors' disempowering treatment of her as an adult, the verb 's'occuper de' recurs in requests that beg assistance for a helpless person: 'je le prie de vouloir bien **s'occuper de** moi'; 'mes parents ne **s'occupent pas de** moi'. Ultimately, however, the sense we are left with is that Claudel is becoming resigned to her fate, despite the fact that the loss of hope that we glimpse in the opening lines fills her—and her reader—with horror: '[l'asile] d'aliénés d'où elle ne sortira peut-être jamais'. As though the writing of the letter is a process of realization, she finally concedes that even the doctor who signed the documents necessary to have her locked away for what would become the rest of her life, is 'si occupé' that it is unlikely he will be able to help her.

The affective power of breakdown

If the signs of dissimulation, and the construction of an illusion of plausibility, can be read as signs of mental illness, and therefore claims that are universally ignored by the sane majority, then how can we read this writing in terms of its reason for existing? Can we approach such a text and find truth instead of fiction? This is possible if we concede that many of the statements made are straightforwardly correct from almost any perspective, for example: 'je suis incarcérée [...] comme une criminelle'; 'mes parents ne s'occupent pas de moi et ne répondent à mes plaintes que par le mutisme le plus complet'; 'C'est affreux d'être abandonnée de cette façon'; 'ma sœur s'est emparée de mon héritage'. These compelling statements are lost in the mire of paranoia that provides the structuring principle behind the writing of the text, and those who really inflict this suffering are so close to the author of these words that, rather than biting the hand that feeds her, responsibility for the 'chagrin qui [l]'accable' is projected onto another person who had long ago decided to leave her alone: Rodin, and by extension his 'bande' who continue to influence those who should be allies.

Following a piece of writing that partially achieves an effect of plausibility, a most revealing postscript is attached to this letter. This is the part of the letter that strikes the reader as disinhibited: the unbridled expression of pure affect, the articulation of the most basic desires, partially concealed and partially revealed in the first section of the letter. Feelings of rage, fear, desperation, and dark cynicism spill on to the page without order or structure. These sentences or fragments lack punctuation, or are incorrectly punctuated. The most poignant truth evinced by these words, tacked on to another piece of writing that appears to be rather better considered, is that Claudel here puts down on paper an unwitting prophecy that would become her destiny. She knows that she is being lied to: 'On prétend que l'on va me laisser enfermée jusqu'à la fin de la guerre', when in fact she would stay there for the rest of her life. Claudel predicts that she will not survive to see the end of the war: 'd'ici-là je serai finie moi-même'. She did live through the war, but she would be finished before ever leaving the asylum.

This postscript reverses the effect of submission to the addressee that is rather laboured in the main part of the letter, initially by opening with the 'je' we might have expected at the beginning. It is at this point in the text that the absolute breakdown of the dissimulatory system occurs. Claudel writes: 'Je dois vous mettre en garde', selecting the verb 'devoir' which implies obligation, and which also reveals an attitude of urgency towards the situation, previously kept painstakingly at bay. It is the addressee, 'Dr Michaux', who is made the object of the opening clause; the writing 'je', unable to defuse an all-pervasive and devastating fear, takes it upon herself to act against the very serious threat posed by the indistinct figure or group, 'on'. This use of the nonspecific pronoun 'on' is reminiscent of Hersilie Rouy's exclamation: 'le terrible *on* se taira-t-il?'.[54] It also reflects Lamotte's most fragile moments of 'torture', in which the imprecise threat posed by 'on' is that of an agent of suffering and constraint, rather than external forces of help and emancipation. When such a group is portrayed as vague and indistinct, the impression given is of potentially limitless power.

[54] Rouy (1883: 317).

In the following sentence, the 'je' is presented as the object of the verb 'abuser', providing a concrete connection with the image of her sculptures being used and abused in the first letter discussed. The reference to 'fausses promesses', once again a claim with a prophetic quality since the promises made to Claudel would turn out to be ungrounded, reveals a sense of 'déception', with all the strength of its double signification in French, leaving the writer both deceived and disappointed.

The only punctuation marks in the whole short excerpt are exclamation and question marks, the remaining persuasive devices available to the author being exclamatory and interrogative. Perhaps aware that the letter will fail to convince and will fall on deaf ears, as have other communications, this is a final strategy of resistance that acts as an attempt to move its addressee to action. The final two sentences hang alone, almost as distinct paragraphs, and are completely unpunctuated, leaving a strikingly beautiful impression of pure flow of affect. By failing to offer closure with a simple mark of punctuation, or alternatively the ability to leave the text's meaning open, the text refuses to be reduced to an economy of plausibility, respectability, and social conformity.

What she must endure is 'à faire frémir', and the selection of a verb that implies a physical quaking is indicative of the strength of feeling attached to the horrifyingly present experience of being in real fear, and yet being disbelieved. And this fear is so profound because the threat is unknown and unknowable: 'l'influence secrète des étrangers', a power by analogy with the 'on' previously invoked that is absolute. The ones who really keep her imprisoned, such as 'maman', are held in the grip of these stronger powers, as though it is impossibly painful to acknowledge that such cruelty could be inflicted by the person who brought you into the world. As the figure of the 'implorante' begs her addressee, 'veuillez tout de même ne pas m'abandonner', Claudel begs her reader to pick up her story and give it a place in history.

These letters represent yet another example of the 'undecidable' nature of writing by psychiatric patients. The ideas propounded are ordered, as are the beliefs of the paranoiacs described in textbooks of psychiatry, but they also escape the reduction initially imposed because the flow of affect attached to real experiences cannot be contained. Her text suggests that, if Camille Claudel was such a danger to society and to herself that her indefinite detention was warranted, the attitude of disbelief inherent in psychiatric analysis clearly did not encourage her to abandon her 'morbid' beliefs. All that this achieved was a failed attempt to construct an acceptable face of sanity through dissimulation, and it made her all the more intransigent in beliefs that ultimately only harmed her. Many of her claims are true from any perspective: it is awful to be abandoned, and, far from displaying a manifest lack of insight, Claudel in these excerpts demonstrates that she is completely conscious of what is happening to her. Those same textual effects that have her marked out as unsound of mind are the very impressions that reveal the heart of the psychotic experience for the individual suffering it. The sense of isolation and despair in the first letter examined is to some extent self-imposed, as a reaction to the maddening experience of trying to exist in a world that did not give due credit to women artists. It is, however, the experience of incarceration that produces the pure misery of the second letter, which is all the more pitiful for its pathetic attempt to regain a hold on sanity. Within these texts, sanity and insanity hold forth side by side, and each challenges the comfortable knowledge of our own safe position of reason outside of mental illness, and outside the asylum.

These texts invite the reader to oppose the readings offered by 'sane' psychiatrists, and to interpret something other than fictional delusion in the author's treatment of her subject matter. They tell us that being a brilliantly creative woman, in a society that would never allow you to stand on an equal footing with men, could be a mentally shattering experience. Far from stressing the predisposing factors in an individual such as Camille Claudel, the flexible interpretation of delusional ideas as metaphorical expressions of a disappointing reality has shown that when 'real life' is as bad as it was for her, there is a real motivation, as with Rouy's adoption of a new family story, to abandon it and to create your own empowering version of this. Women like Claudel have a very serious point to make about how society created an environment in which their lives would end in tragedy, and for their potential contribution to fall by the wayside. Claudel's story tells us a great deal about her experience as a woman, as an artist, and as a person who suffered mentally, at the mercy of her own ideas and a wider set of power structures that remained deaf to the truth of her utterances until the end of her life. The specificity of her experience, and of those who have a similar story to tell, lies in the fact that she was disempowered by a suspicious and doubting system—a paranoid one—when she and others like her should have been heard. It is for this reason that the narrative of female insanity needs now to take its place in the history of psychiatry.

Conclusion

The verdict reached in the case of Camille Claudel, that the paradoxical nature of the text in question should be acknowledged and validated, can in the final analysis be extended to all the texts we have examined. Two broad conclusions suggest themselves in the final evaluation. The first is that we are left in every case with a negative outcome, in that the stories we have closely scrutinized have told of protagonists who spent years of their lives in painful isolation and effective imprisonment, failed by a system that was conceived with the aim of healing their mental distress. The second, however, is more positive: we are also left with four documents that stand as permanent testimonies to the experience of being a female psychiatric patient in the late nineteenth and early twentieth centuries in France, in which the voice of protest articulated by the patient represents a significant emancipatory attempt that achieved an important measure of success. Each of the individuals discussed has left an important legacy that is testament to her vitality in the face of adversity. Camille Claudel's artistry has at last been given the recognition it deserves; Hersilie Rouy single-handedly wrote her way out of incarceration, and died a free woman; Marie Esquiron demonstrated convincingly that her insight into her own case was as valid as any man's; and Pauline Lair Lamotte achieved a level of mental stability and reintegration into family life that would have been inconceivable earlier in her life, and in her animated dialogue with Janet she also articulated an important voice of protest against the totalizing discourse of psychiatry. Despite their sufferings and failings, these women gained important personal victories over the injustices of their era, even if unfortunately for some of them this recognition has come too late.

Psychiatric medicine, with some enlightened exceptions, functioned as an extension of a society that oppressed women, particularly women who deviated from the narrow path of bourgeois feminine normality. The construction of delusional stories has been read as a compensatory defence adopted in reaction to a social situation that annihilated an individual's aspirations. It has been repeatedly proposed here that it is a misleading and unproductive critical exercise to characterize madness as meaningless. Rather, there is arguably much that can be read as meaningful, when placed in an illuminating context, in the utterances of the 'insane': Rouy's delusions translate into the idea, 'My existence is legitimate', and are a metaphorical reversal of the experience of perceived annihilation by society; Esquiron's *Mémoire* is a first-class piece of rhetoric, and her 'extravagant' behaviour functioned as a means of resisting the infantilizing treatment she received; Lair Lamotte has produced a creative exploration of a colourful and empowering internal world, which disrupts the limitations of the real world, and challenges the reasoning strategies of those who observed her; and Claudel's delusions of persecution are a means of asserting, 'I am important enough to persecute', in compensation for the lack of recognition she received in wider society.

By 1930, thirteen years after the death of Rodin, Claudel had come no closer to relinquishing her fiercely held feelings of persecution by her former lover:

Tout cela au fond sort du cerveau diabolique de Rodin. Il n'avait qu'une idée c'est que lui, étant mort, je prenne mon essor comme artiste et que je devienne plus que lui: il fallait qu'il arrive à me tenir dans ses griffes après sa mort comme pendant sa vie. Il fallait que je sois malheureuse lui mort comme vivant. Il a réussi en tous points car pour être malheureuse, je le suis![1]

This reveals the extent of the devastating, psychotic mental disturbance evinced by the texts we have studied. These writings have been read as pathologically introspective, and it has frequently been noted that malicious motives are wrongly attributed to external forces in order to account for personal misery. This connecting of personal suffering to specific outside agents is usually misguided in its intensity, but the suffering is real and the act of blaming is not invalid.

The stories related here have effectively been read as metaphorical representations of the real persecution women suffered in a society hostile to their attempts to evade its confines and limitations. For many who preferred a path other than the narrow one offered by 'normal' family life, the price of choosing a different way of life, as we have seen, was simply too great, and the obstacles too damaging. Bruno Bettelheim's analysis of children's fairy tales provides a useful parallel to

---

[1] Camille Claudel to Paul Claudel, 3 March 1930 (Rivière 2003: 298).

draw on when considering patients' writings, for in both forms of text it is the internal world that predominates:

The content of the chosen tale usually has nothing to do with the patient's external life, but much to do with his inner problems, which seem incomprehensible and hence unsolvable. [...] The unrealistic nature of these tales (which narrow-minded rationalists object to) is an important device, because it makes obvious that the fairy tales' concern is not useful information about the external world, but the inner processes taking place in the individual.[2]

Similarly, the material related in the four texts we have examined is only partially reliable in concrete historical terms. Importantly, however, when read as metaphorical representations of inner crisis, they reveal much about the pathogenic structures that existed in wider society. The four individuals studied and brought to light here rose up as voices of resistance against the perpetuation of these structures, and despite the fact that their own personal successes were limited, the critical stand taken in relation to psychiatric treatment was a crucial precursor to the feminist revision that would come many years later. And arguably these voices of criticism are more compelling because they arose from a place of subjective experience—rather than theoretical observation—which lends authenticity to stories that might otherwise be viewed as straightforwardly delusional.

The concentration on the text of the patient has, I would contend, gone some way towards shifting the focus of scholarly attention away from the medical specialist. The addition of the patient's perspective to the rhetorical analysis of clinical discourse provides a more complete account of the real, everyday debate that occurred as an integral part of the clinical encounter. It is to be hoped that this enquiry could stimulate further research into the many psychiatric memoirs produced by male patients, and indeed literary representations of psychotic writing or madness in fiction. It would also potentially be useful to broaden the time frame of the present study, and to incorporate a more detailed examination of writings by female eccentrics who were not incarcerated, but who claimed to have been dealt a raw deal by society. This could extend the textual corpus to include the writings of authors such as Maria-Stella Chiappini (1830), Sophie Adélaïde (1887), and Emilie-Herminie Hanin (1934), as well as Céline Renooz.

---

[2] Bettelheim (1977: 25).

The present analysis has provided a modest, but crucial and long overdue, reassessment of the voice of the patient in psychiatric writing. The aim has been not to iron out the textual difficulties posed by writing motivated by and inflected with mental disturbance, but rather to lay bare the truths such writing reveals about the suffering subject who lies behind its composition. In response to Caminero-Santangelo's assertion that the madwoman cannot speak, we have shown that, despite the double bind that frustrated her attempt at self-expression, she did speak. She did not speak in ways that necessarily make immediate sense to us, and indeed her discourse may have frustrated her cause, but this observation only highlights the importance of the process of searching for meaning in textual utterances. Although the writing of the 'aliénée' was not in every case successfully subversive of the societal structures in place, her voice still represents resistance embodied in textual form. The psychiatrist Lévy-Valensi, commenting on the famous text of the 'aliéné' Terre-Neuve du Thym, wrote: 'Dès la première ligne, on s'aperçoit que c'est l'œuvre d'un aliéné, bien que son auteur s'en défende et aussi parce qu'il s'en défend.'[3] So it would seem that for the patient, judged mad *despite* the fact that she protested, but also *because* she protested, the double bind in which she had been placed meant that there was no linguistic space in which she could express her reality, and be believed. In re-examining the patient's utterances and finding them to be meaningful, we must concede that there is indeed a great deal more truth in delusion than Freud, or any of us, can comfortably admit.

---

[3] Lévy-Valensi (1911). Cited in new edition to Terre-Neuve du Thym (1990: 14).

Bibliography

Adélaïde, S. 1887. *Histoire contemporaine* (Paris: Ollendorff).

Agoult, M. de Flavigny. 1846. *Nélida* (Paris: Amyot).

Allouch, J. 1994. *Marguerite, ou l'Aimée de Lacan* (Paris: E.P.E.L.).

American Psychiatric Association. 1987. *Diagnostic and Statistical Manual of Mental Disorders*, 3rd rev. edn (Washington, DC: American Psychiatric Association).

Antoine, G. 1988. *Paul Claudel ou l'Enfer du génie* (Paris: Robert Laffont).

Appignanesi, L. 2008. *Mad, Bad and Sad: A History of Women and the Mind Doctors from 1800 to the Present* (London: Virago).

Apte, M. 1903. 'Les Stigmatisés: étude historique et critique sur les troubles vaso-moteurs chez les mystiques', medicine thesis, University of Paris.

Avila, St Teresa of. 1999. *Way of Perfection*, ed. E. A. Peers (London: Sheed and Ward).

—— 2002. *The Life of the Holy Mother Teresa of Jesus*, ed. E. A. Peers, 3 vols (London: Burnes and Oates).

Ayral-Clause, O. 2002. *Camille Claudel: A Life* (New York: Harry N. Abrams).

Bardwick, J. 1971. *The Psychology of Women: A Bio-Cultural Conflict* (New York: Harper and Row).

Barthes, R. 1973. *Le Plaisir du texte* (Paris: Seuil).

Baruk, H. 1951. 'La condamnation de la psychochirurgie actuelle. Réponse à M. Henri Ey. Problèmes physiologiques, médicaux, moraux et légaux', *Annales médico-psychologiques* 4: 97–105.

Bateman, A., and J. Holmes. 1995. *Introduction to Psychoanalysis: Contemporary Theory and Practice* (London: Routledge).

Beauvoir, S. de. 1976. *Le Deuxième sexe*, 2 vols (Paris: Gallimard).

Berrios, G. E. 1993. 'European Views of Personality Disorders: A Conceptual History', *Comprehensive Psychiatry* 34: 14–30.

Bertrand, M. 2002. 'La neurochirurgie fonctionnelle d'affections psychiatriques sévères', *Comité Consultatif National d'Ethique*, available at http://www.ccne-ethique.fr/docs/fr/avis071.pdf. Accessed 1 February 2010.

Bettelheim, B. 1977. *The Uses of Enchantment: The Meaning and Importance of Fairy Tales* (New York: Random House).

Bidelman, Patrick K. 1975. *The Feminist Movement in France*, thesis, Michigan State University.

Blackburn, S., and K. Simmons (eds) 1999. *Truth* (Oxford: Oxford University Press).

Blavier, A. 1982. *Les Fous littéraires* (Paris: Henri Veyrier).

Bouté, G. 1995. *Camille Claudel: Le miroir et la nuit* (Paris: Éditions de l'amateur–Éditions des catalogues raisonnés).

Bowie, M. 1991. *Lacan* (London: Fontana).

Breton, A. 1924. 'Manifeste du Surréalisme', in *Œuvres complètes*, ed. Étienne-Alain Hubert et al. (Paris: Gallimard): 311–46.

——1925. 'Lettre aux Médecins-Chefs des Asiles de Fous', *La Révolution Surréaliste*, 3: n.p.

——and P. Éluard. 1930. 'L'immaculée conception', in *Œuvres complètes*, ed. É.-A. Hubert et al. (Paris: Gallimard): 839–84.

Brierre de Boisment, A. 1854. 'De la réforme du traitement des aliénés', *Annales médico-psychologiques* 6: 1–13.

Broc, A. 1863. 'Observations et réflexions critiques sur la mégalomanie ou folie des grandeurs', medicine thesis, University of Montpellier.

Burton, É. 1882. *Mémoires d'une feuille de papier écrits par elle-même* (Paris: Ollendorff).

Burton, R. 2004. *Holy Tears, Holy Blood: Women, Catholicism, and the Culture of Suffering in France, 1840–1970* (Ithaca: Cornell University Press).

Caldwell Lathrop, C. 1890. *A Secret Institution* (New York: Bryant).

Camille Claudel (1864–1943), catalogue d'exposition (Tokyo: 1987).

Caminero-Santangelo, M. 1998. *The Madwoman Can't Speak, or Why Insanity Is Not Subversive* (Ithaca: Cornell University Press).

Cassar, J. 1987. *Dossier Camille Claudel* (Paris: Librairie Séguier/Archimbaud).

Castel, R. 1976. *L'Ordre psychiatrique: L'âge d'or de l'aliénisme* (Paris: Les éditions de minuit).

Chambers, R. 1983. 'Récits d'aliénés, récits aliénés. Nerval et John Perceval', *Poétique* 53: 72–90.

Champfleury. 1852. *Les Excentriques* (Paris: Lévy frères).

Champigneule, B. 1967. *Rodin* (Paris: Somogy).

Chesler, P. 1974. *Women and Madness* (London: Allen Lane, 1974).

Chiappini, M. 1830. *Maria-Stella ou Échange criminel d'une demoiselle du plus hau trang contre un garçon de la condition la plus vile* (Paris: chez les principaux libraires).

Claridge, G., R. Pryor, and G. Watkins. 1990. *Sounds from the Bell Jar: Ten Psychotic Authors* (London: Macmillan).

Claude, H. 1925. 'Les psychoses paranoïdes', *L'Encéphale* 3: 137–49.

Claudel, P. 1905. 'Camille Claudel statuaire', in *Œuvres en prose* (Paris: Gallimard–Bibliothèque de la Pléiade): 272–6.

——1951. 'Ma Sœur Camille', in *Œuvres en prose* (Paris: Gallimard–Bibliothèque de la Pléiade): 276–85.

Clément, C., and H. Cixous. 1975. *La Jeune née* (Paris: Union générale d'éditions).

——and S. Kakar. 1993. *La Folle et le saint* (Paris: Seuil).

Congrès français et international du droit des femmes (Paris: E. Dentu, 1889).

Curinier, C. E. 1905. *Dictionnaire national des contemporains* (Paris: Office général d'édition).

Cutting, G. 1994. 'Michel Foucault's hänomenologie des Krankengeistes', in R. Porter and M. S. Micale (eds), *Discovering the History of Psychiatry* (Oxford: Oxford University Press): 331–47.

Delacroix, H. 1938. *Les Grands mystiques chrétiens* (Paris: Alcan).

Delbée, A. 1982. *Une femme* (Paris: Presses de la Renaissance).

Derrida, J. 1967. 'Cogito et histoire de la folie', in *L'Écriture et la différence* (Paris: Seuil): 51–97.

Diderot, D. 1972. *Le Neveu de Rameau* (Paris: Gallimard).

Dudovitz, R. 1990. *The Myth of Superwoman: Women's Bestsellers in France and the United States* (London: Routledge).

Duras, C. de. 1824. *Ourika* (Paris: Ladvocat).

Dwyer, E. 1988. *Homes for the Mad* (New Brunswick, NJ: Rutgers University Press).

Edelman, N. 1995. *Voyantes, guérisseuses et visionnaires en France 1785–1914* (Paris: Albin Michel).

Ellenberger, H. 1958. 'Phenomenology and Existential Analysis', in E. May and H. Ellenberger (eds), *Existence* (New York: Basic Books).

Esquirol, J.-É. 1838. *Des maladies mentales considérées sous les rapports médical, hygiénique et médico-légal*, 2 vols (Paris: Baillière).

Esquiron, M. 1893. *Mémoire adressé à Monsieur le Ministre de la Justice par Madame Esquiron, née de Gasté, Séquestrée dans la Maison de santé de M. le docteur Goujon, 90, rue de Picpus, à Paris, Où elle réfute elle-même l'imputation d'aliénation mentale et le rapport de MM. les aliénistes Mottet, Magnan et Voisin* (Paris: Imprimerie de Hénon).

Fabre-Pellerin, B. 1988. *Le Jour et la nuit de Camille Claudel* (Paris: Lachenal et Ritter).

——2005. *Camille Claudel: le tourment de l'absence* (Paris: Les Carnets de psychanalyse).

Falret, J. 1866. *De la folie raisonnante ou folie morale* (Paris: Imprimerie Martinet).

——1890. *Les Aliénés et les asiles d'aliénés: assistance, législation et médecine légale* (Paris: Baillière).

Fauvel, A. 2002. 'Le crime de Clermont et la remise en cause des asiles en 1880', *Revue d'Histoire Moderne et Contemporaine* 49: 195–216.

Felman, S. 1975. 'Women and Madness: The Critical Phallacy', *Diacritics* 5: 2–10.

——1978. *La Folie et la chose littéraire* (Paris: Seuil).

Finch, A. 2000. *Women's Writing in Nineteenth-Century France* (Cambridge: Cambridge University Press).

Finn, M. 2003. 'Retrospective Medicine, Hypnosis, Hysteria and French Literature', in George Rousseau et al. (eds), *Framing and Imagining Disease in Cultural History* (Basingstoke: Palgrave): 173–89.

Flaubert, G. 1857. *Madame Bovary* (Paris: Mothy frères).

Fontaine, A. 1852. *Un théorème de la philosophie des corps* (Brussels: Imprimerie Vanbuggenhoudt).

Fontaine, J.-P. 2005. *Les Mystères de l'Yonne* (Paris: Editions de Borée).

Fordham, F. 1981. *An Introduction to Jung's Psychology*, 3rd edn (Harmondsworth: Penguin).

Forrester, J. 1980. *Language and the Origins of Psychoanalysis* (London: Macmillan).

—— and L. Appignanesi. 2000. *Freud's Women* (London: Penguin).

Foucault, M. 1961. *Folie et déraison: histoire de la folie à l'âge classique* (Paris: Plon).

—— 1963. *Naissance de la clinique: une archéologie du regard clinique. Histoire et philosophie de la biologie et de la médecine* (Paris: Presses Universitaires de France).

—— (ed.) 1973. *Moi, Pierre Rivière, ayant égorgé ma mère, ma sœur et mon frère . . . : un cas de parricide au XIXe siècle* (Paris: Gallimard).

—— 1976. *La Volonté de savoir: histoire de la sexualité*, 3 vols (Paris: Gallimard), vol i.

Fournet, J. 1854. 'Le traitement moral de l'aliénation, soit mentale, soit morale, à son principe et son modèle dans la famille', *Annales médico-psychologiques* 6: 521–9.

Foville, A. 1871. 'Étude clinique de la folie avec prédominance du délire des grandeurs', *Mémoires de l'Académie de médecine* 29: 318–452.

Freud, S. 1893–5. 'Studies on Hysteria', in *The Standard Edition of the Complete Psychological Works of Sigmund Freud*, ed. and trans. James Strachey et al., 24 vols (London: Vintage, 1953), ii.

—— 1900–1. 'The Interpretation of Dreams' (First Part and Second Part), in *The Standard Edition of the Complete Psychological Works of Sigmund Freud*, ed. and trans. James Strachey et al., 24 vols (London: Vintage, 1953), iv–v.

—— 1905. 'Fragment of an Analysis of a Case of Hysteria', in *The Standard Edition of the Complete Psychological Works of Sigmund Freud*, ed. and trans. James Strachey et al., 24 vols (London: Vintage, 1953), vii. 7–122.

—— 1909. 'Family Romances', in *The Standard Edition of the Complete Psychological Works of Sigmund Freud*, ed. and trans. James Strachey et al., 24 vols (London: Vintage, 1953), ix. 235–41.

—— 1911. 'The Case History of Schreber', in *The Standard Edition of the Complete Psychological Works of Sigmund Freud*, ed. and trans. James Strachey et al., 24 vols (London: Vintage, 1953), xii. 3–82.

—— 1914. 'On Narcissism: An Introduction', in *The Standard Edition of the Complete Psychological Works of Sigmund Freud*, ed. and trans. James Strachey et al., 24 vols (London: Vintage, 1953), xiv. 67–102.

—— 1915. 'A Case of Paranoia Running Counter to the Psycho-Analytic Theory of the Disease', in *The Standard Edition of the Complete Psychological*

Works of Sigmund Freud, ed. and trans. James Strachey et al., 24 vols (London: Vintage, 1953), xiv. 261–72.

——1919. 'The Uncanny', in *The Standard Edition of the Complete Psychological Works of Sigmund Freud*, ed. and trans. James Strachey et al., 24 vols (London: Vintage, 1953), xvii. 219–52.

——1930. 'Civilization and Its Discontents', in *The Standard Edition of the Complete Psychological Works of Sigmund Freud*, ed. and trans. James Strachey et al., 24 vols (London: Vintage, 1953), xxi. 64–145.

Fusnot, C. 1854. *Vérités positives. Rapports entre les vérités physiques et les vérités morales* (Brussels: Mahieu).

Gagneur, M.-L. 1870. *Les Forçats du mariage* (Paris: A. Lacroix, Verboeckhoven et Cie).

——1872. *Le Divorce* (Paris: Librairie de la bibliothèque démocratique).

Gallop, J. 1985. 'Keys to Dora', in C. Bernheimer and C. Kahane (eds), *In Dora's Case: Freud-Hysteria-Feminism* (New York: Columbia University Press): 200–20.

Gaudichon, B., et al. (eds) 1984. *Camille Claudel (1864–1943)* (Paris: Catalogue d'exposition).

Gelder, M., et al. (eds) 2001. *The Shorter Oxford Textbook of Psychiatry* (Oxford: Oxford University Press).

Genette, G. 1972. 'Discours du récit', in *Figures III* (Paris: Seuil): 67–273.

Gilbert, S., and S. Gubar. 1979. *The Madwoman in the Attic: The Woman Writer and the Nineteenth-Century Imagination* (London: Yale University Press).

Gill, M. 2009. *Eccentricity and the Cultural Imagination in Nineteenth-Century France* (Oxford: Oxford University Press).

Girard, P., and D. L. L. Parry. 2002. *France since 1800* (Oxford: Oxford University Press).

Goldstein, J. 1987. *Console and Classify: The French Psychiatric Profession in the Nineteenth Century* (Cambridge: Cambridge University Press).

Greer, G. 1999. *The Female Eunuch* (London: Flamingo).

Gregory, R. L. (ed.) 1987. *The Oxford Companion to the Mind* (Oxford: Oxford University Press).

Grévisse, M. 1993. *Le Bon usage: grammaire française*, 3rd edn (Paris: Duculot).

Grunfeld, F. 1989. *Rodin: A Biography* (Oxford: Oxford University Press).

Guelfi, J., et al. (eds) 2002. *Psychiatrie*, 8th edn (Paris: Presses Universitaires de France).

Gyp. 1886. *Autour du divorce* (Paris: C. Lévy).

Hamona, R. 2008. 'Madeleine Lebouc: se faire un corps sanctifié par la religion catholique', *L'Evolution psychiatrique* 73: 41–52.

Hanin, E.-H. 1934. *Super-despotes* (Paris: Imprimerie Amédée-Chiroutre).

Harsin, J. 1992. 'Gender, Class, and Madness in Nineteenth-Century France', *French Historical Studies* 17: 1048–70.

Hart, K. 2004. *Revolution and Women's Autobiography in Nineteenth-Century France* (New York: Rodopi).

Hawthorne, J. 1983. *Multiple Personality and the Disintegration of Literary Character* (London: Arnold).

Hendrik van den Berg, J. 1955. *The Phenomenological Approach to Psychiatry* (Springfield, IL: Charles C. Thomas).

Holmes, D. 1996. *French Women's Writing 1848–1994* (London: Athlone).

Hubert, S. J. 2002. *Questions of Power: The Politics of Women's Madness Narratives* (London: Associated University Presses).

Inge, W. R. 1899. *Christian Mysticism* (London: Methuen).

Irigaray, L. 1977. 'Pouvoir du discours/subordination du féminin', in *Ce sexe qui n'en est pas un* (Paris: Éditions de Minuit): 65–82.

Jakobson, R. 1971. 'Two Aspects of Language and Two Types of Aphasic Disturbances', in R. Jakobson and M. Halle (eds), *Fundamentals of Language* (Paris: Mouton): 67–96.

James, T. 1995. *Dream, Creativity, and Madness in Nineteenth-Century France* (Oxford: Clarendon).

Janet, P. 1894. *L'État mental des hystériques* (Paris: Alcan).

——1926. *De l'angoisse à l'extase: études sur les croyances et les sentiments*, 2 vols (Paris: Alcan).

Jeanneret, M. 1980. 'La folie est un rêve: Nerval et le docteur Moreau de Tours', *Romantisme* 27: 59–75.

Jésus-Marie, B. de. 1931. 'A propos de la "Madeleine" de Pierre Janet', *Études carmélitaines* 1: 20–61.

——1931. 'A propos de la "Madeleine" de Pierre Janet', *Études carmélitaines* 2: 43–136.

Jomiaux, Madame. 1895. *Affaire Jomiaux-Abbay. Voir d'outre tombe!!! Mémoire...* (Brussels: Société générale d'imprimerie).

Jousselin, E.-H. 1895. *Les Planètes rocheuses, les Erreurs de la vie* (Paris: Imprimerie Chamerot and Renouard).

Jung, C. G. 1907. 'The Psychology of Dementia Praecox', in *The Psychogenesis of Mental Disease*, trans. R. F. C. Hall, *The Collected Works of C. G. Jung*, 20 vols (London: Routledge), 3: 1–151.

Kelsey, M. T. 1976. *The Other Side of Silence: A Guide to Christian Meditation* (New Jersey: Paulist Press).

Kristeva, J. 1969. *Séméiotiké: Recherches pour une sémanalyse* (Paris: Seuil).

——1977. *Polylogue* (Paris: Seuil).

——2001. *Melanie Klein*, trans. Ross Guberman (New York: Columbia University Press) [Originally published in French as *Le Génie féminin: Melanie Klein* (Paris: Librairie Arthème Fayard, 2000)].

Lacan, J. 1975a. *De la psychose paranoïaque dans ses rapports avec la personnalité suivi de premiers écrits sur la paranoïa* (Paris: Seuil).

Lacan, J. 1975b. *Livre XX Encore (1972–1973)*, ed. J.-A. Miller, Le séminaire de Jacques Lacan (Paris: Seuil).

—— 1981. *Livre III, Les Psychoses (1955–1956)*, ed. J.-A. Miller, Le séminaire de Jacques Lacan (Paris: Seuil).

—— Lévy-Valensi, and P. Migault. 1931. 'Écrits "inspirés": schizographie', *Annales médico-psychologiques* 2: 508–22.

Lachaux, G. 1893. 'De la dissimulation des idées de grandeur dans le délire chronique à évolution systématique', medicine thesis, University of Paris.

Laing, R. D. 1967. *The Politics of Experience and the Bird of Paradise* (Harmondsworth: Penguin).

—— 1990. *The Divided Self* (London: Penguin).

Laplanche, J., and J.-B. Pontalis. 1988. *The Language of Psychoanalysis*, trans. Donald Nicholson-Smith (London: Karnac) [Originally published in French as *Vocabulaire de la psychanalyse* (Paris: Presses Universitaires de France, 1967)].

Lasègue, C. 1852. 'Du délire des persécutions', *Archives générales de médecine* 28: 129–50.

—— and J. Falret. 1877. 'La folie à deux', *Extrait des archives générales de médecine* 1–41.

Legrand du Saulle, H. 1871. *Le Délire des persécutions* (Paris: Plon).

Legué, G., and G. de la Tourette (eds) 1886. *Autobiographie de Sœur Jeanne des Anges* (Paris: Delahaye).

Lejeune, P. 1971. *L'Autobiographie en France* (Paris: Librairie Armand Colin).

—— 1975. *Le Pacte autobiographique* (Paris: Seuil).

—— 1993. *Le Moi des demoiselles: enquête sur le journal de jeune fille* (Paris: Seuil).

—— 1998. 'Autobiographie et contrainte', in *Les Brouillons de soi* (Paris: Seuil): 125–39.

Le Roy Ladurie, E. 1975. *Montaillou, village occitan de 1294–1324* (Paris: Gallimard).

Leuret, F. 1834. *Fragmens psychologiques sur la folie* (Paris: Crochard).

—— 1841. 'Notice sur M. Esquirol', *Extrait de la Gazette Médicale de Paris*: 2.

Lévy-Valensi, J. 1911. 'Une forme littéraire du délire d'interprétation', *L'Encéphale* 9 [cited in new edition of *Terre-Neuve du Thym* 1990: 14. No original page reference].

Lhermitte, F., and J.-F. Allilaire. 1984. 'Camille Claudel: malade mentale', in R.-M. Paris (ed.), *Camille Claudel, 1864–1943* (Paris: Gallimard): 155–208.

Lieberman, J. A. 1995. 'Treatment of Schizophrenia: Trends and Outlook', *Psychiatric Times* 12, [online]. Available at http://www.psychiatrictimes.com/p950627.html. Accessed 2 February 2005.

Lloyd, R. 2000. 'The Nineteenth Century: Shaping Women', in S. Stephens (ed.), *A History of Women's Writing in France* (Cambridge: Cambridge University Press): 120–46.

—— and B. Nelson (eds) 2000b. *Women Seeking Expression: France 1789–1914* (Melbourne: Monash).

Macalpine, I., and R. Hunter. 1956. *Schizophrenia 1677: A Psychiatric Study of an Illustrated Autobiographical Record of Demoniacal Possession* (London: Dawsons).

Magnan, V. 1871. *Étude expérimentale et clinique sur l'alcoolisme: alcool et absinthe: épilepsie absinthique* (Paris: Renon et Maulde).

——1874. *De l'alcoolisme, des diverses formes du délire alcoolique et de leur traitement* (Paris: Delahaye).

——1893. *Recherches sur les centres nerveux: alcoolisme, folie des héréditaires dégénérés, paralysie générale, médecine légale*, 2 vols (Paris: Masson), vol ii.

—— and P.-M. Legrain. 1895. *Les Dégénérés* (Paris: Reuff).

Maître, J. 1986. 'Thérèse Martin: "Histoire d'une âme": code institutionnel et créativité subjective dans un récit de vie', *Cahiers de sémiotique textuelle* 8–9: 23–42.

——1989a. 'Biographies à thèse: les trois vies de Pauline Lair Lamotte', *Cahiers de sémiotique textuelle* 16: 81–90.

——1989b. 'A l'écoute de Madeleine Lebouc', *L'Évolution psychiatrique*, 54: 451–9.

——1993. *Une inconnue célèbre: la Madeleine Lebouc de Janet* (Paris: Anthropos).

——1994. *L'Autobiographie d'un paranoïaque: l'abbé Berry (1878–1947) et le roman de Billy 'Introïbo'* (Paris: Anthropos).

——1997. *Mystique et féminité. Essai de psychanalyse sociohistorique* (Paris: Editions du Cerf).

——2001. 'Anorexies religieuses: Anorexie mentale', *Revue française de psychanalyse* 65: 1551–60.

Marcé, L. V. 1864. 'De la valeur des écrits des aliénés au point de vue de la sémiologie et de la médecine légale', *Journal de médecine mentale* 4: 85–95; 189–203 (suite).

Masson, J. 1997. *Against Therapy*, 2nd edn (London: Harper Collins).

Matlock, J. 1991. 'Doubling out of the Crazy House: Gender, Autobiography and the Insane Asylum in Nineteenth-Century France', *Representations* 34: 167–95.

——1994. *Scenes of Seduction: Prostitution, Hysteria, and Reading Difference in Nineteenth-Century France* (New York: Columbia University Press).

McGovern, C. 1986. 'The Myths of Social Control and Custodial Oppression', *Journal of Social History* 20: 3–23.

McGovern, U. (ed.) 2002. *Chambers Biographical Dictionary* (Edinburgh: Chambers Harrap).

Merriman, J. M. 1985. 'The Miracle Baby', in J. M. Merriman (ed.), *For Want of a Horse: Chance and Humor in History* (Lexington, MA: Stephen Greene Press): 53–7.

Metcalf, A. 1876. *Lunatic Asylums: And How I Became an Inmate of One* (New York: Ottoway).

Metcalf, U. 1818. *The Interior of Bethlehem Hospital* [pamphlet cited in R. Porter 2002. *Madness: A Brief History* (Oxford: Oxford University Press): 161].

Michel, L. 1886. *Mémoires de Louise Michel écrits par elle-même* (Paris: F. Roy).

Minkowski, E. 1934. *Le Temps vécu: études phénoménologiques et psychopathologiques*, ed. J. L. L. D'Artrey (Paris: Saint-Amand).

——1970. *Lived Time: Phenomenological and Psychopathological Studies*, trans. N. Metzel (Evanston, IL: Northwestern University Press).

Mitchell, J. 2000. *Psychoanalysis and Feminism: A Radical Reassessment of Freudian Psychoanalysis* (London: Penguin).

Moi, T. 1985. 'Representation of Patriarchy: Sexuality and Epistemology in Freud's Dora', in C. Bernheimer and C. Kahane (eds), *In Dora's Case: Freud-Hysteria-Feminism* (New York: Columbia University Press), 181–99.

Montmorand, M. de. 1920. *Psychologie des mystiques catholiques orthodoxes* (Paris: Alcan).

Moreau de Tours, J.-J. 1845. *Du hachisch et de l'aliénation mentale. Études psychologiques* (Paris: Masson).

——1859. *La psychologie morbide dans ses rapports avec la philosophie de l'histoire* (Paris: Masson).

——1888. 'La raison dans la folie', *Annales d'hygiène publique et de médecine légale* 20: 170–4.

Morel, B. A. 1857. *Traité des dégénérescences physiques, intellectuelles et morales de l'espèce humaine et des causes qui produisent ces variétés*, 2 vols (Paris: Baillière).

——1860. *Traité des maladies mentales* (Paris: Masson).

Murat, L. 2001. *La Maison du docteur Blanche* (Paris: Lattès).

Murisier, E. 1901. *Les Maladies du sentiment religieux* (Paris: Alcan).

Nerval, G. de. 1855. 'Aurélia', in *Œuvres de Gérard de Nerval*, ed. Henri Lemaître (Paris: Éditions Garnier frères), 747–824.

Nevinson, C. R. W. 1937. *Paint and Prejudice* (London: Methuen).

Nuytten, B. (dir.) 1989. *Camille Claudel* (Paris: Christian Fechner Films).

Ott, M. 1854. 'De la folie générale et de la folie partielle', *Annales médico-psychologiques* 6: 317–38.

Packard, E. 1866. *Marital power exemplified in Mrs. Packard's trial, and self-defence from the charge of insanity; or, Three years' imprisonment for religious belief, by the arbitrary will of a husband, with an appeal to the government to so change the laws as to afford legal protection to married women* (Hartford: published by the author).

Parant, V. 1888. *La Raison dans la folie: étude pratique et médico-légale sur la persistance partielle de la raison chez les aliénés et sur leurs actes raisonnables* (Paris: Octave Doin).

Paris, R.-M. 1984. *Camille Claudel* (Paris: Gallimard).

——and A. de la Chapelle. 1990. *L'Œuvre de Camille Claudel, catalogue raisonné* (Paris: Éditions d'art et d'histoire Arhis/Éditions Adam Biro).

Pheterson, G. 1986. 'Alliances between Women: Overcoming Internalized Oppression and Internalized Domination', *Signs* 12: 146–60.

Pickering, M. 1993. *Auguste Comte: An Intellectual Biography* (Cambridge: Cambridge University Press).

Pinel, C. 1864. 'Quelques mots sur les asiles d'aliénés et la loi de 1838', *Journal de médecine mentale* 4: 144–58.

Pinel, P. 1800. *Traité médico-philosophique sur l'aliénation mentale, ou la manie* (Paris: Richard, Caille et Ravier).

Pinel, S. 1836. *Traité complet du régime sanitaire des aliénés* (Paris: Mauprivez).

Pingeot, A. (ed.) 1988. *'L'Âge mûr' de Camille Claudel* (Paris: Éditions de la réunion des musées nationaux).

——2002. 'Affirmation of the Republican Idea', in G. Duby and J.-L. Daval (eds), *Sculpture from Antiquity to the Present Day* (Köln: Taschen): 916–46.

Plas, R. 2000. *Naissance d'une science humaine: la psychologie* (Rennes: Presses Universitaires de Rennes).

Porter, R., and M. S. Micale (eds) 1994. *Discovering the History of Psychiatry* (Oxford: Oxford University Press).

——2002. *Madness: A Brief History* (Oxford: Oxford University Press).

Preez, A. du. 2004. 'Putting on appearances: Mimetic representations of hysteria', *de arte* 69: 47–61.

Prendergast, C. 1986. *The Order of Mimesis: Balzac, Stendhal, Nerval, Flaubert* (Cambridge: Cambridge University Press).

Prestwich, P. 1993. 'Women and Madness in a Nineteenth-Century Parisian Asylum', in S. Neuman and G. Stephenson (eds), *Reimagining Women: Representations of Women in Culture* (Toronto: University of Toronto Press): 111–24.

Prichard, J. C. 1835. *A Treatise on Insanity* (London: Sherwood, Gilbert and Piper).

Proust, A., and G. Ballet. 1897. *L'Hygiène du neurasthénique* (Paris: Masson).

Queneau, R. 1938. *Les Enfants du limon* (Paris: Gallimard).

Rachilde. 1889. *Monsieur Vénus* (Paris: F. Brossier).

——1928. *Pourquoi je ne suis pas féministe* (Paris: Editions de France).

Réja, M. 2000. *L'Art chez les fous: le dessin, la prose, la poésie* (Paris: L'Harmatton) [Originally published in 1907 and reproduced in facsimile in the Collection psychanalyse et civilisations: série trouvailles et retrouvailles].

——1895. *La Force* (Paris: Société d'éditions scientifiques).

Renooz, C. 1888. 'Une révélation', *La Religion laïque et universelle*: 267.

Rey, H. 1994. *Schizoid Modes of Being* (London: Free Association Books).

Ribot, T. 1888. *Les Maladies de la volonté* (Paris: Alcan).

Ribot, T. 1896. *La Psychologie des sentiments* (Paris: Alcan).

Rigoli, J. 2001. *Lire le délire* (Geneva: Arthème Fayard).

Ripa, Y. 1983. 'Contribution à une histoire des femmes, des médecins et de la folie à l'âge d'or de l'aliénisme français, 1838–1860' (unpublished doctoral thesis, University of Paris VII).

——1986a. 'L'affaire Hersilie Rouy', *L'Histoire* 87: 74–81.

——1986b. *La Ronde des folles: femme, folie et enfermement au XIXe siècle (1838–1870)* (Paris: Aubier).

Rivière, A., et al. (eds) 2001. *Camille Claudel: Catalogue Raisonné*, 3rd edn (Paris: Adam Biro).

——and B. Gaudichon (eds) 2003. *Camille Claudel: correspondance* (Paris: Gallimard).

Roche, A., and L. Soulayrol. 1998. 'Le cas de Hersilie Rouy, maladie mentale, ou internement abusif?', *Le Coq-héron* 152 (whole issue).

Rogues de Fursal, J. 1905. *Les Écrits et les dessins dans les maladies nerveuses et mentales (essai clinique)* (Paris: Masson).

Rose, J. 1985. 'Dora: Fragment of an Analysis', in C. Bernheimer and C. Kahane (eds), *In Dora's Case: Freud-Hysteria-Feminism* (New York: Columbia University Press): 128–48.

Roubinovitch, J., and E. Toulouse. 1897. *La Mélancolie* (Paris: Masson).

Roudinesco, E. 1982. *La Bataille de cent ans: histoire de la psychanalyse en France 1: 1885–1939*, 2 vols (Paris: Seuil), vol i.

Rouy, H. 1883. *Mémoires d'une aliénée* (Paris: Ollendorff).

Royer, C. 1900. *La Constitution du monde. Dynamique des atomes. Nouveaux principes de philosophie naturelle* (Paris: Schleicher).

Sand, G. 1832. *Indiana* (Paris: J.-P. Roret).

——1833. *Lélia* (Paris: H. Dupuy).

——1856. *Histoire de ma vie* (Paris: Michel Lévy).

Sandon, L. 1865. *Plaidoyer de Me Léon Sandon, avocat, ancien avocat général, contre les médecins Tardieu, Blanche, Parchappe, Foville, Baillarger & Mitivié, prononcé à Paris, devant la Première Chambre, Le 9 Mai 1865* (Brussels: Imprimerie de A. Mertens).

Sayers, J. 2002. 'Marion Milner, Mysticism and Psychoanalysis', *International Journal of Psychoanalysis* 83: 105–20.

Schor, Naomi. *Breaking the Chain: Women, Theory and French Realist Fiction* (New York: Columbia University Press, 1985).

Schreber, D. 1955. *Memoirs of My Nervous Illness*, ed. I. Macalpine and R. Hunter (London: Dawsons).

Séglas, J. 1892. *Des Troubles du langage chez les aliénés* (Paris: J. Reuff).

——and G. Brouardel. 1893. 'Auto-accusateurs et persécutés et possédés', *Extrait des archives de neurologie* 82: 1–13.

Seine, Conseil général. 1893. *Mémoires de M. le préfet de la Seine & de M. le préfet de police et procès-verbaux des délibérations* (Imprimerie municipale).

Selling, L. S. 1940. *Men against Madness* (New York: Greenberg).

Semelaigne, R. 1930–32. *Les Pionniers de la psychiatrie française avant et après Pinel,* 2 vols (Paris: Baillière).

Sérieux, P., and J. Capgras. 1909. *Les Folies raisonnantes: le délire d'interprétation* (Paris: Alcan).

——and ——1910. 'Roman et vie d'une fausse princesse', *Journal de psychologie normale et pathologique* 7: 193–225.

Sheringham, M. 2000. 'Changing the Script: Women Writers and the Rise of Autobiography', in S. Stephens (ed.), *A History of Women's Writing in France* (Cambridge: Cambridge University Press): 185–203.

——1993. *French Autobiography: Devices and Desires* (Oxford: Clarendon).

Showalter, E. 1978. *A Literature of Their Own* (Princeton: Princeton University Press).

——1979. 'Towards a Feminist Poetics', in Mary Jacobus (ed.), *Women Writing and Writing about Women* (London: Croom Helm): 22–41.

——1981. 'Feminist Criticism in the Wilderness', *Critical Inquiry* 8: 179–205.

——1987. *The Female Malady: Women, Madness and English Culture* (London: Virago).

Silvestre, C. 1968. 'Le traité médico-philosophique sur l'aliénation mentale de Philippe Pinel et la philosophie des lumières' (unpublished doctoral thesis, University of Paris).

Simon, P.-M. 1888. 'Les écrits et les dessins des aliénés', *L'Anthropologie criminelle et des sciences pénales* 3: 318–55.

Sirey. 1882–6. *Code Civil,* Les Codes Annotés De Sirey, 3rd edn, 2 vols (Paris: Imprimerie et librairie générale de jurisprudence Marchal et Billard), vol i.

Slama, B. 1980. 'Femmes écrivains', in J.-P. Aron (ed.), *Misérable et glorieuse: la femme du XIXe siècle* (Paris: Fayard): 214–43.

Smith, L. 1879. *Behind the Scenes; or, Life in an Insane Asylum* (New York: Culver).

Smith Allen, J. 1999. 'The Language of the Press: Narrative and Ideology in the Memoirs of Céline Renooz, 1890–1913', in D. de la Motte and J. M. Przyblyski (eds), *Making the News: Modernity and the Mass Press in Nineteenth-Century France* (Boston: University of Massachusetts Press): 279–301.

——2000a. *Poignant Relations: Three Modern French Women* (London: John Hopkins University Press).

——2000b. 'Writing the Body and Women's Madness: The Historiographical Implications of *l'écriture féminine* in Céline Renooz's "Une Révélation" (1888)', in R. Lloyd and B. Nelson (eds), *Women Seeking Expression: France 1789–1914* (Melbourne: Monash Romance Studies): 194–205.

Soulayrol, L. 1988. 'Mémoires d'une aliénée par Hersilie Rouy: le sujet dans la folie: comparaison entre la perception du XIXe siècle et le point de vue psychanalytique' (medicine thesis, University of Marseille).

Staël, G. de. 1807. *Corinne, ou l'Italie* (Paris: H. Nicolle).

Stephens, Sonya (ed.) *A History of Women's Writing in France* (Cambridge: Cambridge University Press, 2000).

Strindberg, A. 1895. *Le Plaidoyer d'un fou* (Paris: Mercure de France, 1964).

—— 1898. *Inferno* (Paris: Mercure de France, 1966).

Swain, G. 1997. *Le Sujet de la folie: naissance de la psychiatrie* (Paris: Calmann-Lévy).

Swiffen, J. A. 2002. 'Treating Psychosis: Madness and Ethics in Nerval, Desnos and Lacan' (unpublished doctoral thesis, University of Cambridge).

Szasz, T. 1961. *The Myth of Mental Illness: Foundations of a Theory of Personal Conduct* (New York: Hoeber-Harper).

—— 1994. *Cruel Compassion: Psychiatric Control of Society's Unwanted* (New York: Wiley).

Teissier, Marie Andrieux Saint-Rémy, veuve. 1899. *Les Dieux anarchistes. Annales de l'universellisme* (Paris: Durville).

Terre-Neuve du Thym, B. 1821. *Les Farfadets, ou Tous les démons ne sont pas de l'autre monde* (Grenoble: Jérome Millon, 1990).

Tomes, N. 1994. 'Feminist Histories of Psychiatry', in Porter 1994: 348–83.

Trélat, U. 1861. *La Folie lucide étudiée et considérée au point de vue de la famille et de la société* (Paris: Delahaye).

Tristan, F. 1838. *Pérégrinations d'une paria* (Paris: A. Bertrand).

Underhill, E. 1911. *Mysticism* (London: Methuen).

Unwin, Timothy (ed.) 1997. *The Cambridge Companion to the French Novel: From 1800 to the present* (Cambridge: Cambridge University Press).

Vandermeersch, P. 1994. ' "Les mythes d'origine" in the History of Psychiatry', in Porter, R., and M. S. Micale (eds), *Discovering the History of Psychiatry* (Oxford: Oxford University Press): 219–31.

Waller, Margaret, *The Male Malady: Fictions of Impotence in the French Romantic Novel* (New Brunswick, NJ: Rutgers University Press, 1993).

Weiner, D. B. 1994. ' "Le geste de Pinel": The History of a Psychiatric Myth', in Porter, R., and M. S. Micale (eds), *Discovering the History of Psychiatry* (Oxford: Oxford University Press): 232–47.

Wordsworth, A. 1987. 'Derrida and Foucault: Writing the History of Historicity', in G. Bennington et al. (eds), *Post-Structuralism and the Question of History* (Cambridge: Cambridge University Press): 116–25.

Wright, E. (ed.) 1992. *Feminism and Psychoanalysis: A Critical Dictionary* (Oxford: Blackwell).

Zeldin, T. 1973. *France 1848–1945: Ambition, Love and Politics*, 2 vols (Oxford: Clarendon), vol i.

—— 1977. *A History of French Passions: Intellect, Taste and Anxiety* (Oxford: Clarendon), vol i.

REFERENCE WORKS

Dictionnaire de biographie française (Paris: Librairie Letouzey et Ané, 1959).
Encyclopædia universalis, 16 vols (Paris: Encyclopædia Universalis France, 1968).
Grand dictionnaire universel du XIXe siècle, 17 vols, (Paris: Slatkine, 1982).
Grand Larousse encyclopédique, 10 vols (Paris: Librairie Larousse, 1960).
Le Nouveau Petit Robert: dictionnaire de la langue française (Paris: Dictionnaires Le Robert, 1993).
La Sainte Bible, trans. Louis Segond (Paris: La Maison de la Bible, 1935).

ARCHIVE MATERIAL

Archives de l'Assistance publique–Hôpitaux de Paris.
Pauline Lair Lamotte
Hôpital de l'Hôtel-Dieu, registre d'entrées, année 1894, cote 1Q2/296.
Hôpital Bichat, registre d'entrées, année 1894, cote 1Q2/12.
Hôpital Necker, registre d'entrées, année 1895, cote 1Q2/122.
Hôpital de la Salpêtrière, registre d'entrées, années 1895–1898, cote 1Q2/183.
Hôpital de la Salpêtrière, registre d'entrées, années 1901–1903, cote 1Q2/186.

Hersilie Rouy
Hôpital de la Salpêtrière, registre d'entrées des aliénées d'office, no. 21468, années 1854–5, cote 6Q2/22 (feuillet 52) and no. 22225, années 1855–6, cote 6Q2/24 (feuillet 35).

Archives de Paris.
Marie Esquiron
Section I, Sources Généalogiques, Rubrique 2: État civil de 1860 à 1902, 5 Mi 3 1593 à 2080, Actes de naissance, mariage et décès, 1893–1902, Répertoire méthodique.
Section III, Archives Judiciaires, Rubrique 5, Tribunal civil de la Seine, III.5.1, 'Répertoire des décisions du tribunal de première instance, puis de grande instance de la Seine et du tribunal de grande instance de Paris'. The series D.U⁵ contains records of the following: 'Délibérations, jugements et ordonnances, répertoires et audienciers, an IV–1967'.
Section IV, Archives Fiscales, Rubrique 3, Contributions directes et cadastre, IV.3.3.D.1P⁴ 1 à 1237, Calepins des propriétés bâties, 1852–1900. Infor-mation on Esquiron's address is held under the serial number D.1P⁴ 142.
Fichier des successions déclarées, 1893–1940, serial numbers D.Q⁷ 39021–39271.

Bibliothèque historique de la ville de Paris.

Céline Renooz

The memoirs of Céline Renooz, which includes a copy of her article 'Une révélation', may be found among her papers held at this library, in a file entitled 'Prédestinée: Autobiographie de la femme cachée', Fonds Marie Bouglé, papiers Céline Renooz, boîte 16, dossier 'Ma vocation scientifique', part 5, 'Le retour', fol. 4.

Index